DK EYEWITNESS TOP 10 TRAVEL GUIDES

LONDON

ROGER WILLIAMS

DORLING KINDERSLEY PUBLISHING, INC.
LONDON • NEW YORK • MUNICH
MELBOURNE • DELHI
WWW.DK.COM

Left **Old English Garden, Battersea Park** Right **Tower Bridge**

DORLING KINDERSLEY PUBLISHING, INC.

www.dk.com

Reproduced by Colourscan, Singapore
Printed and bound in Italy by Graphicom

First US Edition, 2002
2 4 6 8 10 9 7 5 3 1

Published in the United States by Dorling
Kindersley Publishing, Inc., 95 Madison
Avenue, New York, New York 10016

**Copyright 2002 © Dorling
Kindersley Limited, London
A Penguin Company**

ALL RIGHTS RESERVED UNDER INTERNATIONAL
AND PAN-AMERICAN COPYRIGHT CONVENTIONS.
NO PART OF THIS PUBLICATION MAY BE
REPRODUCED, STORED IN A RETRIEVAL SYSTEM, OR
TRANSMITTED IN ANY FORM OR BY ANY MEANS,
ELECTRONIC, MECHANICAL, PHOTOCOPYING,
RECORDING OR OTHERWISE, WITHOUT PRIOR
WRITTEN PERMISSION OF THE COPYRIGHT OWNER.
PUBLISHED IN GREAT BRITAIN BY DORLING
KINDERSLEY LIMITED

A CATALOGUE IN PUBLICATION record IS
AVAILABLE FROM THE LIBRARY OF CONGRESS

US ISBN 0-7894-8351-3

Within each Top 10 list in this book, no
hierarchy of quality or popularity is implied.
All 10 are, in the editor's opinion, of roughly
equal merit.

Floors are referred to throughout in
accordance with British usage; ie the "first
floor" is the floor above ground level.

Contents

London's Top 10

**The information in this
DK Eyewitness Top 10 Travel Guide is checked annually.**
Every effort has been made to ensure that this book is as up-to-date as possible at the time
of going to press. Some details, however, such as telephone numbers, opening hours,
prices, gallery hanging arrangements and travel information are liable to change. The
publishers cannot accept responsibility for any consequences arising from the use of this
book, nor for any material on third party websites, and cannot guarantee that any website
address in this book will be a suitable source of travel information. We value the views and
suggestions of our readers very highly. Please write to:
Senior Publishing Manager, DK Eyewitness Travel Guides,
Dorling Kindersley, 80 Strand, London WC2R 0RL.

Left **Houseboat, Regent's Canal** Right **Riverside Walk, Southbank**

Left **Lamb and Flag pub, Covent Garden** Right **View from Parliament Hill**

LONDON'S
TOP 10

LONDON'S TOP 10

TOP 10 London Highlights

A city of infinite color and variety, London is both richly historic, tracing its roots back over 2000 years, and unceasingly modern, at the forefront of fashion, music and the arts. There is a fantastic amount to interest and entertain the visitor here: a selection of the best of the best is explored in the following chapter.

1 British Museum
The oldest museum in the world, it contains a rich collection of treasures and artifacts from every corner of the globe *(see pp8–11)*.

National Gallery and Portrait Gallery 2
The nation's most important art collections are held in these two galleries, which hold some of the finest paintings in the world *(see pp12–15)*.

3 London Eye
This gigantic observation wheel (the largest ever built) is opposite the Houses of Parliament, on the South Bank, and offers great views of the city *(see pp16–17)*.

4 Tate Modern and Tate Britain
London's two Tate galleries house a superb collection of international art. Modern focuses on contemporary work after 1900, and Britain on national art from 1500 to the present *(see pp18–21)*.

5 Natural History Museum
The enormous and varied collection here explores both the geology of the Earth and the incredible range of life it supports *(see pp22–3)*.

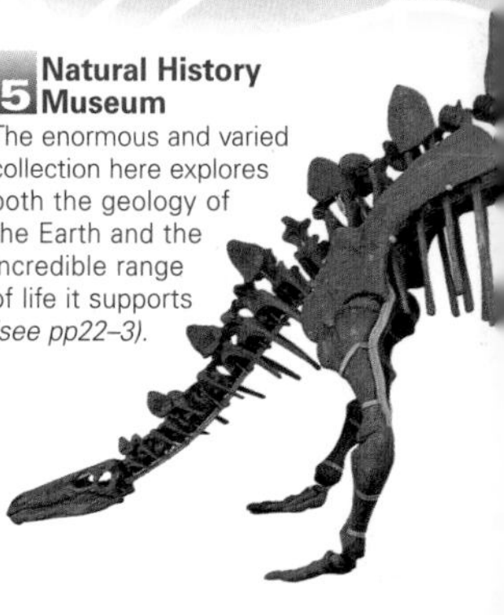

Map labels: Camden High · Regent's Park · St. John's Wood · Maida Vale · Edgware Road · Marylebone Road · Marylebone · Notting Hill · Paddington · Oxford Street · Mayfair · Bayswater Road · Notting Hill Gate · Kensington Gardens · Hyde Park · Park Lane · Holland Park · Knightsbridge · Brompton Rd · Green Park · St James · Kensington · Cromwell Road · Chelsea · King's Rd · Fulham Rd · Victoria · Pim · Wellington Road · Hampstead Rd

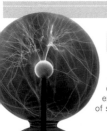

6 Science Museum
A huge museum with fascinating exhibits that demonstrate and explain the wonders of science *(see pp24–5)*.

Buckingham Palace 7
The official home of the Queen, Buckingham Palace is one of the city's most recognizable landmarks, where the changing of the Queen's guard happens every day *(see pp26–7)*.

8 Westminster Abbey and Parliament Square
This royal abbey has, since 1066, been the place where all Britain's monarchs have been crowned *(see pp32–5)*.

9 Tower of London
Steeped in bloody history, the Tower has been a royal palace, fortress and prison, as well as the home of the Crown Jewels *(see pp36–9)*.

Finsbury
nsbury
Holborn
vent rden
City
South Bank
Southwark
minster
Lambeth

1 ———— miles ⌐0⌐ km ————1

10 St. Paul's Cathedral
Sir Christopher Wren's Baroque masterpiece, St. Paul's still dominates the City skyline and has been the setting of many great ceremonial events *(see pp40–43)*.

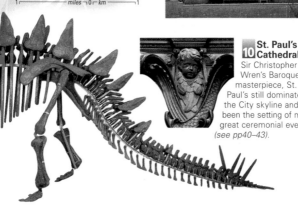

TOP 10 British Museum

The world's oldest museum has no fewer than 6 million items spanning 1.8 million years of world civilization. The collection was started with the bequest of a physician and antiquarian, Sir Hans Sloane, in 1753. In the 18th and 19th centuries travelers and emissaries, such as Captain James Cook, Lord Elgin, Lord Curzon and Charles Townley, added treasures from around the world. The present, Classical style building was completed around 1850. The courtyard Library was added later. In 2000 this opened as a new public space, the Great Court (see p11).

The British Museum façade

- There are two cafés and restaurants.

  Picnics can be eaten in the forecourt by the main entrance.

- Highlights' tours give an introduction to the collection.

  The British Museum shop sells reproduction artifacts.

- Great Russell St WC1
- Map L1
- 020 7323 8000
- www.thebritish museum.ac.uk
- Open 10am–5:30pm daily (selected galleries 10am–8:30pm Thu & Fri). Great Court: open 9am–6pm Mon, 9am–9pm Tue, Wed & Sun, 9am–11pm Thu–Sat
- Guided tours at 10:30am, 11:30am, 12:30pm, 1:30pm, 2:30pm & 3:30pm daily

Top 10 Exhibits

1. Elgin Marbles
2. Mummified Cat
3. Ram in a Thicket
4. Mildenhall Treasure
5. Rosetta Stone
6. Portland Vase
7. Rameses II
8. Mixtec-Aztec Mosaic Mask
9. Kwakwaka'wakw
10. Amitabha Buddha

1 Elgin Marbles

This spectacular 5th-century BC frieze from the Parthenon *(below)* was made under Pericles and shows a procession in honor of the goddess Athena. It was obtained in 1779 by Lord Elgin, Ambassador to Constantinople.

2 Mummified Cat

Cats and sacred cows were mummified in Ancient Egypt. This cat comes from Abydos and dates from around 30 BC. Many Egyptian deities took on animal shapes, as seen on wall paintings and other artifacts.

Key to Floorplan

	Basement
	Ground floor
	First floor

3 Ram in a Thicket

Decorated with shells and gold leaf, this priceless ornament comes from Ur in Sumer, one of the world's earliest civilizations. Games and musical instruments have also been found.

4 Mildenhall Treasure
Some of the greatest early English treasures are 34 silver plates from the 4th century, found at Mildenhall in Suffolk. Their lively decorations include sea gods, satyrs and ancient characters.

5 Rosetta Stone
In 196 BC Egyptian priests wrote a decree on this tablet in both Greek and Egyptian hieroglyphics. Found in 1799, it proved crucial in deciphering Egyptian pictorial writing.

6 Portland Vase
Sold by Britain's ambassador to Naples, Sir William Hamilton, to the Duchess of Portland, this exquisite 1st-century blue-and-opaque glass vase comes from a tomb in Rome, and was probably made by a Greek craftsman.

7 Rameses II
This is all that remains of the colossal granite statue of Rameses II (c1275 BC) from his memorial temple at Thebes. The statue was acquired in the late 18th century by Charles Townley, British ambassador to Rome.

8 Mixtec-Aztec Mosaic Mask
Made by Mixtec artisans for the Aztec royal court in Mexico, this mosaic mask (below) is believed to be of the god Quetzalcoatl, and dates from the 15th century.

9 Kwakwaka'wakw
The large, carved and painted wood thunderbird from North America was used as an anvil for breaking coppers (a form of currency) at potlatches (ceremonies of Pacific Coast peoples in which chiefs destroyed their worldly goods).

10 Amitabha Buddha
This impressive stoneware Buddha dates from around AD 585, during the Chinese Sui Dynasty, when Buddhism became the state religion.

Museum Guide

Visitor guides with full maps are on sale at the information desk in the Great Court, or you can plot your route on computer (Compass) in the library. Otherwise start to the left of the main entrance with the Assyrian, Egyptian, Greek and Roman galleries. Upstairs, the North Wing ethnography galleries provide a change from Classical material, as do the early British, medieval and Renaissance collections.

For more London museums See pp48–9

Left **Classical portico, British Museum** Right **Lindow Man**

British Museum Collections

1 Ancient Near East
Some 6,000 years of history start with the spectacular carved reliefs from the Assyrian palace of Nineveh.

2 Egyptian Antiquities
Mummies and sarcophagi are among 70,000 objects in one of the world's greatest collections.

3 Greek and Roman Antiquities
Highlights from the Classical world (c.3000 BC to c.AD 400) include the Elgin marbles and exquisite Greek and Roman vases.

Ancient Greek vase

Floorplan

4 Japanese and Oriental Antiquities
Buddhist limestone reliefs from India, Chinese antiquities, Islamic pottery and a Japanese collection so large it has to be shown on a rotating basis.

Native Canadian gull mask

5 Ethnography
An incredible 350,000 objects from indigenous peoples around the world. A new Africa gallery is scheduled to open in 2003.

6 Prehistory and Early Europe
Covering a long period from prehistoric cave paintings to Roman finds, this large collection includes Lindow Man, a 2,000-year-old body found preserved in a peat bog.

7 Medieval and Modern Europe
An incredible array of fine decorative arts ranging from medieval jewelry and Renaissance clocks to early 20th-century pottery.

8 Coins and Medals
A comprehensive collection of more than 750,000 coins and medals dating from the 7th century BC to the present day.

9 Prints and Drawings
Priceless prints and drawings from the Renaissance form part of this collection, which is shown in regularly changing exhibitions.

10 The Joseph Hotung Great Court Gallery
A small gallery for temporary exhibitions attached to the old British Library reading room.

For more London museums See pp48–9

Top 10 Library Readers

1. Karl Marx (1818–83) German revolutionary
2. Mahatma Gandhi (1869–1948), Indian leader
3. Oscar Wilde (1854–1900), playwright and wit
4. Virginia Woolf (1882–1941), Bloomsbury novelist
5. W.B. Yeats (1865–1939), Irish poet and playwright
6. Thomas Hardy (1840–1928), English novelist
7. George Bernard Shaw (1856–1950), Irish playwright
8. E.M. Forster (1879–1970), English novelist
9. Rudyard Kipling (1865–1936) Poet, novelist and chronicler of Empire
10. Leon Trotsky (1879–1940), Russian revolutionary

The Great Court

A magnificent new glass-roofed addition now encloses the heart of the British Museum. Opened in December 2000, the new Great Court was designed by architect Norman Foster around the domed Reading Room of the British Library, which was built in 1857. Holding one of the world's most important collections of books and manuscripts, the library has been the workplace of some of London's greatest writers and intellectuals. The Library is now located in St Pancras (see p107) and the Great Court contains a shop, café, restaurant and study center.

Portico detail

Rooftop View of the Great Court
The top of the British Library Reading Room dome protrudes from the new glass canopy of the Great Court. The public can now use the room to access information about the museum by computer.

Glass canopy, Great Court

TOP 10 National Gallery

The National Gallery has around 2,000 pictures, from the early Renaissance to the Impressionists (1260–1900), which form one of the greatest art collections in the world. Containing the main European schools of painting, with examples by all their most important painters, the collection was acquired from John Julius Angerstein in 1824, and moved to the present building (which is also home to the National Portrait Gallery, see pp14–15) in 1838. The Sainsbury Wing opened in 1991 to house the excellent Renaissance collection.

National Gallery façade

🔵 There is a spacious café and a good restaurant.

🔵 The Sainsbury Wing has an excellent art bookshop.

Guided tours and audio guides are available.

Explore the collection on screen in the Micro Gallery in the Sainsbury Wing.

• Trafalgar Square WC2
• Map L4
• 020 7747 2885
• www.nationalgallery.org.uk
• Open 10am–6pm daily (10am–9pm Wed). Sainsbury Wing exhibitions open until 10pm on Wed
• Free
• Guided tours at 11:30am and 2:30pm daily (also 6:30pm Wed)

Top 10 Paintings

1 Virgin and Child with St Anne and John the Baptist
2 The Arnolfini Portrait
3 The Ambassadors
4 The Wilton Diptych
5 Rokeby Venus
6 Mystic Nativity
7 Christ at Supper
8 Young Woman Standing at a Virginal
9 A Woman Bathing in a Stream
10 Bathers at La Grenouillière

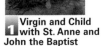

1 Virgin and Child with St. Anne and John the Baptist

This full-size drawing for a painting, known as a cartoon (from *cartone*, a large sheet of paper), is one of the masterpieces of the Renaissance, by Leonardo da Vinci (1452–1519).

2 The Arnolfini Portrait

One of the most famous paintings from the extensive Flemish collection is this unusual and masterly portrait of an Italian banker and his wife in Bruges *(above)*. Jan van Eyck (1389–1441) brought oil painting to a new and colorful height.

3 The Ambassadors

Full of symbols and hidden meaning, this painting by Hans Holbein (1533) has a foreshortened skull in the foreground.

Key to Floorplan

▨	North wing
▨	East wing
▨	West wing
▨	Sainsbury wing

5 Rokeby Venus
Painted in Rome to replace a lost Venetian painting, the *Rokeby Venus (left)* is the only nude by Diego Velázquez (1599–1660), court painter to Spain's Philip IV.

6 Mystic Nativity
Feminine grace has never been depicted better than by the painter Sandro Botticelli (1445–1510). Painted in a centennial year, *Mystic Nativity* reflects his own anxieties, with an inscription from *Revelation*.

9 A Woman Bathing in a Stream
This portrait by Rembrandt (1606–69) was painted when his technical powers were at their height, and shows his striking brushwork and mastery of earthy colors.

Trafalgar Square entrance

7 Christ at Supper
A master of light and shade, Caravaggio (1573–1610) painted without preliminary drawings and with enormous energy, using contemporary costumes and settings to produce a vivid realism.

10 Bathers at La Grenouillière
Claude Monet (1840–1926), the original Impressionist, explored the effect of light on water at La Grenouillière *(above)*, a popular bathing spot on the Seine, where he worked alongside Auguste Renoir.

4 The Wilton Diptych
A highlight of Gothic art, this exquisite English royal painting *(below)*, by an unknown artist, shows Richard II being recommended to the Virgin by saints John the Baptist, Edward and Edmund.

8 Young Woman Standing at a Virginal
Peace and calm rule the works of the Dutch painter Jan Vermeer (1632–75). Many of his interiors *(above)* were painted in his home in Delft, but it has never been possible to identify his models.

Gallery Guide
The gallery is divided into four areas. The Sainsbury Wing contains the Early Renaissance collection, with paintings from 1260 to 1510. The West Wing displays works from 1510 to 1600, the North Wing 1600–1700, and the East Wing 1700–1900. Although the main entrance is on Trafalgar Square, the Sainsbury Wing makes a more sensible starting point.

London's Top 10

For more London galleries See pp50–51

🔟 National Portrait Gallery

This is one of the most unexpectedly pleasing galleries in London. Unrelated to the neighboring National Gallery, it opened in 1856. Well known names can be put to some not-so-well-known faces, and there are some fascinating paintings from the time of the Tudors to the present day. Royalty is depicted from Richard II (1367–1400) to Queen Elizabeth II, and the collection also holds a 1554 miniature, the oldest self-portrait in oils in England. The gallery runs annual prizes for both painting and photography.

Royal coat of arms, main gallery entrance

🍴 **The Portrait Restaurant** has great views across Trafalgar Square, down Whitehall to Parliament.

📖 The gallery bookshop stocks fashion, costume, history and biography titles.

The ground-floor gift shop has good postcards.

Free concerts at 7pm on Fridays, and free lectures at 7pm on Thursdays.

- *St Martin's Place WC2*
- *Map L3*
- *020 7312 2463*
- *www.npg.org.uk*
- *Open 10am–6pm Sat–Wed, 10am–9pm Thu–Fri*
- *Free*

Top 10 Portraits

1. Queen Elizabeth
2. Shakespeare
3. The Brontës
4. The Whitehall Mural
5. George Gordon, 6th Lord Byron
6. Horatio Nelson
7. Alfred Lord Tennyson
8. The Beatles
9. Germaine Greer
10. Margaret Thatcher

1 Queen Elizabeth

This anonymous portrait is one of several of Elizabeth I, who presided over England's Renaissance (1533–1603). The Tudor rooms are the most satisfying in the gallery, and they contain two cases of miniature paintings, a popular genre of the time.

2 Shakespeare

This is the only portrait of Britain's most famous playwright known with certainty to have been painted during his lifetime (1564–1616).

3 The Brontës

Found in a drawer in 1914, this portrait of the great literary sisters, Charlotte, Emily and Anne Brontë, from York-shire, was painted by their brother, Branwell. He appears as a faint image behind them.

Key to Floorplan

Ground floor

First floor

Second floor

The Whitehall Mural
4 This cartoon of Henry VII and his son Henry VIII by Hans Holbein (1537) was drawn for a large mural in the Palace of Whitehall, lost when the palace burnt down in 1698.

George Gordon, 6th Lord Byron **5**
This painting of Lord Byron (1788–1824), by Thomas Phillips, depicts the poet and champion of liberty in Albanian dress. He died fighting with Greek insurgents against the Turks.

Horatio Nelson
6 This 1799 portrait *(below)* by Guy Head depicts Nelson after the Battle of the Nile. Apart from Queen Victoria and the Duke of Wellington, he was painted more often than any other British figure in history.

Alfred Lord Tennyson
7 This picture of the poet laureate is by one of the pioneers of photography, Julia Margaret Cameron (1815–79). She was given a camera at the age of 48 and was noted for her memorable portraits of Tennyson, the naturalist Charles Darwin and the essayist Thomas Carlyle.

The Beatles
8 Photographic portraits took on a new lease of life in the 1960s, when photographers themselves became stars. Norman Parkinson, who took this picture of the Beatles, was one of *Vogue*'s favorite fashion photographers.

Germaine Greer
9 The feminist author of *The Female Eunuch* is brilliantly captured *(below)* by Portuguese artist Paula Rego, who spent a year as artist-in-residence at the Gallery.

Margaret Thatcher
10 Today's famous are more likely to sit for a photographer than a painter. This revealing portrait of the former British prime minister by Helmut Newton allows you to study her in a way you would never dare in real life.

Gallery Guide

The gallery's three floors are arranged chronologically. Take the escalator to the second floor and start with the stunning Tudor and Stuart galleries (1–8). Men and women of arts, science and industry from the 18th and early 19th century are in the other galleries (9–20). The first floor has eminent Victorians and early photographs. The Balcony Gallery contains contemporary photographs and portraits.

For more London galleries **See pp50–51**

TOP 10 The London Eye

An amazing feat of engineering, this giant observation wheel is the highest in the world, and offers fascinating views over the whole of London. Towering over the Thames opposite the Houses of Parliament, it was built to celebrate the Millennium year, and has proved enormously popular. Its 32 enclosed capsules each hold 25 people and offer total visibility in all directions. The capsules take 30 minutes to turn through the circle and from the top, on a clear day, you can see as far as 25 miles (40 km).

Observation capsule

🍮 There are two coffee shops in County Hall.

💷 Advance reservations advisable, but some tickets are available from the ticket hall each day.

You can rent binoculars in the ticket hall.

After-dark "flights" make the city look romantic.

• South Bank SE1
• Map N5
• 0870 5000 600
• www.ba-londoneye.com
• Open April–mid Sept: 9:30am–10pm daily; mid Sept–Mar: 10am–8pm daily. Closed for 2 weeks during winter
• Ticket prices vary
• Timed tickets are on the hour and half-hour, and boarding can take up to 30 minutes.

Top 10 Sights

1. Houses of Parliament
2. Wren Churches
3. Canada Tower
4. Tower 42
5. British Telecom Tower
6. Windsor Castle
7. Heathrow
8. Alexandra Palace
9. Crystal Palace
10. Queen Elizabeth II Bridge

3 Canada Tower

London's tallest building is at Canary Wharf *(see p153)* in the heart of Docklands, the East London business and finance center. It stands in the middle of the Isle of Dogs, in a great meander in the river, formerly occupied by the West India Docks.

1 Houses of Parliament

The London Eye rises high above the Houses of Parliament *(see p34)* on the far side of the Thames. From here you can look down on Big Ben and see the Commons Terrace, where Members of Parliament and the House of Lords drink, dine and discuss policy by the river.

2 Wren Churches

The dome of St. Paul's *(see pp40–43)* stands out as the star of the City churches. Pricking the sky around it are the spires of Wren's other 31 churches, such as St. Bride's, the tallest, on which wedding cakes have been modeled.

4 Tower 42
Built for the National Westminster Bank, this was the tallest building in London until overtaken by Canada Tower. The fact that it stands out shows that the City is still relatively unspoiled by high-rise buildings.

5 British Telecom Tower
Built for the Post Office in 1961–5, this 620-ft (190-m) tower *(left)* is a television, radio and telecommunications tower. At the height of terrorist activity in the 1970s, the revolving restaurant at the top was closed and has never re-opened.

9 Crystal Palace
This BBC transmission mast to the south of the city *(below)* is near the site of the 1851 Great Exhibition "Crystal Palace" that was moved here in 1852 and burned down spectacularly in 1936.

10 Queen Elizabeth II Bridge
On a clear day you can just make out the lowest downstream crossing on the Thames, a huge suspension bridge at Dartford, some 20 miles (32 km) away. Traffic flows north in a tunnel under the river, south over the bridge.

6 Windsor Castle
Windsor Castle sits by the Thames to the west of London *(below)*. The largest occupied castle in the world, it is still a favorite residence of the royal family.

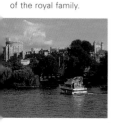

7 Heathrow
To the west of the city, London's main airport is one of the busiest international airports in the world. The Thames acts as a kind of runway, as planes line up overhead to begin their descent.

8 Alexandra Palace
The world's first high-definition television broadcasting service was transmitted by the BBC from Alexandra Palace on November 2, 1936. There is an ice hockey rink and exhibition halls here.

Millennium Legacy

The British Airways London Eye was one of a number of nationwide projects designed for the Millennium. The focus in London was on the enormous Millennium Dome, a spectacular structure built in Greenwich to house a national exhibition. Other projects were Tate Modern *(see pp18–19)* and the Millennium Bridge, the Waterloo Millennium Pier, the Great Court at the British Museum *(see pp8–11)* and the opening up of Somerset House *(see p99)*.

🔟 Tate Modern

Affiliated with Tate Britain (see pp20–21), London's most exciting new gallery is housed within the old Bankside power station, on a prime riverside site opposite the City. Large enough for huge installations, its 88 galleries provide a light, airy space in which to display the Tate's extensive collection of international modern art. This includes major works by Dalí, Picasso, Matisse, Rothko and Warhol as well as work by many acclaimed contemporary artists.

Bankside power station, now home to Tate Modern

🍽 There is a great view from the Café on level 7. The Café on level 2 overlooks the gardens. The Espresso Bar on level 4 has a riverside balcony.

📚 With more than 10,000 titles, the Turbine Hall bookshop claims to be the largest art bookshop in London.

Daily events of cinema, video, talks and tours are advertised in the main hall.

- Bankside SE1
- 020 7887 8008
- www.tate.org.uk
- Map R4
- Open 10am–6pm Sun–Thu, 10am–10pm Fri–Sat. Closed 24–26 Dec
- Free (admission charge for temporary exhibitions)

Top 10 Exhibits

1. Fountain
2. Marilyn Diptych
3. The Bath
4. Three Dancers
5. Forms Without Life
6. Light Red over Black
7. Summertime No. 9A
8. The Kiss
9. Composition (Man and Woman)
10. England

1 Fountain
Any object can be selected at random and described as a work of art, according to Marcel Duchamp (1887–1968). His urinal, entitled *Fountain*, set the tone for the absurd streak that runs through contemporary art.

3 The Bath
After mixing with Nabis, Fauvists and Intimistes, the French painter Pierre Bonnard (1867–1947) refused to follow fellow artists in abstraction, and in 1915 returned to "pure" painting. His quiet interiors and family scenes have a luminous quality.

4 Three Dancers
One of the 20th-century's most important painters, Pablo Picasso (1881–1973) was noted for the different painting styles that he mastered as he pushed back the bounds of Modern Art. The *Three Dancers*, one of several Picassos at the Tate, came from his Metamorphic phase.

2 Marilyn Diptych
The pioneer of Pop Art, New-York based Andy Warhol (1927–87) produced this icon to a major 20th-century film star *(above)*. His use of everyday objects, rather than objects of beauty, was a fundamental idea of the movement. Warhol also made art films designed to be shown in galleries.

5 Forms Without Life

Leader of the contemporary "Britpack" of artists, Damien Hirst (b1965) curries publicity by working with dead animals. *Forms Without Life*, a display of beautiful shells, represents the dilemma between collection, knowledge and life.

Light Red over Black 6

Part of the series *Ten Very Large Paintings*, by American Abstract Expressionist painter Mark Rothko (1903–70), swathes of pure color create a mood of contemplation *(right)*.

7 Summertime No. 9A

The American Jackson Pollock (1912–56) was the pioneer of Action Painting. He carried out his first "drip" painting in 1947, by pouring paint directly on to huge canvases tacked to the floor. *Summertime No. 9A* is from 1948 *(below)*.

8 The Kiss

The great sculptor of the French Romantic school, Auguste Rodin (1840–1917) produced this statue and others such as *The Thinker* from a series of some 200 figures he designed for the Musée des Arts Décoratifs in Paris.

9 Composition (Man and Woman)

One of the most distinctive sculptors of the 20th century, the Swiss artist Alberto Giacometti (1901–66) has always been popular at the Tate, which has several of his works, including this piece from 1927 *(below)*. Created while he was looking at Cubism, it explores different ways of representing the human form.

Key to Floorplan

▓	Level 3
▓	Level 4
▓	Level 5

on level 2 concourse

10 England

This piece is by the performing art duo of Gilbert Proesch (b1943) and George Passmore (b1944), who have a world-wide reputation and are among several British artists who have work on display in Tate Modern and Tate Britain.

Gallery Guide

The main entrance is down a ramp into the huge Turbine Hall below ground level, on level 1, where the coat check, information and main shop are. You can also enter the gallery on the ground floor, level 2, by the Café or by the Millennium Bridge. The main themed galleries are on levels 3 (nude/action/body; history/memory/society) and 5 (still life/object/real life; landscape/matter/environment). Temporary exhibitions are housed on level 4, and level 7 has a café.

For more London galleries See pp50–51

19

Tate Britain

Opened in 1894 as the national gallery of British art, the magnificent collection at London's first Tate gallery ranges from 1500 to the present day. Its founder was Henry Tate (1819–99) who made his fortune from sugar. The collection contains works by all Britain's major painters, and was greatly added to by J.M.W. Turner. The new Centenary Development allows all the key artists to be shown in depth. Paintings often move between the Tate's other galleries across the country.

Tate Britain's grand portico

🍽 Good basement café.

Excellent Restaurant, with good wine list.

🎬 Free guided tours, talks and films every day of the week.

Audio guides only £1 for main collection (£3 for temporary exhibitions).

Comprehensive art bookshop.

Free cloakroom.

• Millbank SW1
• Map E5
• 020 7887 8000
• www.tate.org.uk
• Open 10am– 5.50pm daily. Closed 24–26 Dec
• Free (admission charge for most temporary exhibitions)

Top 10 Paintings

1. Norham Castle, Sunrise
2. Flatford Mill
3. Wooded Landscape with a Peasant Resting
4. Three Ladies Adoring a Term of Hymen
5. Mare and Foals in a River Landscape
6. Elohim Creating Adam
7. A Scene from the Beggar's Opera
8. Sancta Lilias
9. Pink and Green Sleepers
10. Three Studies for a Figure at the Base of a Crucifixion

1 Norham Castle, Sunrise
J M W Turner (1775–1851) was the great genius of English landscape painting. This work typifies his use of abstraction and luminosity of color.

2 Flatford Mill
This scene is from England's other great landscape painter, John Constable (1776–1837). His scenes were set mostly in Suffolk and London, where he became obsessed with cloud formations.

3 Wooded Landscape with a Peasant Resting
Thomas Gainsborough (1727–88) was a portrait and landscape painter and a favorite of the Royal Family. His family groups in landscapes are among the finest "Conversation pieces" in English art. An artistic interpretation of his native Suffolk, this is one of his earliest landscapes, painted in 1747.

4 Three Ladies Adoring a Term of Hymen
Joshua Reynolds (1723–92) was the first president of the Royal Academy and a painter in the "Grand Manner" – as typified by this painting *(above)*. He raised the international status of British art.

5 Mare and Foals in a River Landscape

Liverpool-born and self-taught, George Stubbs (1724–1806) moved to London in 1759 and became the country's greatest painter of horses. This painting *(above)* is one of his finest.

6 Elohim Creating Adam

Born in London and taught at the Royal Academy School, poet, mystic, illustrator and engraver William Blake (1757–1827) claimed to be guided by visions. *Elohim Creating Adam (below)* is typical of his work, of which the Tate has a large collection.

7 A Scene from the Beggar's Opera

This lively, colorful painting is by William Hogarth (1697–1764). Born in Smithfield, he was a cartoonist and engraver as well as a painter, and one of the finest chroniclers of London life.

10 Three Studies for a Figure at the Base of a Crucifixion

Leading light of the Soho arts scene, Francis Bacon (1910–1992) was uncompromising in his view of life. When first shown, this series of paintings caused an immediate sensation, shocking audiences with their savage imagery. They have become some of his best-known works *(below)*.

Gallery Guide

The main galleries are all on the ground floor, and organized by theme, rather than by date. On the east side of the building themes covered are Artists and Models and Home and Abroad. On the west side you will find the Literature and Fantasy and Public and Private galleries. Particularly British visions are the 19th-century Pre-Raphaelites and the artists sent to the front line to capture the 20th-century's wars. Be sure to visit the Clore Gallery, which extends to part of the upper floor, to see Turner's sketchbooks and paintings. Temporary exhibitions are held in six new galleries on the lower floor, and there is nearly always an interesting temporary exhibition on.

8 Sancta Lilias

Dante Gabriel Rossetti (1828–82) was a leading member of the Pre-Raphaelite Brotherhood, a group of painters who harked back to the romance of the Middle Ages in their attempts to bring a moral and literary austerity into their art.

9 Pink and Green Sleepers

One of several 20th-century artists from Yorkshire, Henry Moore (1898–1986) was an outstanding sculptor whose work is on public display around London. This drawing was made during World War II *(above)*.

For more London galleries See pp50–51

TOP 10 Natural History Museum

There are some 70 million specimens in the Natural History Museum's fascinating collection. Originally the repository for items brought home by Charles Darwin and Captain Cook's botanist, Joseph Banks, it combines traditional displays with many innovative, hands-on exhibits, and is one of London's most popular museums. A new Darwin Centre will provide space to put more of the collection on display. Still a hothouse of research, the museum employs 300 scientists and librarians.

Tyrannosaurus Rex
1 Star of the Dinosaur Gallery is the giant robotic *Tyrannosaurus rex*. It moves, roars and even smells, and at 13 ft (4 m) tall and 23 ft (7 m) long, it is three-quarters the size of the real thing. Nearby, roaring *Deinonychus* noisily eats a *Tenontosaurus*.

Main entrance

🍴 Try the Life galleries Restaurant, or the other two cafés and snack bar.

🚶 A number of different tours are available, including a visit to the outdoor Wildlife Garden. Details at the Life galleries information desk.

• Cromwell Road SW7
• Map B5
• 020 7942 5000
• www.nhm.ac.uk
• Open 10am–5:50pm Mon–Sat, 11am–5:50 Sun. Last admission 5:30pm
• Free

Top 10 Exhibits
1 Tyrannosaurus Rex
2 Earthquake Simulator
3 Journey Through the Globe
4 No. 1 Crawley House
5 Model Baby
6 Water Cycle Video Wall
7 Fossils
8 Origin of the Species
9 Gemstones
10 Borehole

Earthquake Simulator
2 The Power Within looks at volcanoes and earthquakes. You can stand in a Japanese supermarket and experience the 1995 Kobe earthquake *(below)*.

Journey Through the Globe
3 Approach the Earth galleries by an escalator that travels through a giant globe. The model is made of iron, zinc and copper to symbolize the Earth's composition.

No. 1 Crawley House
4 Perhaps the most hair-raising display is housed in No. 1 Crawley House, a gallery which shows just how many of the 1.3 million known kinds of arthropods, or creepy-crawlies, share our homes.

5 Model Baby

A giant model of an unborn baby in the Human Biology galleries explores the sounds we hear in the womb. Other hands-on exhibits test abilities and reactions and show how physical characteristics are inherited.

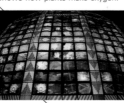

6 Water Cycle Video Wall

A semi-spherical video wall in the Ecology Gallery shows the water cycle and how it links all life on the planet. A walk-through leaf shows how plants make oxygen.

9 Gemstones

The museum's extensive collection of gemstones, rocks and minerals includes the brilliant red Rhodochrosite from the USA. The Earth's Treasury Gallery investigates how quartz keeps time and how carbon becomes diamonds.

10 Borehole

A 490-ft (150-m) borehole drilled beneath the museum reveals its fascinating contents in the Earth galleries, where fossil fuels and renewable energy sources are explored.

Key to Floorplan

- Ground floor
- First floor
- Second floor

Museum Guide

The museum is set out in two distinct halves: the Life galleries, which focus on evolution, and include the Dinosaur Gallery, and the Earth galleries, with their geological displays. The main entrance, which leads to the imposing central hall with its grand staircase and carved terracotta animals, leads to the four floors of the Life galleries. The Earth galleries occupy the former Geological Museum, and can be reached from either the main entrance or by a separate entrance on Exhibition Road.

7 Fossils

Marine reptiles that lived at the time of the dinosaurs have survived in some remarkable fossils, such as the pregnant female *Ichthyosaur*, found in a Dorset garden, which lived 187–178 million years ago.

8 Origin of the Species

This armadillo was found by Charles Darwin (1809–1892) in 1833, and forms part of a step-by-step guide to his theory of natural selection. A collection of Darwin's drawings and paintings is also on display.

For more London museums See pp48–9

🔟 Science Museum

Full of exciting interactive exhibits, this hi-tech museum explores the fascinating world of science through centuries of scientific and technological development. It shows British inventiveness leading the world in the Industrial Revolution, with spinning looms and steam engines, navigation and early flight. It also has displays on space-age science and cutting-edge technologies, as well as a large medical collection housed in the Wellcome Wing.

Science Museum façade

🍴 There is a restaurant, several cafés and a picnic area where you can eat your own food.

ℹ️ Visitor information touch screens throughout the museum give details of exhibits.

The bookshop is an excellent place to buy innovative gifts.

• *Exhibition Road SW7*
• *Map B5*
• *020 7942 4455*
• *www.science museum.org.uk*
• *Open 10am–6pm daily*
• *Free (separate charge for Virtual Voyages and IMAX cinema)*

Top 10 Exhibits

1. Virtual Voyages
2. The Secret Life of the Home
3. Apollo 10 Command Module
4. Harle Sykes Red Mill Engine
5. Puffing Billy
6. Babbage's Difference Engine
7. Dish of E-coli
8. On Air
9. Flight Lab
10. Digitopilis

3 Apollo 10 Command Module

The Apollo 10 Command Module, which went around the moon in May 1969, is on display, along with a replica of the Apollo 11 Lunar Lander. Buzz Aldrin and Neil Armstrong stepped onto the moon from the original in July 1969.

1 Virtual Voyages

Virtual Voyages are 20-minute science-themed stories with special effects in a multi-sensory environment. There is also an IMAX cinema, where 3D films are shown.

2 The Secret Life of the Home

This gallery contains a wacky variety of household gadgets and gizmos, from washing machines to burglar alarms.

4 Harle Sykes Red Mill Engine

This immaculate steam engine *(above)* can sometimes be seen up and running. It's just one exhibit in the East Hall's Power and Space gallery, which includes one of James Watt's original 1788 rotative steam engines.

5 Puffing Billy
Puffing Billy (left) is the world's oldest remaining steam locomotive. It was built in England in 1813 and used to transport coal. George Stephenson's famous 1829 *Rocket*, the first locomotive engine to pull passenger carriages, is also on display.

6 Babbage's Difference Engine
The computing and mathematics galleries on the second floor display a model of the *Difference Engine No. 2*. Designed by Charles Babbage (1791–1871), it was the forerunner of the modern computer.

9 Flight Lab
The Flight Lab *(below)* has a number of interactive models and games showing how aircraft fly. Real aircraft on display include Amy Johnson's *Gipsy Moth* (1930), and the first British jet.

10 Digitopilis
This futuristic gallery in the Wellcome Wing looks at digital sound and vision. Networking People shows how digital networks can be used in our daily lives. Artificial intelligence is also explored.

7 Dish of E. coli
Health Matters is a multimedia look at medicine. Aids, cancer and heart disease are reviewed, by patients, doctors and alternative practitioners. Take a look at *E. coli* bacteria, a modern killer.

8 On Air
A radio and sound studio on the third floor houses all the equipment used in broadcasting *(left)*. Using computer simulation, children over 12 can compile a mix of sounds and play them back.

Key to Floorplan

▓	Basement
▓	Ground floor
▓	First floor
▓	Second floor
▓	Third floor
▓	Fourth floor
▓	Fifth floor

Museum Guide

The museum is on five floors. Heavy machinery, in the Power and Space gallery, is on the ground floor. Telecommunications, time, agriculture and weather are on the first floor. Chemistry, nuclear physics and computing are on the second floor, and heat, optics health and flight are on the third. The small fourth floor contains the Glimpses of Medical History gallery and the fifth floor the Science and Art of Medicine and Veterinary History galleries.

For more London museums **See pp48–9**

Buckingham Palace

London's most famous residence, and one of its best recognized landmarks, Buckingham Palace was built as a town house for the first duke of Buckingham in 1705. Between 1824 and 1830, George IV commissioned John Nash to extend the house into a substantial palace, which was first occupied by Queen Victoria in 1837. The extensive front of the building was completed by Sir Aston Webb in 1913. The Palace is now home to the present Queen and some of the State Rooms are open to the public during summer. Many royal parks and gardens in London are also accessible to the public (see pp28–9).

Decorative lock on Palace gates

Top 10 Highlights

1. Changing of the Guard
2. The Balcony
3. Queen's Gallery
4. Grand Staircase
5. Throne Room
6. Picture Gallery
7. State Ballroom
8. Royal Mews
9. Palace Garden
10. Brougham

Victoria Monument

🕐 Time your visit to coincide with the Changing of the Guard *(see below)*.

- Buckingham Palace SW1
- Map J6
- 020 7799 2331
- www.royalresidences.com/frBPalace.htm
- State Apartments: open Aug–Sep: 9:30am–4:30pm daily. Admission: adults £11.00; over 60s £9.00; under 17s £5.50; under 5s free
- Royal Mews: open Jul–Oct: 9:30am–4:15pm Mon–Thu; Oct–Jul noon–4pm. Admission: adults £4.60; over 60s £3.60; under 17s £2.60; under 5s free
- Queen's Gallery: reopens early 2002

1 Changing of the Guard

The Palace guards, in their familiar red tunics and tall bearskin hats, are changed at 11am each morning (10am on Sundays, and alternate days in winter). The guards march to the Palace from the nearby Wellington Barracks.

2 The Balcony

On special occasions, the Queen and other members of the Royal Family step on to the Palace balcony to wave to the crowds gathered below.

3 Queen's Gallery

Currently undergoing major redevelopment, the gallery exhibits paintings and drawings from the Royal Collection, photographs from the Royal Archive, and also furniture, textiles and decorative art.

4 Grand Staircase

The Palace's main entrance leads into the Grand Hall. From here the magnificent Grand Staircase, with gilded balustrades, rises to the first floor where the State Rooms are located.

5 Throne Room

This houses the thrones of Queen Elizabeth and Prince Philip used for the coronation. Designed by John Nash, the room has a highly ornamented ceiling and magnificent chandeliers.

6 Picture Gallery

The largest room in the Palace has a barrel-vaulted glass ceiling and contains a number of paintings from the Royal Collection, including works by Rembrandt *(above)*, Rubens and Van Dyck.

7 State Ballroom

Banquets for visiting heads of state are held here. The most glittering social event of the year is in November, when 1,200 members of the Diplomatic Corps arrive in full court dress.

8 Royal Mews

Caring for 30 horses, including the Windsor Greys, which pull the royal coach on state occasions, these are the finest working stables in Britain. The collection of coaches, landaus and carriages includes the magnificent gold State Coach, which was built in 1762.

10 Brougham

Every day a horse-drawn Brougham carriage sets out to collect and deliver royal packages around London, including the Palace's weekly copy of *Country Life*.

9 Palace Garden

The extensive Palace garden includes a four-acre lake with resident flamingoes. There are four Royal garden parties held here each year, to which over 9,000 guests are invited *(below)*.

Palace Life

The official business of the monarchy takes place in the Palace, which has a staff of around 300. The Duke of Edinburgh, Duke of York, Prince Edward and the Princess Royal all have offices here. The most senior member of the Royal Household is the Lord Chamberlain. The Master of the Household and 200 domestic staff organize many functions in the Palace every year, including 22 Investitures for recipients of awards which are given by the Queen.

For more on royal London See pp54–5

TOP 10 Royal Parks and Gardens

Buckingham Palace overlooks two of London's most central Royal Parks – St. James's and Green Park – and is just a short walk from Hyde Park and Kensington Gardens. Along with the other London parks, these provide year-round pleasure and an invaluable retreat for all who live, work and visit the city. Many offer facilities for tennis, riding and boating, as well as opportunities for other activities. Picnicking in the park while a band plays is one of London's greatest summer joys.

Statue of Peter Pan in Kensington Gardens

⏰ Most of the larger parks have a number of open-air cafés, restaurants and ice-cream stands.

Parks open at dawn and close at sunset (around 9:30pm in summer). Don't get caught in the middle of large parks just as the sun goes down.

Open-air concerts, festivals and other events are regularly held in Hyde Park, Regent's Park and St. James's Park in the summer months.

• Royal Parks HQ,
The Old Police House,
Hyde Park, London W2
• Map C4
• 020 7298 2000

Top 10 Green Spaces

1. Hyde Park
2. St. James's Park
3. Kensington Gardens
4. Regent's Park
5. Green Park
6. Greenwich Park
7. Richmond Park
8. Primrose Hill
9. Bushy Park
10. Grosvenor Square

1 Hyde Park
One of the most popular features of this huge London park *(above) (see p74)* is its lake, the Serpentine, with boats for rent and a swimming area. Horses can be rented and ridden in the park. Speakers' Corner, near Marble Arch, is the place to go if you want to get up on a soapbox and address the crowds who gather there.

2 St. James's Park
London's most elegant park *(below)* was laid out in the 18th century by Capability Brown. Its lake is home to some 40 varieties of water-fowl. It has an attractive café and, in summer, lunchtime concerts are given on the bandstand *(see p113).*

3 Kensington Gardens
A continuation of Hyde Park, Kensington Gardens *(below)* was opened to the public in 1841. The recently opened Princess Diana Memorial Gardens play-ground has proved a great hit with children.

For more on royal London **See pp54–5**

Regent's Park
4 Surrounded by the Classical terraces of John Nash, Regent's Park is home to an open-air theatre and London Zoo. The fragrant Queen Mary's Rose Garden is a delight *(above) (see p129)*.

Green Park
5 Popular with office workers, this small park *(below)* is a sea of daffodils in spring. It was once part of the grounds of St. James's Palace.

Greenwich Park
6 The 0° longitude meridian passes through the Old Royal Observatory, located on a hill in this leafy family park. There are great views down to the Royal Naval College *(below)*, the river and across London *(see p147)*.

Richmond Park
7 Covering an area of 2,350 acres, this is by far the largest Royal Park. Herds of roe and fallow deer *(below)* roam freely across the heath. In late spring, the Isabella Plantation is a blaze of colorful rhododendrons. The Royal Ballet School is based in the White Lodge, originally built for George II in 1727.

Primrose Hill
8 North of Regent's Park, Primrose Hill offers spectacular views of the city skyline from its 216-ft (66-m) summit. Once a popular venue for duels, this small park was saved from development in 1841 when it was taken over by the Crown Commissioners.

Bushy Park
9 Chestnut Sunday in May, when the trees' blossoms are out, is the time to come to Bushy Park, near Hampton Court. Like Richmond, this park is run by the Royal Parks Constabulary, game-keepers and wardens.

Grosvenor Square
10 The hub of high society from the early 18th century until World War II, Grosvenor Square is the only London square that is owned by the Crown. On its west side stands the imposing American Embassy.

Sport for Kings

Much of the land of London's Royal Parks was taken from the Church by Henry VIII in the 1530s, during the Reformation. He was a passionate hunter and filled Hyde, Green and St. James's parks with deer. Henry also hunted in Greenwich Park, London's oldest, having been founded in 1433.

From the late 17th century, parks were land-scaped and gardens laid out. In 1689 William and Mary ordered the planting of Kensington Gardens. In 1811 the Prince Regent and Nash built the private estate that became Regent's Park.

Following pages **View from Trafalgar Square to Houses of Parliament**   29

10 Westminster Abbey

A glorious example of Medieval architecture, on a truly grand scale, this Benedictine abbey church stands on the south side of Parliament Square (see pp34–5). Founded in the 11th century by Edward the Confessor, it survived the Reformation and continued as a place of royal ceremonials. Queen Elizabeth's coronation was held here in 1953 and Princess Diana's memorial service in 1997. Royals, deans, statesmen, poets and writers are all buried or remembered here.

3 Poet's Corner

This corner of the transept contains memorials to many literary giants, including Shakespeare and Dickens.

The Abbey's nave

🎵 Hear the choir sing at services at 5pm every weekday, 3pm on Saturdays and at the three Sunday services.

Listen to free organ recitals at 5:45pm every Sunday.

Guided tours and audio guides are available.

- Broad Sanctuary SW1
- Map L6
- 020 7222 5152
- Abbey: open 9:30am–3:45pm Mon–Fri, 9:20am–1:45pm Sat. Closed Sun. Museum & Pyx Chamber: open 10:30am–4pm daily. Chapter House: open Oct–Mar: 10am–4pm daily; Apr–Aug: 9:30am–5pm daily; Sep: 10am–5pm daily
- Admission: adults £6.00; concessions £3.00; under 11s free

Top 10 Sights

1. St. Edward's Chapel
2. Nave
3. Poet's Corner
4. Lady Chapel
5. Coronation Chair
6. Tomb of Elizabeth I
7. The Choir
8. Tomb of the Unknown Warrior
9. Chapter House
10. Cloisters

1 St. Edward's Chapel

The shrine of Edward the Confessor (1003–66), last of the Anglo-Saxon kings, lies at the heart of the Abbey. He built London's first royal palace at Westminster, and founded the present Abbey.

4 Lady Chapel

The fan vaulting above the nave of this eastern addition to the church is spectacular Late Perpendicular *(above)*. Built for Henry VII (1457–1509), it includes two side aisles and five smaller chapels and is the home of the Order of the Bath *(see p36)*.

2 Nave

At 102 ft (32 m), this is the tallest Gothic nave in England. Built by the great 14th-century architect Henry Yevele, it is supported externally by flying buttresses.

5 Coronation Chair

This simple chair was made in 1300 for Edward I. It was placed in front of the high altar screen on the 13th-century mosaic pavement when used for coronations.

6 Tomb of Elizabeth I

England's great Protestant queen (1553–1603) is buried on one side of the Lady Chapel, her Catholic rival Mary Queen of Scots (beheaded in 1587) on the other. A contemporary notice regrets the religious intolerance of their era.

7 The Choir

The all-boy Westminster Abbey Choir School, the only school in England devoted entirely to choristers, produces the choir which sings here every day. The organ was installed in 1937 and first used at the coronation of George VI.

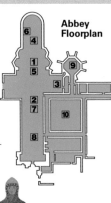

Abbey Floorplan

10 Cloisters

The heart of the former Benedictine monastery now contains a brass-rubbing center. On its north side are the only remaining parts of the Norman church, the Pyx Chambers (the former vestry) and the Undercroft, which contains a museum.

Abbey History

A Benedictine monastery was established by St. Dunstan (AD 909–988) on what was the marshy Isle of Thorney. King Edward the Confessor re-endowed the monastery, and founded the present church in 1065. William the Conquerer was crowned here soon after in 1066. Henry III's architect Henry Yevele enlarged the church in 1376, building the huge nave. The eastern end of the church was extended by Henry VII who had the Lady Chapel built. Finally, in 1734–45, the twin towers on the west front were designed by Nicholas Hawksmoor.

8 Tomb of the Unknown Warrior

The last person to be buried in the Abbey was this unknown soldier from World War I. He represents Britain's war dead.

9 Chapter House

This octagonal building with a 13th-century tiled floor *(above and left)* is where the Abbey's monks gathered. The House of Commons met here between 1257 and 1542. Run by English Heritage, it also has an entrance in Dean's Yard.

For more London places of worship **See pp46–7**

🔟 Parliament Square

The spiritual and political heart of the city, the Palace of Westminster was built here a thousand years ago as a royal household, seat of government and abbey. The square was planned as part of the rebuilding program following a fire that destroyed the Palace in 1834. Usually known as the Houses of Parliament, the new Palace of Westminster stands opposite Westminster Abbey. On the north side of the square, Parliament Street leads to Whitehall and No.10 Downing Street, the Prime Minister's residence.

Detail above Central Hall window

🍴 The basement cafe in Central Hall is a good place for a snack.

🕐 To avoid the lines for the Strangers' Galleries go after 6pm Mon–Thu.

• Parliament Sq SW1
• Map M6
• The Strangers' Galleries in the two chambers at the Houses of Parliament have limited seating for visitors during debates. Times are posted outside St. Stephen's gate, or phone 020 7219 4272
• Tours can be arranged through MPs (overseas visitors should phone 020 7219 4750)

Top 10 Sights

1. Westminster Abbey
2. Houses of Parliament
3. Big Ben
4. Westminster Hall
5. St. Margaret's Church
6. Winston Churchill Statue
7. Central Hall
8. Dean's Yard
9. Jewel Tower
10. Statue of Oliver Cromwell

1 Westminster Abbey
See pp32–3.

3 Big Ben
The huge Clock Tower of the Palace of Westminster is popularly known as Big Ben. However, the name actually refers to the clock's 14-ton bell, named after Sir Benjamin Hall, who was Chief Commissioner of Works when it was installed in 1858.

4 Westminster Hall
Westminster Hall *(left)* is about all of the original palace that remained after the 1834 fire. For centuries the high court sat beneath its marvellous hammerbeam roof.

2 Houses of Parliament
A Gothic revival building from 1870 by Sir Charles Barry and Augustus Welby Pugin, the Houses of Parliament cover 8 acres and have 1,100 rooms around 11 courtyards. The Commons Chamber *(right)* is where Members of Parliament sit and debate policy.

7 Central Hall

This large assembly hall, built in a Beaux Arts style, was funded by a collection among the Methodist Church who wanted to celebrate the centenary of their founder John Wesley (1703–91).

8 Dean's Yard

Buildings around this secluded square were used by monks before the Dissolution of the Monasteries in the 1530s which closed their school here. A new Westminster School was founded by Elizabeth I in 1560 and it remains one of Britain's top public schools.

Plan of the Square

9 Jewel Tower

Built in 1336 to safeguard the treasure of Edward III, this is an isolated survivor of the 1834 fire. A small museum about the history of parliament is housed inside.

10 Statue of Oliver Cromwell

Oliver Cromwell (1599–1658) presided over England's only republic, which began after the Civil War. He was buried in Westminster Abbey, but when the monarchy was restored in 1660, his corpse was taken to Tyburn and hanged as though he were a criminal.

Parliament

The 659 publicly elected Members of Parliament sit in the House of Commons, where the Prime Minister and his or her government sits on the right-hand side of the Speaker, who ensures the House's rules are obeyed. The opposing "shadow" government sits on his left. The neighboring House of Lords is for an unelected upper chamber which has more than 1,000 members and limited powers. The Prime Minister has a weekly audience with the Queen, who today has only a symbolic role.

5 St. Margaret's Church

Winston Churchill was among many eminent figures to marry in this 15th-century church. William Caxton (1422–91), who set up the first printing press in England, and Sir Walter Raleigh, who established the first British colony in America, are both buried here. Charles I is also remembered *(right)*.

6 Winston Churchill Statue

This powerful statue of Britain's wartime leader (1874–1965), dressed in his famous overcoat, is one of several statues in the square. These include prime minister Benjamin Disraeli (1804–81), American president Abraham Lincoln (1809–65), and many other statesmen and soldiers.

⑩ Tower of London

London's great riverside fortress is usually remembered as a place of imprisonment, but it also has a more glorious past. Originally a moated fort, the White Tower, it was built for William I (the Conqueror) and begun around 1080. Enlarged by later monarchs – including Henry VIII, who famously sent two of his wives to their deaths on Tower Green – it became home to the city arsenal, the Crown Jewels, a menagerie and the Royal Mint.

3 Yeoman Warders

Some 40 Yeoman Warders guard the Tower. Former non-commissioned military officers with Long Service and Good Conduct Medals, they live in the Tower and wear uniforms dating from Tudor times.

Royal Fusiliers' Museum

🍴 Enjoy a meal at the Tower's café or restaurant.

⏱ Allow at least two hours for your visit.

- Tower Hill EC2
- Map H4
- 020 7709 0765
- Open Mar–Oct: 9am–5pm Mon–Sat, 10am–5pm Sun; Nov–Feb: 9am–4pm Tue–Sat, 10am–4pm Sun & Mon.
- Admission: adults £11.30; children 5–15 £7.50 (under 5s free); family tickets (5 people) £34; concessions £8.50

Top 10 Features

1. The White Tower
2. Imperial State Crown
3. Yeoman Warders
4. Henry III's Throne
5. Chapel of St. John the Evangelist
6. Ravens
7. Royal Armouries
8. Tower Green
9. Traitors' Gate
10. Lion Tower

1 The White Tower

The heart of the fortress is a sturdy keep, 90 ft (30 m) tall with walls 15 ft (5 m) thick. It was constructed under William I, and completed in 1097. In 1240 it was white-washed inside and out, hence its name.

2 Imperial State Crown

This is the most dazzling of a dozen crowns in the Jewel House. It has 2,800 diamonds, and the sapphire at its top is from the reign of Edward the Confessor (r.1042–66). The crown was made for the coronation of George VI in 1937.

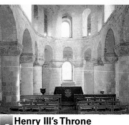

4 Henry III's Throne

Henry III (r.1216–72) richly embellished the Tower and its chapels. His own private chamber still survives in the Wakefield Tower, where you can also see his throne.

5 Chapel of St. John the Evangelist

The finest Norman place of worship in London (*left*), which remains much as it was when it was built, is on the upper floor of the White Tower. In 1399, in preparation for Henry IV's coronation procession, 40 noble knights held vigil here. They then took a purifying bath in an adjoining room and Henry made them the first Knights of the Order of the Bath.

6 Ravens

When ravens leave the Tower of London, the saying goes, the Tower will fall down. There are eight ravens in residence, looked after by a Ravenmaster.

7 Royal Armouries

The Tower's Armoury was greatly expanded under Henry VIII, who formed the basis of this important national collection, now shared with a museum in Leeds.

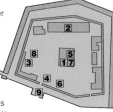

Plan of the Tower

10 Lion Tower

Wild animals presented to monarchs were kept in a menagerie here from the time of Henry III until 1835, when they were transferred to the new London Zoo *(see p129).* The treasury and crown jewels were also once kept here, protected by the wild animals.

8 Tower Green

The place of execution for nobility, including Lady Jane Grey (1554) and Henry VIII's wives Katharine Howard (1542) and Anne Boleyn (1536).

9 Traitors' Gate

The oak and iron watergate in the outer wall *(above)* was used to bring many prisoners to the Tower, and became known as Traitors' Gate.

Tower History

William I's White Tower, built by Gundolph, Bishop of Rochester, was intended to defend London against attacks – and to be a visible sign to the native Anglo-Saxon population of the conquering Normans' power. Henry III (r.1216–72) built the inner wall with its 13 towers and brought the Crown Jewels here. The city arsenal was kept here, and under Henry VIII (r.1509–47) the Royal Armouries were improved. James I (r.1603–25) was the last monarch to stay in residence. All coinage in Great Britain was minted in the Outer Ward of the Tower until 1810 when the Royal Mint was established nearby, on Tower Hill.

For more on royal London See pp54–5

Left **Bell Tower** Center **Apartment in the Bloody Tower** Right **Beauchamp Tower**

🔟 Tower Prisoners

1 Bishop of Durham
The first political prisoner to be held in the White Tower was Ralph de Flambard, Bishop of Durham. Locked up by Henry I in 1100, he was seen as responsible for the unpopular policies of Henry's predecessor, William II.

2 Henry VI
During the Wars of the Roses, between the rival families of York and Lancaster, Henry VI was kept in Wakefield Tower for five years, until restored to power in 1470.

3 The Little Princes
The murder of the two boy princes, Edward, 12 and Richard, 10, in 1483, gave the Bloody Tower its name. It is thought their uncle, Richard III, was responsible.

4 Sir Thomas More
Henry VIII's chancellor Thomas More's refusal to approve the King's marriage to Anne Boleyn led to his imprisonment in the Bell Tower. He was beheaded in 1535.

Chapel of St. Peter ad Vincula

5 Henry VIII's Wives
Some of the tower's most famous victims, such as the beheaded wives of Henry VIII, Anne Boleyn and Katharine Howard, were buried in the Chapel Royal of St. Peter ad Vincula.

Sites of imprisonment

6 The Dudley Family
Lord Dudley and his four brothers were imprisoned (before their execution) in the Beauchamp Tower for supporting Lady Jane Grey's 1554 claim to the throne.

7 Lady Jane Grey
In 1554 Lady Jane Grey was queen for nine days. Aged 17, she was held in the jailer's house on Tower Green and later executed by order of Queen Mary I.

8 Catholic Martyrs
Under the reign of Elizabeth I (1558–1603), many Catholics were executed. Most, including Jesuits, were held in the Salt Tower.

9 John Gerard
He escaped from the Cradle Tower with a fellow prisoner in 1597, using a rope strung over the moat by an accomplice in a boat.

10 Rudolf Hess
The tower's last prisoner was Hitler's deputy. He was held in the Queen's House in 1941, having come to England to ask for peace.

For more on royal London See pp54–5

Top 10 Jewels

1. Imperial State Crown
2. St. Edward's Crown
3. Imperial Crown of India
4. Queen Victoria's Crown
5. Royal Sceptre
6. Jeweled State Sword
7. George V's Crown
8. The Sovereign's Ring
9. The Sovereign's Orb
10. The Sovereign's Sceptre

The Crown Jewels

The lavish, bejeweled items that make up the sovereign's ceremonial regalia, are all in the care of the Tower of London. The collection dates from 1661 when a new set was made to replace those destroyed by parliament following the execution of Charles I in 1649. St. Edward's crown was the first subsequent crown to be made, of pure gold, and is the oldest of the 12 crowns here. Other coronation jewels on display include a gold, jewel-studded orb, made in 1661, and a sceptre containing the 530-carat Star of Africa, the biggest cut diamond in the world. The Sovereign's Ring, made for William IV, is sometimes called "the wedding ring of England".

Sovereign's Sceptre

Imperial State Crown
Heavily encrusted with 2,868 diamonds, 17 sapphires, 11 emeralds, 5 rubies and 273 pearls, this crown was designed for the coronation of George VI in 1937.

Queen Elizabeth II wearing the Imperial State Crown, coronation day, June 2, 1953

🔟 St. Paul's Cathedral

This is the great masterpiece of Sir Christopher Wren, who rebuilt the City's churches after the Great Fire of 1666. Completed in 1708, it was England's first purpose-built Protestant cathedral, and has many similarities with St. Peter's in Rome, notably in its enormous ornate dome. It has the largest swinging bell in Europe, Great Paul, which strikes every day at 1pm. The hour bell, Great Tom, strikes the hour and marks the death of royalty and senior churchmen. The cathedral has a reputation for music, and draws its choristers from St. Paul's Cathedral School.

St. Paul's semicircular South Porch

🥣 Soup and snacks in the Crypt Café.

🎵 The most popular service is the choral evensong (usually at 5pm daily) when you can hear the choir.

Guided tours and audio guides are available.

- St. Paul's Cathedral, Ludgate Hill EC4
- Map R2
- 020 7236 4128
- www.stpauls.co.uk
- Open 8:30am–4pm Mon–Sat
- Admission: adults £5; children 6–16 £2.50 (under-6s free); concessions £4; group rates available, call for details
- Guided tours at 11am, 11:30am, 1:30pm, 2pm (fee charged, call for details)

Top 10 Features

1. West Front and Towers
2. Dome
3. Whispering Gallery
4. Quire
5. OBE Chapel
6. High Altar
7. Jubilee Cope
8. Tijou Gates
9. Mosaics
10. Treasury

1 West Front and Towers
The imposing West Front is dominated by two huge towers. The pineapples at their tops are symbols of peace and prosperity. The Great West Door is 29 ft (9 m) high and is used only for ceremonial occasions.

4 Quire
The beautiful stalls and organ case in the Quire are by Grinling Gibbons. Handel and Mendelssohn both played the organ, which dates from 1695.

2 Dome
One of the largest domes in the world *(above)*, it is 365 ft (110 m) high and weighs 65,000 tonnes. The Golden Gallery at the top, and the larger Stone Gallery, both have great views.

3 Whispering Gallery
Inside the dome is the famous Whispering Gallery. Words whispered against the wall can be heard on the opposite side of the gallery.

5 OBE Chapel
At the eastern end of the crypt is a chapel devoted to men and women who received the Order of the British Empire, a military and civil honor established in 1917, and the first to include women.

6 High Altar
The magnificent High Altar *(below)* is made from Italian marble, and the canopy is from a sketch by Wren. The large candlesticks are copies of a 16th-century pair made for Cardinal Wolsey.

7 Jubilee Cope
This beautiful cope was made by Beryl Dean for the silver jubilee of Elizabeth II in 1977. Made of silk organza, its rich gold and silk embroidery illustrates St. Paul's and 76 other London churches.

8 Tijou Gates
The French master metal worker, Jean Tijou, designed these ornate wrought iron gates *(detail above)* in the North Quire Aisle, along with the Whispering Gallery balcony and other cathedral metalwork.

9 Mosaics
Colorful mosaic ceilings were installed in the Quire and Ambulatory *(above)* in the 19th century. They are made with irregular cubes of glass, set at angles so that they sparkle.

Cathedral Floorplan

10 Treasury
St. Paul's lost most of its gold and silver in a robbery in 1810. The ceremonial items now on display in the Treasury (in the crypt) are from churches across the city. There are also models of the cathedral and some of Wren's designs.

St. Paul's History

The first known church dedicated to St. Paul was built on this site in AD 604. Made of wood, it burned down in 675 and a subsequent church was destroyed by Viking invaders in 962. The third church was built in stone. Following another fire in 1087, it was rebuilt under the Normans as a much larger cathedral, with stone walls and a wooden roof. This was completed in 1300. In 1666 Christopher Wren's plans to restore the building had just been accepted when the Great Fire of London burned the old cathedral to the ground.

For more London places of worship **See pp46–7**

Left **View up the Nave** Right **Lord Nelson memorial**

St. Paul's Monuments

1 Tomb of Christopher Wren
St. Paul's architect, Sir Christopher Wren (1632–1723), has a plain tomb in the OBE chapel. Its inscription reads, "*lector, si monumentum requiris, circumspice* – Reader, if you seek his monument, look around you".

2 Wellington's Tomb
Britain's great military leader and prime minister, Arthur Wellesly, 1st Duke of Wellington (1769–1852), lies in the crypt. He also has a monument in the nave.

3 Nelson's Tomb
Preserved in brandy and brought home from Trafalgar, sea hero Admiral Lord Nelson (1758–1805) is in the center of the crypt.

4 John Donne's Tomb
The metaphysical poet John Donne (1572–1631) was made Dean of St. Paul's in 1621. His tomb is in the South Quire Aisle.

American Memorial, detail

5 Gallipoli Memorial
One of many war memorials in the cathedral, this one is dedicated to those who died in the 1915 Gallipoli campaign.

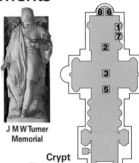

J M W Turner Memorial

Crypt Floorplan

6 William Howard Russell Memorial
Russell (1821–1907) is one of many war correspondents remembered in the OBE chapel.

7 The Worshipful Company of Stonemasons Memorial
This City guild's plaque near Wren's tomb reads, "Remember the men who made shapely the stones of Saint Paul's Cathedral".

8 Turner's Tomb
The great landscape painter J.M.W. Turner (1775–1851) is buried in the OBE chapel.

9 American Memorial
Behind the High Altar, the American Memorial Chapel's roll of honor lists the US servicemen killed while stationed in Britain during World War II.

10 Fire-Watchers Memorial
In the Nave, this remembers those who saved the church from destruction during the 1940 Blitz.

Top 10 Moments in St. Paul's History

1. Prince Charles' and Lady Diana's wedding (1981).
2. Elizabeth II's Silver Jubilee (1977).
3. Winston Churchill's funeral (1965).
4. Martin Luther King preaches (1964).
5. Festival of Britain launched (1951).
6. Cathedral bombed (1940).
7. Queen Victoria's Diamond Jubilee (1897).
8. Duke of Wellington's funeral (1852).
9. Nelson's funeral (1806).
10. First service (1697).

St. Paul's Role in History

St. Paul's belongs to the nation and to London. It is run by a Dean and Chapter of five priests, including the Archdeacon, who is responsible for the City of London's 30 parishes. Annual services for the City guilds have taken place here for a thousand years. One of the cathedral's main functions is as a place of national mourning

Wedding of Prince of Wales, 1501, St Paul's

and celebration. In the 19th century 30,000 filled the cathedral for the funeral of the Duke of Wellington. Queen Victoria's Jubilee was a spectacular occasion held on the steps of the cathedral. The Prince of Wales and Lady Diana Spencer chose to be married here rather than the royal Westminster Abbey to show that they were the people's prince and princess.

Nelson's Funeral
Such was Admiral Nelson's popularity that he was afforded a full state funeral *(left)*. His body was carried up the Thames from Greenwich Hospital to St. Paul's by barge.

Wedding of Prince Charles and Lady Diana Spencer, 1981

Execution of Charles I outside Banqueting House

 Moments in London's History

1 43 CE: Roman Invasion

When the Romans arrived in Britain, they built a bridge across the Thames from Southwark and encircled Londinium with a wall, part of which is still visible in the City *(see pp134–9)*. Their forum was in Cornhill and their amphitheatre lies beneath the Guildhall.

Roman invasion of Britain

2 1066: Norman Conquest

The next successful invasion of Britain came from northern France. It was led by William the Conqueror, Duke of Normandy, who was crowned King of England in the newly completed Westminster Abbey *(see pp32–3)* on Christmas Day 1066.

3 1240: First Parliament

The first parliament sat in Westminster and became a seat of government separate from the mercantile City, which continued to expand on the former Roman site.

4 1534: The Reformation

A quarrel between Henry VIII and Pope Clement VII over the king's divorce led to Henry breaking with Rome and declaring himself head of the church in England. Today, the sovereign remains the head of the Church of England.

5 1649: Charles I Executed

Charles I's belief in the divine right of kings led to civil war. The royalist cause was lost and the king was beheaded in 1649. After 11 years of Puritanism, his son Charles II returned to the throne to preside over the Restoration.

6 1666: Great Fire of London

Much of the city, including the medieval St. Paul's and 87 parish churches, were destroyed in the fire, which raged for five days. Afterwards Sir Christopher Wren replanned the entire city, including the cathedral *(see p40)*.

7 1863: First Underground

Originally designed to link the main London railway termini, the Metropolitan Line was the world's first underground railway. When it opened, the carriages were little more than trucks.

The Great Fire of London

Bomb damage near St. Paul's Cathedral

8 1875: Embankments Built
Built on either side of the river, the Embankments were among the great engineering works of the Victorians. They were designed by Sir Joseph Bazalgette to contain a vast new sewage system to take waste to pumping stations outside London.

9 1940–41: The Blitz
Between September 1940 and May 1941, German air raids left 30,000 Londoners dead. The bombers destroyed much of the Docks, the East End and the City. The House of Commons, Westminster Abbey and the Tower of London were all hit. Many Londoners sought shelter in Underground stations at night.

10 1992: Docklands Development
Docks that were once hives of activity began to be deserted in the 1960s as trade moved to a modern container port at Tilbury. In the 1980s, regeneration of the area began, notably around the West India Dock, where Canary Wharf was built in 1992. A new City airport was created on the site of the former Royal docks.

Top 10 Cultural Highlights

1 Shakespeare Arrives
The first mention of William Shakespeare (1564–1616) as a London dramatist was recorded in 1585.

2 Rubens Knighted
The Dutch painter Peter Paul Rubens was knighted by Charles I in 1629 after painting the Banqueting House ceiling.

3 Purcell's Appointment
The greatest English composer of his age, Henry Purcell was appointed organist at Westminster Abbey in 1679.

4 Handel's Water Music
George Friedrich Handel's *Water Music* was composed for a performance on George I's royal barge in 1711.

5 Great Exhibition
In 1851, the expanding Empire was celebrated in an exhibition held in a massive glass structure in Hyde Park.

6 J.M.W. Turner Bequest
Turner's paintings were left to the nation on condition that they be seen by the public free of charge *(see pp20–21)*.

7 Royal Opera Highlight
In 1892 Gustav Mahler conducted the first British performance of Wagner's *Ring* at the Royal Opera House.

8 First Radio Broadcast
The BBC made its first broadcast on New Year's Day 1927.

9 Festival of Britain
In 1951, the Festival of Britain was held at the South Bank to mark the centenary of the Great Exhibition.

10 Royal National Theatre
The Royal National Theatre company was founded in 1963 at the Old Vic under Laurence Olivier (later Lord Olivier).

Left **Carving, Westminster Abbey** Center **Brompton Oratory interior** Right **Cherub, St. Bride's**

Churches

St. Martin-in-the-Fields

1 Westminster Abbey
See pp32–3.

2 St. Paul's Cathedral
See pp40–43.

3 St. Martin-in-the-Fields
Known for its royal connec-tions, St. Martin's is the only church to have a royal box. There has been a church on the site since the 13th century, but the handsome present building was designed by James Gibbs in 1726. Coffee shop in the crypt. ✪ *Trafalgar Square WC2 • Map L4 • Open 9am–5pm Mon–Sat, services only Sun • Free*

4 Southwark Cathedral
This priory church was elevated to a cathedral in 1905. It has many connections with the area's Elizabethan theatres, and with Shakespeare, who is commemorated in a memorial and a stained-glass window. US college founder John Harvard, who was bapti-zed here, is rememberd in The Harvard Chapel. ✪ *Montague Close SE1 • Map G4 • Open 8am–6pm Mon–Fri, 9am–5pm Sat & Sun • Free*

Southwark Cathedral stained glass

5 Temple Church
This unusual circular church was built in the 12th century for the Knights Templar, a crusading order. Effigies of the knights are embedded in the floor. A chancel was added later, and a reredos was designed by Christopher Wren. Gutted by fire in World War II, it was rebuilt in 1958. ✪ *Middle Temple Lane EC4 • Map P2 • Open 10am–4pm Wed–Sat • Free*

Gatehouse, St. Bartholemew-the-Great

6 St. Bartholemew-the-Great
A survivor of the Great Fire, this is London's only Norman Church apart from St. John's chapel in the Tower of London. It was founded in 1123 by a courtier of Henry I, and its solid pillars and Norman choir have remained unal-tered. The 14th-century Lady Chapel, restored by Sir Aston Webb in 1890, once housed a printing press where Benjamin Franklin worked *(see p138)*.

7 Brompton Oratory

This very un-English, Italianate church was established by a Catholic convert, John Henry Newman (1801–90). He introduced England to the Oratory, a religious institute of secular priests founded in 16th-century Rome. The building, designed by Herbert Gribble, opened in 1884, with many of its treasures imported from Italy. ✆ *Brompton Rd SW7 • Map C5 • Open 6:30am–8pm daily • Free*

Italianate interior of Brompton Oratory

8 Westminster Cathedral

The main Roman Catholic church in England is in a fearless Byzantine style, designed by John Francis Bentley and completed in 1902. It has an 87-m (285-ft) campanile, which can be climbed for a great view of the city. Mosaics and colored marble decorate the interior, which has the widest nave in Britain. ✆ *Ashley Place SW1 • Map E5 • Open 7am–7pm daily • Free*

9 St. Bride's

There has been a church on this site since Roman times, a fact discovered during excavations after the church was bombed during World War II. Sir Christopher Wren's fine church has a wonderful tiered spire that was copied for a wedding cake by a Fleet Street baker, Mr. Rich, starting a trend. This is traditionally the journalists' church and memorial services are held here.

10 All Souls

This distinctive building, with a semi-circular portico and stiletto spire, was designed by John Nash, creator of Regent Street. After the BBC built their headquarters next door, it became the home of religious broadcasts. ✆ *Langham Place W1 • Map J1 • Open 9:30am–6pm Mon–Fri, 9am–9pm Sun • Free*

Memorial tablet at All Souls

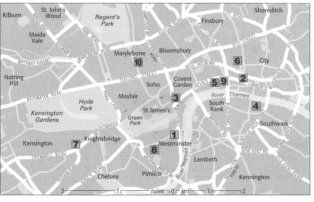

Left **Theatre Museum** Right **London Transport Museum**

🔟 Museums

Victoria and Albert Museum

1 British Museum
The oldest museum in the world, and one of London's most fascinating, contains treasures and artifacts from all over the world *(see pp8–11)*.

2 Natural History Museum
Life on Earth and the Earth itself are vividly explained here using hundreds of traditional and interactive exhibits *(see pp22–3)*.

3 Science Museum
This exciting museum traces centuries of scientific and technological development, with impressive and educational displays *(see pp24–5)*.

4 Victoria and Albert Museum
This museum of decorative arts is one of London's great pleasures,

National Maritime Museum

with 145 astonishingly eclectic galleries. One of the highlights is the huge Dress Collection, with exhibits dating from 1600 to the present day. The museum also has collections of jewelery, ceramics, metalwork, glass, paintings, prints, sculpture and rooms full of Indian and Far Eastern treasures *(see p119)*.

5 Museum of London
This comprehensive museum located near the Barbican Centre *(see p137)* provides a detailed account of London life from prehistoric times to the present day. It is particularly strong on Roman Londinium, but also has a large model re-creating the Great Fire of 1666, as well as reconstructed period interiors and street scenes *(see p136)*.

6 National Maritime Museum
The world's largest maritime museum, perfectly located in part of Wren's Royal Naval Hospital, has much to offer. The 1803 Battle of Trafalgar is re-enacted, and Admiral Nelson's fatally pierced tunic is on display. Antarctic expeditions are recalled and there is a collection of boats, from coracles to royal barges. State-of-the-art simulators give an idea of modern navigation and what it was like when the *Titanic* went down *(see p147)*.

Imperial War Museum

7 In this museum, which is housed in part of the former Bethlehem ("Bedlam") Hospital for the Insane, a clock in the basement moves remorselessly on, recording the world's war dead – a figure that has now reached 100 million. Six million of them are commemorated in the Holocaust Exhibition. Other displays include evocative re-creations of World War I trench warfare and the life of Londoners during the World War II Blitz. Now it is "total war" that we have to contemplate, and this, too, is explored *(see p83)*.

Imperial War Museum

Design Museum

8 Based in a clean white 1930s building beside Tower Bridge, this museum is devoted to modern design. The permanent collection offers a nostalgic look at mass-produced everyday objects, while on a separate floor there are temporary displays and bright ideas from around the world providing a taste of what is to come. ◉ Butler's Wharf SE1 • Map H4 • Open 11:30am–6pm Mon–Fri, 10:30am–6pm Sat & Sun • Admission charge

Austin Mini in the Design Museum

London Transport Museum

9 In this light and airy former flower-market building, the history of London's transport system is illustrated with posters, photographs and examples of early buses, tubes and horse-drawn vehicles. There are also educational hands-on "KidZones" for children *(see p100)*.

Theatre Museum

10 Filling the museum's sub-terranean galleries, the collection documents the history of British theatre from Shakespeare's time up until the present, with a wealth of memo-rabilia, paintings and prints of famous thespians. It also holds educational workshops, events and perfor-mances *(see p100)*.

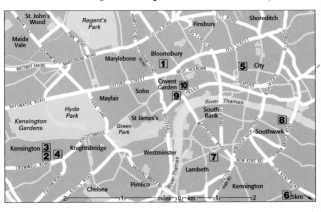

For children's museums **See pp68–9**

Left **The National Gallery** Right *Satan Smiting Job with Sore Boils* by William Blake, Tate Britain

🔟 Art Galleries

1 The National Gallery and National Portrait Gallery

Located next door to each other at the top of Trafalgar Square, these comprehensive galleries make up the core of Britain's art collection *(see pp12–15)*.

The Umbrellas by Renoir, National Gallery

2 Tate Modern

Housed in a huge converted power station on the south bank of the Thames, this exciting new gallery covers modern art from 1900 to the present day *(see pp18–19)*.

3 Tate Britain

The other Tate gallery in London, focusing on work from 1500 to 1900, has the greatest collection of British art in the world *(see pp20–21)*.

4 Courtauld Institute Gallery

From Fra Angelico to Van Gogh, this is a complete art course in one manageable gallery. The core of the collection is the country's finest Impressionist and Post-Impressionist works, amassed by a textile magnate, Samuel Courtauld (1876–1947). Many of them are instantly recognisable: Monet's *The Bar at the Folies-Bergère*, Toulouse Lautrec's dancing *Jane Avril*, Gauguin's *Te Rerioa* and Manet's *Déjeuner sur L'Herbe*. Visit Somerset House's fountain courtyard and riverside terrace café for a drink afterwards *(see p99)*.

5 Wallace Collection

This wonderful Victorian mansion belonged to Sir Richard Wallace (1818–90). In 1897, his widow bequeathed the house and their amazing art collection to the nation. Covering two floors, the 25 public rooms are beautifully furnished with one of the best private collections of French 18th-century pictures, porcelain and furniture in the world. The paintings are rich and voluptuous – notable works include Nicolas Poussin's *A Dance to the Music of Time* and Frans Hals' *The Laughing Cavalier*. There are English portraits by Gainsborough and Reynolds *(see p129)*.

The Laughing Cavalier by Frans Hals, Wallace Collection

Vermeer's *The Guitar Player*, Kenwood House

exhibitions draw the crowds, and it is often necessary to reserve a ticket in advance. The traditional Summer Exhibition, which anyone can apply to enter, is also extremely popular (see p113).

9 Queen's Gallery, Buckingham Palace
Established in 1962 to display works from the Royal Collection, this fascinating gallery reopens in 2002 for the Queen's Jubilee year after renovation (see p26).

10 Kenwood House
This majestic mansion with interiors designed by Robert Adam has a small but important collection comprising 17th-century Dutch and Flemish works, 18th-century English portraits, and a small French Rococo section. There are statues by Henry Moore and Barbara Hepworth in the extensive grounds (see p142).

6 Dulwich Picture Gallery
If you have time, this suburban gallery is well worth a short train journey. Britain's oldest art gallery, which had a face-lift for the Millennium, was opened in 1817. The important collection includes Murillo's *Flower Girl*, Poussin's *Triumph of David* and Rembrandt's *Girl at the Window* (see p148).

7 Saatchi Gallery
Exhibits in this 1920s building are never on loan: they all belong to advertising tycoon Charles Saatchi. He has become the most influential contemporary arts patron in Britain by supporting and promoting Damien Hirst and other *enfants terribles* of the modern art scene. Three exhibitions are staged each year. ⊗ *98a Boundary Road NW8 • Tube St John's Wood • Open noon–6pm Thu–Sun • Admission charge*

8 Royal Academy
Although it has no permanent exhibition, the Royal Academy's continual big-name temporary

Left **Dickens' house** Right **Carlyle's House interior**

🔟 Famous Residents

1 Sherlock Holmes
The famous but fictitious detective created by Arthur Conan Doyle first appeared in 1891. He still gets regular fan mail sent to his equally fictitious address of 221b Baker Street (the museum is next to No. 239, *see p130*).

2 Charles Dickens
The great Victorian novelist and social campaigner (1812–70) lived in Doughty Street for two years from 1837. The house is his only surviving London home, and he thought it "a frightfully first-class family mansion, involving awful responsibilities" *(see p108)*.

3 Dr. Johnson
"When a man is tired of London, he is tired of life," said Dr. Samuel Johnson (1709–84). He lived in the City from 1748 to 1759 and much of his famous dictionary was compiled here, with six copyists working in the garrett. His companion James Boswell reported on the social comings and goings in the house.
⊗ *Dr. Johnson's House, 17 Gough Square EC4 • Map P2 • Open 11am–5:30pm Mon–Sat • Admission charge*

Freud's famous couch

Sherlock Holmes, London's famous detective

4 John Keats
The London-born Romantic poet (1795–1821) lived in Hampstead from 1818 to 1820 before leaving for Italy to try to cure his fatal tuberculosis. After falling in love with his neighbor's daughter, Fanny Brawne, he wrote his famous and beautiful *Ode to a Nightingale* in the garden *(see p141)*.

5 Sigmund Freud
The Viennese founder of psychoanalysis (1856–1939) spent the last year of his life in a north London house *(see p136)*. A Jew, he had fled the Nazis, bringing his celebrated couch with him *(see p141)*.

6 Lord Leighton
Yorkshire-born Frederick Leighton (1830–96) was the most successful painter in Victorian London and president of the Royal Academy. He had this exotic house built for him in 1899 *(see p121)*.

7 Thomas Carlyle

The Scottish historian and essayist Thomas Carlyle, famous for his history of the French Revolution, lived in London from 1834. ✒ *Carlyle's House, 24 Cheyne Row SW3 • Map C6 • Open Apr–Oct: 11am–5pm Wed–Sun • Admission charge*

8 The Duke of Wellington

Charles Wellesley, 1st Duke of Wellington (1769–1852), lived at Apsley House, which has the unique address of No. 1 London. It was his home from 1817, after his victories in the Napoleonic Wars *(see p114)*.

9 Georg Friedrich Handel

The great German-born composer first visited London in 1710 and settled here permanently in 1712. ✒ *Handel House Museum, 25 Brook St W1 • Map D3 • Open 10am–6pm Tue–Sat (10am–8pm Thu), 12–6pm Sun • Admission charge*

10 William Hogarth

The great painter of London life (1697–1764, *see pp20–21*) was used to the gritty life of the city and called his house near Chiswick "a little country box by the Thames". ✒ *Hogarth's House, Hogarth Lane W4 • Open Apr–Oct: 1–5pm Tue–Fri, 1–6pm Sat & Sun; Nov–Mar: 1–4pm Tue–Fri, 1–5pm Sat & Sun • Closed Jan • Free*

Richly decorated interior of Leighton House

Top 10 Blue Plaques

Circular blue plaques displayed on the walls of some London buildings recall famous residents.

1 Wolfgang A. Mozart

The German composer (1756–91) wrote his first symphony, aged eight, while at No. 180 Ebury Street.

2 Benjamin Franklin

The American statesman and scientist (1706–90) lived for a time at No. 38 Craven Street.

3 Charlie Chaplin

The much-loved movie actor (1889–1977) was born at No. 287 Kennington Road.

4 Charles de Gaulle

The exiled general (1890–1970) organized the Free French Forces from No. 6 Carlton Terrace during World War II.

5 Dwight Eisenhower

During World War II the Allied Commander (1880–1969) lived at No. 20 Grosvenor Square, near the US embassy.

6 Mark Twain

The American humorist (1835–1910) lived for a year at No. 23 Tedworth Square.

7 Mahatma Gandhi

The "father" of India's independence movement (1869–1948) studied law in the Inner Temple in 1889.

8 Jimi Hendrix

The American guitarist (1942–1970) stayed in central London at No. 23 Brook Street.

9 Henry James

The American writer (1811–1916) lived in Bolton Street, de Vere Gardens, and in Cheyne Walk, where he died.

10 Giuseppe Mazzini

From 1837 to 1849 the Italian revolutionary and patriot (1805–72) lived at No. 183 Gower Street.

Left **Buckingham Palace** Right **Kensington Palace**

Royal London

1 Buckingham Palace
See pp26–7.

2 Hampton Court
The finest piece of Tudor architecture in Britain, Hampton Court was begun by Henry VIII's ally Cardinal Wolsey in 1514 and later given to the king. It was enlarged first by Henry and then by William and Mary, who employed Christopher Wren as architect. Its many rooms include a huge kitchen, a Renaissance Picture Gallery, the Chapel Royal and sumptuous royal apartments. Set in 60 acres, the gardens, with their famous maze, are as much an attraction as the palace (see p147).

3 Kensington Palace
An intimate royal palace in Kensington Gardens, famous as the home of Princess Diana, the first sovereign residents here were William and Mary in 1689. Queen Victoria was born here in 1837 and opened parts of the palace to the public, including some of the State Apartments. These are still open today, along with a beautiful Royal Ceremonial Dress Collection. The Orangery is delightful for coffee (see p119).

4 St. James's Palace
Although not open to the public, St. James's has a key role in royal London. Its classic Tudor

Tudor gatehouse, St. James's Palace

style sets it in the reign of Henry VIII, although it served only briefly as a royal residence. Prince Charles has offices here (see p113).

5 Kew Palace and Queen Charlotte's Cottage
The smallest royal palace, Kew was built in 1631 and used as a residence by George III and Queen Charlotte. Nearby Queen Charlotte's Cottage was used for picnics and housing a menagerie of exotic royal pets. The palace is set in Kew Gardens (see p147).
⌖ Kew, Surrey • Closed for renovations

Ceiling detail, Banqueting House

6 Banqueting House
Built by Inigo Jones, this magnificent building is particularly noted for its Rubens ceiling. It was commissioned by Charles I, who stepped from this room onto the scaffold for his execution in 1649. ⌖ Whitehall SW1 • Map L4 • Open 10am–5pm Mon–Sat • Admission charge

7 Queen's House

This delightful home in the midst of Greenwich Park was the first Palladian building by Inigo Jones, and home to the wife of Charles I. Beautifully restored to its 17th-century glory, it has a fine interior, and houses part of the National Maritime Museum's extensive art collection. ◈ Romney Road SE10 • Train to Greenwich • Open 10am–5pm daily • Admission charge

8 Royal Mews
See pp26–7.

9 Queen's Chapel

This exquisite royal chapel is open only to its congregation. Built by Inigo Jones in 1627, its furnishings remain virtually intact, including a beautiful altarpiece by Annibale Carracci. ◈ Marlborough Road SW1 • Map K5

10 Clarence House

Designed by John Nash in 1827 for William IV, this royal residence sits beside The Mall. It has long been the home of the Queen Mother, who has kept an almost Edwardian lifestyle going into the 21st century. ◈ Stable Yard SW1 • Map K5 • Closed to the public

Queen's House, Greenwich

Top 10 Royals in Everyday London Life

1 King Charles Spaniel
These were the favorite dogs of King Charles II. Today, the Queen prefers corgis.

2 Queen Anne's Gate
A delightful small Westminster street with a statue of the queen who gave her name to a style of furniture.

3 Regent's Park
The Prince Regent, later George IV, used John Nash for this ambitious urban plan.

4 Duke of York Steps
A statue of the "Grand Old Duke of York", subject of the nursery rhyme, is elevated above these steps off Pall Mall.

5 Victoria Station
All the main London railway termini were built in Victoria's reign. This one serves southern England.

6 Albert Memorial
Prince Albert, beloved consort of Queen Victoria, has a splendid memorial in Kensington Gardens (see p119).

7 George Cross
Instituted in 1940 under George VI, this medal is awarded for acts of heroism by civilians.

8 Princess of Wales Pubs
Several pubs have changed their name to remember Diana, Princess of Wales, "the people's princess".

9 Windsor Knot
The stylish Duke of Windsor, who abdicated the throne in 1938, gave the world a wide tie knot.

10 King Edward Potato
This variety of English potato was named after King Edward VII, who visited Ireland after the 1903 potato famine.

For royal parks and gardens See pp28–9

Left **Colonnade at the ICA** Center **Royal Court Theatre façade** Right **Poster, Sadler's Wells**

🔟 Performing Arts Venues

1 Royal Opera House

One of the greatest opera houses in the world, this theatre is home to the Royal Ballet Company, and hosts international opera productions. Apart from the sumptuous main auditorium, there are the smaller Lindberg and Clore theatres which have music and dance. There are regular backstage tours and occasional big-screen simulcasts of opera in the Piazza *(see p99)*.

The Nutcracker, Royal Opera House

2 The Royal National Theatre

Seeing a play at the national theatre takes you to the heart of London's cultural life. Within the gray blocks of this innovative building, designed by Denys Lasdun in 1976, you can see a musical, a classic or a new play in one of its three theatres: the Olivier, the Lyttleton or the Cottesloe. Check for free shows and exhibitions in the foyer. Reduced price tickets are sold from 10am on the day of the performance ◈ *South Bank SE1 • Map N4 • 020 7452 3000*

3 Barbican Centre

Home of two of the best theatre and music companies in the world: the Royal Shakespeare Company and the London Symphony Orchestra, the Barbican is the City's most important arts complex. Theatre, cinema, concerts, dance and

Golden globe atop the London Coliseum

exhibitions can all be seen here, and there are plenty of restaurants, cafés and bars. The center also contains a library, convention hall and music school *(see p135)*.

4 London Coliseum

London's other principal opera house presents excellent productions sung in English by the English National Opera. Tickets can be a bargain: from £3 for standing to £25 seats. ◈ *St. Martin's Lane WC2 • Map L3 • 020 7632 8300*

5 The Royal Festival Hall

The London Philharmonic Orchestra is one of many world-class orchestras to perform here. Have a coffee at one of the cafés and check out the 1950s interior design with its majestic staircase. ◈ *South Bank SE1 • Map N4 • 020 7960 4201*

6 Sadler's Wells

After winning a reputation as the best dance theater in London in the 1950s, Sadler's Wells now also hosts music and opera. The stunning new building prides itself on its community events as well as its international dance shows (see p144).

7 Royal Albert Hall

This distinctive, circular building was designed to resemble a Roman amphitheater, and has a delicate Classical frieze around the exterior. The excellent acoustic inside makes this a premier venue for every kind of concert, including the "Proms" (see p120).

8 Royal Court Theatre

The cream of new drama can be seen at this charming small theater. Recently refurbished, both the main, and tiny upstairs theater, are important London venues. Play "actor spotting" in the new restaurant and bar. ® Sloane Square SW1 • Map C5 • 020 7565 5000

9 Riverside Studios

With a glorious location by the Thames at Hammersmith, this is a fascinating arts and media center. An eclectic program includes cinema, theater, dance and the visual arts. Works of such innovators as Samuel Beckett and Peter Brook have premiered here. Once BBC studios, Riverside is still used to to make TV shows. The pleasant café and bar are a draw in themselves. ® Crisp Road W6 • Tube Hammersmith • 020 8237 1111

10 ICA

A stately, colonnaded terrace by Nash houses London's hippest gallery, the Institute of Contemporary Arts. The ICA's cutting edge policy on the visual arts includes developing new and challenging digitally-produced works, and Becks, the UK's largest arts prize for students. ® The Mall SW1 • Map K5 • 020 7930 3647

Performance, Royal Albert Hall

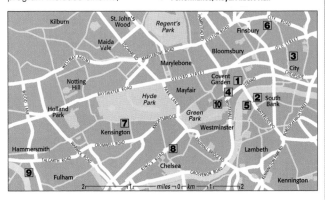

For more theatres See pp60–61

Left **Camden's Jazz Café** Right **Pizza on the Park**

🔟 Live Music Venues

1 Ronnie Scott's
This legendary London jazz club was opened by saxophonist Ronnie Scott (1929–96) in 1959. Intimate lamplit tables surround a tiny stage that has hosted such stars as Miles Davis and Dizzy Gillespie, and continues to attract top names *(see p93)*.

2 100 Club
Atmospheric jazz and blues dive that stays open up to 2am. The Rolling Stones played here, as did the Sex Pistols and other punk bands of the 1970s. Today there is Indie music and early evening dance classes. Membership is not required. ✆ *100 Oxford Street W1 • Map K2 • 020 7636 0933*

3 The Jazz Café
Top jazz and soul performers, as well as great food make this a popular venue. Best views are to be had from the balcony tables. ✆ *5 Parkway NW1 • Map D1 • 020 7916 6060*

4 Astoria
This theatre is now a famous rock venue, playing host to a variety of bands. Its rough-and-

Pizza on the Park

Ronnie Scott's jazz club

ready ambiance attracts a crowd of devoted fans. ✆ *157 Charing Cross Road WC2 • Map L2 • 020 7434 9592*

5 Brixton Academy
This is a great place to see big names from across the music spectrum. Although it holds 4,000, the hall retains an intimate, clubby atmosphere with good views of the performers from across the auditorium. ✆ *211 Stockwell Road SW9 • 020 7771 2000 • Tube Brixton*

6 Dingwalls
See music and comedy at this informal venue, with wooden floors and cosy tables arranged over several levels, overlooking Regent's Canal. ✆ *Camden Lock NW1 • 020 7267 1577 • Tube Camden Town*

7 Pizza on the Park
Famous for its late-night jazz, which ranges from small combos to individual singers performing from a broad jazz repertoire. This is also the top Pizza

Express outlet in the city, and serves good pizzas. ✪ *11 Knightsbridge SW1 • Map C4 • 020 7235 5273*

8 Borderline
One of London's best small clubs, in a basement under the Break for the Border restaurant *(see p93)*, Borderline has hosted many international bands. There's at least one different band every weekday evening. ✪ *Orange Yard, Manette Street W1 • Map L2 • 020 7734 2095*

9 Roadhouse
Retro 1950s decor and a wide range of bands make this a popular venue. Open until late, there is a happy hour each evening and a Ladies' Night every Tuesday, when women get in free and are given a complimentary glass of champagne. ✪ *Jubilee Hall, 35 The Piazza WC2 • Map M3 • 020 7240 6001*

Bar at the Roadhouse

10 Troubadour Coffee House
An atmospheric and laid-back coffee house club devoted to folk music. All the great folk singers of the 1960s played here, and today there is a relaxed, amateur feel to the evenings when singers, poets and comedians perform. ✪ *265 Old Brompton Road SW5 • Map A6 • 020 7370 1434*

Top 10 Nightclubs

1 Fabric
The best dance venue in town, arranged in three rooms filled with sound: 24-hour music licence. ✪ *77a Charterhouse Street EC1 • Map Q1*

2 Hanover Grand
The smartest dance venue in town plays house, R&B and hip-hop. ✪ *6 Hanover Street W1 • Map J2*

3 Stringfellows
Lap dancing for the gold-medallion crowd in London's celebrated club. ✪ *16–19 Upper St. Martin's Lane WC2 • Map L3*

4 Madame Jo-Jo's
Some of the best drag acts in town. ✪ *8–10 Brewer Street W1 • Map K3*

5 Electric Ballroom
Disco funk on three floors until 3am. ✪ *184 Camden High Street NW1 • Map D1*

6 Ministry of Sound
Dance all night to the hippest house and garage tracks. ✪ *103 Gaunt Street SE1 • Tube Elephant & Castle*

7 Africa Centre
Funk, hip-hop and African sounds. Open until 3am. ✪ *38 King Street WC2 • Map M3*

8 The Wag
A mix of DJs and live music on three floors. ✪ *35 Wardour Street W1 • Map K3*

9 Heaven
London's best-known gay venue has several bars and dance floors beneath Charing Cross station. ✪ *Villiers Street WC2 • Map M4*

10 The End
Sophisticated minimalist venue for serious dancing to drum 'n' bass, funk, techno, and house. ✪ *18 West Central Street WC1 • Map M1*

For more late-night venues **See p93**

59

Left **Blood Brothers** Right **Phantom of the Opera**, Her Majesty's Theatre

🔟 West End Shows

1 Les Misérables
Victor Hugo's French classic novel of 1862 was adapted for the stage by Trevor Nunn for the Royal Shakespeare Company in 1985 and it hasn't stopped rolling. With music by Alain Boublil and Claude-Michel Schönberg, "Les Mis" tells the tale of downtrodden poor and the social and political struggles in revolutionary France. It is now at the Palace Theatre, opened in 1891. ✪ Palace Theatre, Shaftesbury Avenue W1 • Map L2 • 020 7434 0909

Les Misérables, Palace Theatre

2 Cats
The longest-running musical in London, Cats is still at the New London Theatre where it opened in 1981. Based on Old Possum's Book of Practical Cats by the poet T.S. Eliot, it is one of the many triumphs of the composer-cum-impresario Andrew Lloyd Webber, whose road to fame and fortune began with Joseph and his Amazing Technicolour Dreamcoat in 1968. ✪ New London Theatre, Drury Lane WC2 • Map M2 • 020 7405 0072

3 Mamma Mia!
By Benny Andersson and Björn Ulvaeus, this fun musical owes much of its success to the nostalgia factor. The story is a romantic comedy, set on a Greek island and based around 22 Abba hits. ✪ Prince Edward's Theatre, Old Compton Street W1 • Map L2 • 020 7447 5400

4 Phantom of the Opera
Andrew Lloyd Webber's 1986 hit musical, The Phantom of the Opera is adapted from Gaston Leroux's tale of Beauty and the Beast and set in the Paris Opera House. A huge international success, it is, perhaps, Lloyd Webber's most famous production. ✪ Her Majesty's Theatre, Haymarket SW1 • Map L4 • 020 7494 5400

5 Buddy
An energetic and hugely entertaining musical, based on the rise to fame of Buddy Holly. Unsurprisingly, it is his music that makes the show. ✪ Strand Theatre, Aldwych WC2 • Map N3 • 020 7930 8800

Cast of Cats

Stars of *Chicago*

6 Lion King
A highly imaginative Disney production, based on the 1994 animated film and brilliantly conjured up on stage. The amazing animal costumes and special effects will wow children and adults alike. Much of the music is by Elton John and Tim Rice. ⓢ *Lyceum Theatre, 21 Wellington Street WC2 • Map N3 • 0870 243 9000*

7 Art
An intelligent comedy, this play by Yasmina Reza revolves around three friends. When one buys a white painting for 200,000 francs, the reaction it provokes exposes some unexpected truths about their friendships.
ⓢ *Wyndham's Theatre, Charing Cross Road WC2 • Map L2 • 020 7369 1746*

8 Chicago
The Bob Fosse hit, set in murderous Chicago, has been packing them in since it arrived from New York in 1998. Despite various changes in international star cast, the dancing and music remain excellent. ⓢ *Adelphi Theatre, Strand WC2 • Map M3 • 020 7344 0055*

9 An Inspector Calls
One of London's longest-running plays, *An Inspector Calls* was written by the Yorkshire playwright J.B. Priestley in 1945. This revival by Stephen Daldry highlights the play's excellence, and shows that it explores enough eternal truths to stand the test of time. ⓢ *Garrick Theatre, Charing Cross Road WC2 • Map L3 • 020 7494 5085*

10 Blood Brothers
A moving, if sentimental, musical by the Liverpudlian playwright Willy Russell. The story revolves around twins separated at birth – one who lives with his poor, natural, mother, the other with his mother's wealthy employer. The consequences when they eventually meet are both comic and tragic. ⓢ *Phoenix Theatre, Charing Cross Road WC2 • Map L2 • 020 7369 1733*

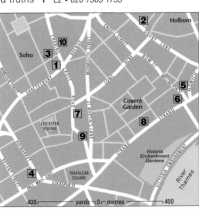

➜ *For more entertainment venues **See** pp56–7*

Left **Sign, George Inn** Right **Outside the George Inn**

⊡10 Pubs

1 The Lamb and Flag
This old-world establishment tucked up an alley looks much as it did in Charles Dickens' day. In the heart of Covent Garden, it can get crowded – during the summer drinkers spill outside into the quiet alley. The 17th-century poet John Dryden was severely beaten up outside the pub, which was known as the Bucket of Blood because of the bareknuckle fights held here *(see p104)*.

2 Dog and Duck
This small, tiled premises is like a cosy front room in the heart of Soho. The Dog and Duck has a tiny bar, where you might bump into art students and designers, and a blackboard with the latest selection of beers from all corners of England *(see p94)*.

Lamb and Flag, Covent Garden

Dog and Duck, Soho

3 Ye Olde Cheshire Cheese
In an alley off Fleet Street, this warren of rooms still seems as if it should have sawdust on the floors. Rebuilt in 1667, after the Great Fire of London, it was a favourite of Dr. Johnson *(see p52)* and other writers. Never too crowded, its intimate corners make a good meeting place, made cozier with fires in winter. ◈ *Wine Office Court EC4 • Map Q2*

4 George Inn
Built in 1676, this is the only galleried coaching inn left in London, and was taken over by the National Trust in 1937. You can enjoy the well-kept beers in its myriad old rooms, with lattice windows and wooden beams, or in the large courtyard *(see p86)*.

5 Jerusalem Tavern
A delightful little pub with cubicles, a small bar and little more than the 18th-century coffee shop it once was. People come here to try out the full range of a tiny but popular brewery, St. Peter's in Suffolk. Light meals are served at lunchtime. ◈ *55 Britton Street EC1 • Map G2*

6 Spaniards Inn

This lovely 16th-century pub north of Hampstead Heath, with a large, attractive beer garden, is steeped in history and romance: the 18th-century highwayman Dick Turpin drank here, along with literary luminaries Keats, Shelley and Byron *(see p145)*.

7 O'Hanlon's

A character pub near Exmouth Market in Clerkenwell is a great find: exotic antiques and casual furniture belie the true worth of its astonishing ales, which the landlord, John O'Hanlon, brews in South London. Inexpensive stews and pies keep the Irish pub tradition going. ◈ 8 Tysoe Street EC1 • Map F2

8 The Grapes

Built in the 1720s, with wooden floors and paneling, The Grapes has survived the modern development of Docklands, retaining its traditional charm and informal atmosphere. The back bar has an open fire and a terrace by the Thames and the excellent upstairs restaurant is renowned for its fish. ◈ 76 Narrow Street E14 • DLR Westferry

9 The Eagle

This large Victorian pub is popular, crowded and lively, with many coming here to eat the excellent, mainly Spanish-based, food. Portions are large and inexpensive, and can be washed down with a good selection of beer and wine *(see p76)*. ◈ 159 Farringdon Road EC1 • Tube Farringdon • No bookings

10 Freedom Brewing Co.

One of only a few brew-pubs in London, this is housed in a large, stylish, brick basement dominated by huge copper vats and pipework. The beer is about as fresh as it comes, and food in the restaurant is good, too. ◈ 41 Earlham Street WC2 • Map L2

Freedom Brewing Co. , Covent Garden

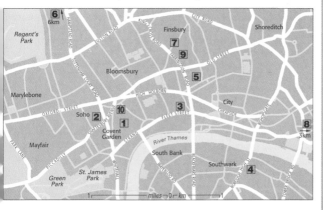

Left **Hamley's** Right **Harrods by night**

TOP 10 Shops and Markets

Liberty's mock-Tudor façade

1 Liberty
This handsome, half-timbered building dates from 1925 and its fine wood-floored and panelled interior is as much a part of the shopping experience as the exclusive goods it contains. Long associated with the Arts and Crafts movement, it employed artists such as William Morris to design its fabrics. Great for men's and women's fashions and original gifts *(see p110)*.

2 Fortnum and Mason
London's most elegant store has hardly noticed the arrival of the 21st century. The ground-floor food hall is famous for its traditional English produce, and lavish picnic hampers can be found, along with wines, in the basement. The upper floors sell well-made traditional British fashions and stylish gifts *(see p116)*.

3 Harrods
London's most famous and exclusive department store is more of an event than a shop. Covering seven bustling floors, it is full of extraordinary things to buy – from wild animals to pianos to children's racing cars – all with equally extraordinary prices. The food hall is rightly famous, and don't miss the tiled meat hall or basement pantry and cheese hall *(see p123)*.

4 Harvey Nichols
Almost a parody of itself, "Harvey Nicks" is where the glamorous shop. There's wall-to-wall designer labels, an extravagant perfume and beauty department and stylish home-ware. The fifth floor is for consuming, with a food hall, sushi bar and the to-be-seen-in Fifth Floor restaurant *(see p123)*.

5 Hamleys
The five stories of London's largest toyshop contain just about anything a child might want, from traditional puppets and games to giant stuffed toys, models, arts and crafts supplies and the latest electronic toys and gadgets. There are also plenty of delights here for the adult who hasn't managed to let go of their childhood *(see p110)*.

Playing with giant teddies, Hamley's

6 Portobello Road

West London's liveliest street starts off selling quality antiques, and continues through to bric-à-brac indoor galleries. As it heads north, there are food stalls, crafts, clothes and music. It is best on Saturday *(see p120)*.

7 Camden Market

A great place to spend a Saturday, this rambling market around Camden Lock takes in several streets and buildings. Street fashion, world crafts... it's as if the 1960s never ended. Sundays are a crush *(see p141)*.

8 Waterstone's Piccadilly

Claimed to be the largest bookshop in Europe, Waterstone's stocks a quarter of a million titles. There's a restaurant, cafés and bars *(see p116)*.

Antique shop, Portobello Road

9 John Lewis

This store has a large and loyal clientele, with departments ranging from kitchenware and haberdashery through furniture, fashion and fabrics to electrical goods. Staff are informed, prices are excellent and the quality is guaranteed *(see p132)*.

10 Tower Records

There is an exceptional range of music in this central store, including imports, vinyl and video. Classics and jazz on the first floor, literature in the basement. It stays open until midnight most of the week *(see p92)*.

Camden's indoor market

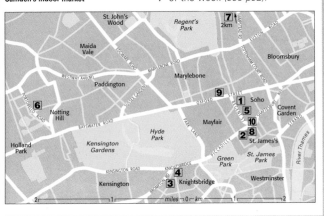

Left **Chelsea Flower Show** Right **Lord Mayor's Show**

Festivals and Events

1 Notting Hill Carnival
This three-day Caribbean festival is Europe's largest carnival, with steel bands and DJ's playing all imaginable kinds of music, street food, brilliant costumes and lively dancers. Children's parades on Sunday, grown-ups' on Monday. ⊗ Notting Hill W11 • Map A3 • Last Sat–Mon in Aug

2 Chelsea Flower Show
As much a society outing as a horticultural event, this is the Royal Horticultural Society's prestigious annual show. Beautiful and imaginative gardens are created especially for the event. ⊗ Chelsea Royal Hospital SW1 • Map C6 • Mid-May • Admission charge

Trooping the Color, Horse Guards Parade

3 Trooping the Color
The Queen celebrates her official birthday on Horse Guards Parade where troops of the Household Division, in their famous red tunics and bearskin hats, put on an immaculate display of marching and drilling before escorting her to Buckingham Palace. ⊗ Horse Guards Parade SW1 • Map L5 • Sat closest to 10 Jun

Extravagant costume, Notting Hill Carnival

4 BBC Promenade Concerts
The most extensive concert series in the world. The famous last concert is relayed live to adjacent Hyde Park, when Land of Hope and Glory rocks the Royal Albert Hall (see p120) to its foundations. ⊗ Royal Albert Hall SW1 • Map B5 • Mid-Jul–mid-Sept

5 Royal Academy Summer Exhibition
Around 1,000 works are selected from the public and academicians for the art world's most eclectic summer show. Works sell for as little as £100. ⊗ Piccadilly W1 • Map J4 • May–Aug • Admission charge

6 Lord Mayor's Show
Every year, the City of London elects a Lord Mayor who processes through the Square Mile in a gilded coach. Military bands, floats and city guildsmen in traditional costume go from Guildhall to the Law Courts. Evening fireworks. ⊗ City of London • Map R2 (Guildhall) • 2nd Sat in Nov

7 Guy Fawkes Night

Effigies of Guy Fawkes, who attempted to blow up parliament in 1605, are burned on bonfires across the country, with accompanying firework extravaganzas. Children make dummy Guys and ask for pennies to pay for their little arsenals. ◎ 5 Nov

8 Chinese New Year

Chinatown (see p87) is taken over by dancing dragons breathing fire during this vibrant, colorful festival. Food and craft stalls are authentically oriental. ◎ Soho W1 • Map L3 • Late Jan–early Feb

9 London Film Festival

Scores of international films are shown in this three-week festival when cinemas, including the National Film Theatre, reduce prices. A booth is set up in Leicester Square to take bookings and distribute programs.
◎ West End • Nov

10 Great British Beer Festival

Organized by the Campaign for Real Ale (CAMRA), this annual festival in a major west London exhibition hall is a chance to sample the best beers and ciders produced in Britain. ◎ Olympia W8 • Aug • Admission charge

Lord Mayor's Show fireworks

Top 10 Sports Events

1 Wimbledon Lawn Tennis Championship

The world's top grass-court championships. ◎ All England Lawn Tennis and Croquet Club, Wimbledon • Jun/Jul

2 London Marathon

42-km (26.3-mile) road race from Greenwich Park to Westminster. ◎ Apr

3 NatWest Trophy Final

The climax of the cricket season. ◎ Lord's NW8 • Jun

4 Oxford and Cambridge Boat Race

The two universities' annual rowing race covers some 6.5 km (4 miles) on the Thames. ◎ Putney to Mortlake • Mar

5 Horse of the Year Show

A six-day event puts show jumpers through their paces. ◎ Wembley Arena • Oct

6 Varsity Match

The Oxford-Cambridge rugby union duel. ◎ Twickenham Rugby Ground • Dec

7 Head of the River Race

A day-long event in which some 400 rowing boats struggle for supremacy. ◎ Mortlake to Putney • Mar

8 Six Nations Rugby

Annual rugby union contest with England, France, Ireland, Italy, Scotland and Wales. ◎ Twickenham Rugby Ground • Feb/Mar/Apr

9 Royal Ascot

All London Society goes to the races in top hats and other glamorous creations ◎ Ascot, Berkshire • Jun

10 Doggett's Coat and Badge

Guildsmen from the Company of Watermen compete in a single sculls race ◎ London Bridge to Chelsea Bridge • Jul

Left **London Zoo** Right **London Dungeon**

🔟 Children's London

1 Science Museum
See pp24–5.

2 Natural History Museum
See pp22–3.

3 Madame Tussaud's
One of London's most popular attractions, this is where you can see everyone from Arnold Schwarzenegger to the Queen. A Spirit of London ride takes you on a whistle-stop tour of the city's history. The famous Chamber of Horrors puts you face-to-face with London's most infamous criminals and has the very guillotine that beheaded Queen Marie Antoinette in the French Revolution. The next-door Planetarium has a 30-minute star show and two interactive exhibits unraveling the mysteries of space. Get there early to avoid the lines (see p129).

Waxwork Royalty, Madame Tussaud's

4 London Zoo
There's a full day out to be had in this 36-acre zoo. Home of the Zoological Society of London, the zoo emphasizes its important international role in conservation and research work. Its cages and enclosures have won awards, such as the aviary designed by Lord Snowdon. The children's zoo is full of things to do, with a pet care center, Animals in Action and Predatory Birds displays (see p129).

5 London Aquarium
Seven watery environments are spread across two floors in this engaging display. They range from freshwater ponds to coral reefs, mangrove swamps to deep mysterious oceans. Sit and watch the sharks and piranhas being fed, or pick up a crab or starfish in the hands-on tidal-pool exhibit (see p84).

Sharks, London Aquarium

6 London Trocadero
The Trocadero entertainment complex in the heart of the West End is a magnet for children. Aside from its shops, restaurants and movie theater, there is a stomach-lifting vertical drop ride, a bowling alley and a bewildering array of hi-tech video games and simulators that will keep them occupied for hours (see p91).

7 Museum of Childhood

Children are invited to spend the day at this East End museum, which has one of the largest toy collections in the world, including dolls, teddies, puppets, games and children's costumes. Activities are organized at weekends (see p154).

8 Coram's Fields

No adults admitted without a child, says the sign on the gate to this 7-acre park dedicated to small children. There's a wading pool, play areas and a city farm with a pets corner and grazing farm animals. ◈ 93 Guilford Street WC1 • Map F2 • Open daily • Free

9 Battersea Park

This large south London park is ideal for children. There are colorful gardens, an adventure playground, boating lake, deer enclosure and a children's zoo (see p150). ◈ Albert Bridge Road SW11 • Map D6 • Zoo: Open Easter to October, and weekends in Winter, Admission charge.

Doll's house, Museum of Childhood

10 London Dungeon

The scariest experience in town celebrates an "orgy of grisly entertainment", with death, torture and violence at every turn. Follow in the bloody footsteps of the Victorian serial killer Jack the Ripper, witness medieval murders, the 17th-century Fire of London, or go to your own execution on Judgment Day. Not for the fainthearted. ◈ 28 Tooley Street, SE1 • Map H4 • Open Apr–mid-July: 10am–5:30pm; mid-July–Aug: 10am–8pm; Sep–Mar: 10am–5:30pm • Admission charge

Entrance sign, London Dungeon

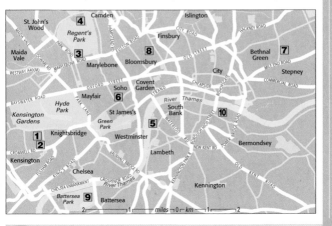

Left **Tower Bridge** Right **St. Katharine's Dock**

🔟 River Sights

1 Lambeth Palace
The Archbishop of Canterbury's official London residence dates from the 13th century, but it is the red-brick Tudor Gatehouse, from 1485, that gives it a distinctive appearance. ◈ *Lambeth Palace Road SE1 • Map F5 • Closed to the public, but tours of the garden given at 2pm Wed and Thu • Admission charge*

Tudor gatehouse, Lambeth Palace

2 Houses of Parliament
See pp34–5.

3 Savoy Hotel
London's first grand hotel was built in 1897. Its Chinese lacquered "ascending rooms" were the first elevators in Europe. Oscar Wilde objected to the newfangled built-in plumbing: he wanted to ring for his hot water like a gentleman.

Adjoining the hotel is the art nouveau Savoy Theatre, built on the site of the medieval Savoy Palace. ◈ *Strand WC2 • Map M3*

4 Millennium Bridge
This stunning, blade-like suspension bridge links Tate Modern on Bankside with St. Paul's and the City opposite. Unfortunately, this new footbridge suffered from excessive movement when it opened to a rush of pedestrians in 2000. Since closed, if new works go well, the bridge will reopen before the end of 2001. ◈ *Map R3*

5 Shakespeare's Globe
This modern reconstruction in oak, thatch and 36,000 handmade bricks is near the site of the original Globe Theatre, which burned down in 1613. The centre of the theatre is uncovered, so performances only happen during part of the year, but there is an interesting exhibition, plus a café and restaurant with river views *(see p83)*.

6 HMS Belfast
The last of the big-gun armored ships, *HMS Belfast* was built in 1938 and saw active service in World War II and Korea. In 1971 she was saved for the nation as an example

Rear of the Savoy Hotel, overlooking the Thames

of an early 20th-century British warship and opened as a museum. Visitors can tour the bridge, the huge engine rooms, the galley and the messdecks, where you get an idea of what life must have been like on board. ◈ *Morgan's Lane, Tooley St SE1 • Map H4 • Open Mar–Oct: 10am–6pm daily; Nov–Feb: 10am–5pm daily • Admission charge*

7 Tower Bridge
London's enduring landmark is a Gothic wonder. A masterly piece of civil engineering, the bridge was built in 1894 with steam pumps to raise its two halves. Guided tours include views from the top *(see p135)*.

8 St. Katharine's Dock
The first and most successful piece of modern Docklands development was this handsome dock beside Tower Bridge. Re-furbished in the 1980s, the area is surrounded by apartments, shops and cafés *(see p137)*.

Cutty Sark tea clipper, Greenwich

9 The Cutty Sark
Built in 1869, this is the last of the record-breaking tea-clippers that brought the leaves to thirsty London. On board you can see how the merchant seamen lived, and exhibits below decks show the history of sail and the Pacific trade routes. ◈ *King William Walk SE20 • Train to Greenwich; DLR Cutty Sark • Open 10am–5pm daily • Admission Charge*

10 Thames Flood Barrier
This huge barrier across the lower reaches of the Thames, just past Greenwich, was built in 1982 to prevent the dangerous combination of wind and tides from flooding the city. The Visitors' Center explains the problem, detailing a long history of flooding in London *(see p154)*.

Thames Flood Barrier

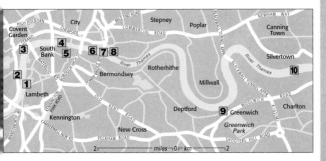

Left **Geoffrey Chaucer** Centre **Oscar Wilde** Right **Martin Amis**

🔟 Literary London

1 Samuel Pepys
The extraordinary Diary of Samuel Pepys (1633–1703) begins on New Year's Day, 1660 and ends on May 31, 1669. He vividly describes contemporary life, the Plague and Great Fire, and an attack on London by the Dutch. The work was written in short-hand and only deciphered in 1825.

2 Dr. Johnson
Samuel Johnson (1709–84) was a towering literary figure who presided over gatherings in pubs, coffee houses and literary clubs, as well as in his own home *(see p52)*, and had opinions on everything. His satirical poem, *London* (1738), attacked poverty in the city and his Parliamentary Sketches and Dictionary made him famous.

Engraving of Dr. Johnson

3 Geoffrey Chaucer
Chaucer (1343–1400) was a diplomat and son of a London vintner. His *Canterbury Tales* is a classic piece of English literature, and follows a group of pilgrims travelling from Southwark to Canterbury. In 17,000 lines the characters tell their rollicking tales.

Peter Ackroyd

4 Oscar Wilde
Dublin-born, Wilde (1854–1900) dazzled London audiences with his plays, and society with his wit. He fell from grace when he was convicted of homosexual activity. His plays, such as *Lady Windermere's Fan* (1892) and *The Importance of Being Earnest* (1895) are frequently revived.

5 Virginia Woolf
Woolf (1882–1941) and her sister Vanessa Bell lived in Gordon Square, where the influential pre-war Bloomsbury Group grew from social gatherings. She developed an impressionistic stream of consciousness in novels such as *Mrs. Dalloway* (1925) and *To The Lighthouse* (1927).

6 John Betjeman
A devoted Londoner, with a fine disdain for bureaucracy, mediocrity and hideous architecture, Betjeman (1906–84) was made Poet Laureate in 1972. His poems are full of gentle wit and humor and he remains one of Britain's favorite poets.

7 Colin MacInnes
MacInnes (1914–76) documented the teenage and black immigrant culture in Notting Hill in the 1950s. *City of Spades* (1957) and *Absolute Beginners* (1959) are set among the coffee bars, jazz clubs, drink and drugs scene at a time of great unrest.

8 Martin Amis
Darling of the London literary scene in the 1970s and 1980s, Amis (b.1949) had a famous literary father, Kingsley, and a precocious talent, having his first book, *The Rachael Papers* (1974), published at the age of 24. London has infused novels such as *Money* (1984) and *London Fields* (1989).

9 Zadie Smith
Her first novel, *White Teeth*, about Asian immigrants in north London, made Smith (b.1975) an overnight sensation in 1999. Wickedly funny, it has remarkably well-drawn portraits of London life.

10 Peter Ackroyd
The biographer of Charles Dickens, Ackroyd (b.1949) turned to fiction to examine the lives of other Londoners, such as the architect Nicholas Hawksmoor and Oscar Wilde. Most ambitiously, he wrote *London: a Biography* (2000).

Zadie Smith

Top 10 London Songs

1 London's Burning
Commemorating the Great Fire of 1666, this is sung in a round, a device popular since Elizabethan days.

2 London Bridge is Falling Down
A traditional song about old London Bridge, which fell into disrepair.

3 Oranges and Lemons
"...say the bells of St. Clement's". This children's song rhymes City churches, and is sung as part of a game.

4 Maybe It's Because I'm a Londoner
The theme song of music-hall duo, Chesney and Allen, it became a patriotic comfort in 1940s' wartime London.

5 The Lambeth Walk
Made popular by the musical *Me and My Girl* in the 1930s, this has been a Cockney favorite ever since.

6 London Pride
An uncharacteristically sentimental song that celebrates the city.

7 England Swings
This hit song came out after a 1966 story in *Time* magazine announced the arrival of "Swinging London".

8 Waterloo Sunset
Pop groups don't usually celebrate London, or Britain, but this 1960s record by The Kinks was an exception.

9 A Nightingale Sang in Berkeley Square
A standard sung by Frank Sinatra and others, it is actually very unusual to hear nightingales in central London.

10 Burlington Bertie
A music-hall song about the life of a Mayfair gentleman in Edwardian London.

For famous London residents See pp52–3

Left **Battersea Park** Right **Thames path, South Bank**

🔟 London on Foot

1 Thames Path, South Bank
Start by the London Eye and walk along the South Bank downstream to London Bridge and the Design Museum beyond Butler's Wharf. This stretch of the Thames Path has enough to distract you all day. ✆ South Bank • Map N5

2 Regent's Canal
It's possible to walk along the whole 8.5-mile (14-km) canal from Paddington to Limehouse. The most accessible part lies between Camden Lock and Regent's Park, where grand houses back on to the water. Further on, in Little Venice, moored "narrowboats" are owned by the wealthy (see p130).

Houseboat, Regents Canal

3 Richmond
Richmond has a lovely aspect on the River Thames. Apart from its royal park (see p29) there is a lot to see and do, with riverside pubs and cafés, and boats to rent. It's a half-hour walk along the towpath to the 17th-century Ham House, owned by the National Trust. In summer you can take a ferry across to Marble Hill House in Twickenham (see p148).

View over London from Hampstead Heath

4 Hampstead Heath
This green grandstand overlooking the city covers 3 sq miles (8 sq km) and is a rural mix of meadows, woods, lakes and ponds for both swimming and fishing. Head off in any direction, and make the Spaniards Inn (see p145) or Kenwood House a stopping-off point (see p142).

5 Hyde Park and Kensington Gardens
Central London's largest green area can tire out any walker. It takes about an hour and a half to walk around, but there are plenty of diversions, from the sculptures by Henry Moore, to cafés, fountains and flower gardens (see p28). ✆ Hyde Park W2 • Map C4 • Open 5am–midnight daily

6 Battersea Park
This lively park is not just for children (see p69). It has a pleasant riverside promenade beside a Buddhist Peace Pagoda, lakeside walks and the Festival Gardens (see p150).

7 Wimbledon Common

It is easy to get lost in this wild public space. Start by the Windmill and go down to Queens Mere Pond or stride out along the cinder horse track to the pine copse of Caesar's Camp, an old Iron Age hill fort *(see p150)*.

8 Blackheath

This treeless expanse, enjoyed by kite flyers, lies behind Greenwich Park *(see p29)*. Donkey rides can be taken around the edge, and on the far side is Blackheath Village. ⊗ *Blackheath SE3 • Train to Blackheath*

9 Wetland Centre

London's major bird sanctuary covers 105 acres in four disused Victorian reservoirs. It has trails, a visitor center and an observatory where you can spot some of the 130 species which come here *(see p150)*.

10 Highgate Cemetery

Filled with grand tombs, many of the rich and famous, this is the best of London's cemeteries. The living have to pay to get in, too, and the cemetery is divided into eastern and western halves, the latter visitable only with a tour *(see p143)*.

Faded grandeur, Highgate Cemetery

Top 10 Outdoor Activities

1 Rowing
Parks with rowing lakes include Hyde Park, Regent's Park and Battersea Park.

2 Ice Skating
The Leisurebox in Queensway is the main indoor venue. Broadgate Ice Rink in the City is an outdoor winter rink.

3 Kite Flying
Hampstead Heath, Primrose Hill and Blackheath are the best places to get a lift.

4 Swimming
There are a number of public indoor pools. ⊗ The *Oasis, Endell Street WC2 • Porchester Baths, Queensway W2 • Chelsea Sports Centre, Chelsea Manor St SW3*

5 Nature Watching
London's open spaces and woodlands are full of plants and wildlife to discover.

6 Skateboarding
Many parks have skateboard facilities. The South Bank's *(see p83)* concrete spaces have a regular clientele.

7 Cycling
Rent bikes from Bikepark in Fulham *(020 7731 7012)* and The London Bicycle Tour Company in Gabriel's Wharf *(020 7928 6838)*.

8 Tennis
For indoors try Islington Tennis Centre, Market Rd N7. Outdoors, Holland Park, Battersea Park or Regent's Park.

9 Skating
With wide paths, Hyde Park is the most popular place to rollerblade.

10 Horse Riding
The best place is the stables at Hyde Park. ⊗ *63 Bathurst Mews W2.*

For royal parks and gardens **See pp28–9**

Left **The People's Palace** Right **Clarke's**

🔟 Best Places to Eat

1 The Sugar Club

"Pacific fusion" is the idea behind New Zealander Peter Gordon's restaurant, but really every dish scrambles – with great success – to combine the most exciting tastes from all over the world. Desserts are particularly impressive. The modern wood decor is as stylish as the restaurant's clientele *(see p95)*.

2 Clarke's

A steady favorite since it opened in 1984, the food here is wonderfully fresh, and basically Mediterranean, with roast and baked dishes to the fore. Set menus mean you have to go with the patronne's taste, but she will take you to places you have not been before. The wine list favors California *(see p125)*.

Clarke's restaurant, Notting Hill

3 Rasa Samudra

Indian curries are almost a national dish in Britain, but this is quite different from the norm. The cooking is stunning, and first-timers will need talking through the unusual menu, which includes delicious fish dishes *(see p111)*.

Sugar Club, West End

4 Club Gascon

Inspired Gallic cooking means you need to make reservations a few weeks in advance. The original idea here is that there are no starter or main courses. Dishes are categorised under half a dozen themed headings, and you put together three of four to make a meal. Each one is a rare combination *(see p139)*.

5 The Eagle

This converted Victorian pub on the edge of the City was the first of London's "gastropubs". Serving high-quality Mediterranean-style cuisine from an open kitchen, it is informal and always busy. The menu largely comprises substantial mains *(see p63)*.

6 Nobu

You don't have to wear Prada or Gucci here, but you will feel more at home if you do. This is the style gurus' hang-out, where impeccable taste ranges from the oak and maple parquet tables to the fabulous Japanese food. Sushi is served in lacquered bowls, sake is served in bamboo flasks. You don't need to make reservations for the sushi bar *(see p117)*.

7 Orrery

Sir Terence Conran is London's most prominent restaurateur. This intimate restaurant is at the peak of perfection and prices. The short menu changes regularly, and is Modern European with a French bias – including the best fish, beef and game *(see p133)*.

8 Rules

London's oldest restaurant (1798), Rules has a wonderful, genuine Belle Epoque atmosphere, and remains a great British institution, not resting on its laurels. It specializes mainly in game – much of it from the northern estates of its owner, John Mayhew *(see p105)*.

9 Wagamama

This basement restaurant is the original of a chain of modern Asian eating houses, offering fast, efficient service. Inexpensive Japanese dishes are served cafeteria-style, with diners eating side-by-side *(see p111)*.

10 St. John

A great restaurant near Smithfield meat market, this is in a converted smokehouse. It serves tasty variations of offal, tripe, tongue, heart and other traditional British dishes which 21st-century Londoners find rather daring. Bar-menu snacks are not expensive *(see p139)*.

Wagamama

Top 10 Places to Eat with a View

1 Oxo Tower
Terrific river views from this South Bank landmark *(see p87)*.

2 Vertigo 42
On the 42nd floor of the City's tallest skyscraper. ◎ *Tower 42, Old Broad St EC2 • Map H3 • 020 7877 7842*

3 The People's Palace
Picture windows look over the river from the Royal Festival Hall's restaurant *(see p87)*.

4 Tate Modern Café: Level 7
Panoramic river views. Changing lunch, afternoon and dinner menus. ◎ *Bankside SE1 • Map R4 • 020 7401 5020*

5 The Portrait
Views over Trafalgar Square and Whitehall. ◎ *National Portrait Gallery, St. Martin's Pl WC2 • Map L4 • 020 7312 2490*

6 Blue Print Café
A breezy restaurant with a spectacular view of London Bridge. ◎ *Butler's Wharf SE1 • Map H4 • 020 7378 7031*

7 The Bridge
A modern brasserie just by the Millennium Bridge. ◎ *1 Paul's Walk EC4 • Map G3 • 020 7236 0000*

8 Shakespeare's Globe
Look over to the City through mullioned windows. ◎ *New Globe Walk SE1 • Map G4 • 020 7902 1576*

9 Top Floor at Smiths of Smithfield
Above a vast warehouse, the dining room has lofty rooftop views *(see p139)*.

10 Coq d'Argent
Fine City sights from this rooftop garden bar and French restaurant. ◎ *1 Poultry EC2 • Map G3 • 020 7395 5000*

For more restaurants **See pp87, 95, 105, 111, 117, 125, 133, 139, 145, 151, 157**

AROUND TOWN

LONDON'S TOP 10

Left **Houses of Parliament** Right **Shakespeare's Globe**

Westminster, the South Bank and Southwark

HERE THERE IS A RICH MIX *of things to do. Sights range from Westminster Abbey and the Houses of Parliament to the Tate's stunning art institutions, the South Bank Complex and Shakespeare's Globe. In between there's the spectacular London Eye and other entertainments around County Hall, former headquarters of the Greater London Council. Two new footbridges due to open – one at Hungerford Bridge, the other at Tate Modern – will help to bring the two sides of the river together.*

🔟 Sights

1	Westminster Abbey	6	Downing Street
2	Tate Modern	7	Cabinet War Rooms
3	London Eye	8	South Bank Complex
4	Houses of Parliament	9	Shakespeare's Globe
5	Tate Britain	10	Imperial War Museum

Statue of Queen Boadicea, near Westminster station

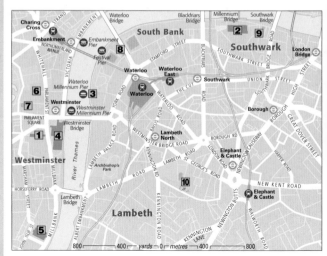

View down Whitehall towards Big Ben

Westminster Abbey
1 London's most venerable and most beautiful church, the scene of coronations and royal weddings and the resting place of monarchs *(see pp32–3)*.

Tate Modern
2 One of the world's great contemporary art galleries. The free Art Bus runs every 20 minutes from nearby Sumner Street to the National Gallery and Tate Britain *(see pp18–19)*.

London Eye
3 The highest observational wheel in the world, offering breathtaking views of the city and beyond. While waiting for a flight, visit the attractions in nearby County Hall – London Aquarium, Namco Station and Dalí Museum *(see pp16–7 and p84)*.

Houses of Parliament
4 The ancient Palace of Westminster is the seat of the two Houses of Parliament – the Lords and the Commons. A Union flag flies on the Victoria Tower when the House of Commons is in session. Night sittings are indicated by a light on the Clock Tower – the tower that houses Big Ben, the 14-ton bell whose hourly chimes are recognized throughout the world *(see pp34–5)*.

Tate Britain
5 The best of British art is held at the Tate and works range from 1500 to the present. Look downstream to see the home of British Intelligence (MI5). This large building, known as Thames House, is built inside a bug-proof "Faraday cage" *(see pp20–21)*.

View from London Eye towards Big Ben and Westminster Abbey

6 Downing Street

The official home and office of Britain's Prime Minister is one of four surviving houses built in 1680 for Sir George Downing (1623–84) who went to America as a boy and returned to fight for the Parliamentarians in the English Civil War. The building contains a State Dining Room and the Cabinet Room, where a group of 20 senior government ministers meets regularly to formulate policy. Next door, No. 11, is the traditional residence of the Chancellor of the Exchequer. Downing Street has been closed to the public for security reasons since 1989. ⊗ *Downing Street SW1 • Map L5 • Closed to public*

No 10 Downing Street

7 Cabinet War Rooms

During the dark days of World War II, Winston Churchill and his War Cabinet met in these rooms beneath the Government Treasury Chambers. They have been kept just as they were left in 1945, with sandbags piled up outside and color-coded phones.

Whitehall and Horse Guards

The wide street connecting Parliament Square and Trafalgar Square takes its name from the Palace of Whitehall built for Henry VIII in 1532. The palace was guarded on the north side at what is now Horse Guards, where the guard is still mounted every morning at 11am (10am on Sundays), with a dismounting inspection at 4pm.

Take a guided audio tour through the rooms where ministers and military leaders plotted the course of the war as bombs fell overhead. ⊗ *Clive Steps, King Charles Street SW1 • Map L6 • Open Apr–Sep: 9:30am–5:15pm daily; Oct– Mar: 10am–5:15pm daily • Admission charge*

8 South Bank Complex

The most accessible arts centre in London still has the air of friendly, egalitarian optimism that brought it into life in the 1950s and 60s. The Royal Festival Hall's three concert halls have diverse programs, while the Hayward Gallery is a major venue for large art exhibitions. The National Film Theatre, run by the British Film Institute, puts on a full program of movies. The Royal National Theatre's three theatres (Olivier, Cottesloe and Lyttleton) are further east along the riverside *(see p56)*. ⊗ *South Bank Centre SE1 • Map N4*

Left **Cabinet War Rooms** Right **Hayward Gallery**

Exhibits in the Imperial War Museum

9 Shakespeare's Globe

To see a Shakespeare play at the reconstructed Globe is a magical experience. Seated in three tiers, open to the skies, the audience is encouraged to heckle and shout as they did in Shakespeare's day. Except when a matinee is playing, visitors to the exhibition next door are given guided tours of the theatre by staff *(see p70)*. ✪ *New Globe Walk, Bankside SE1 • Map R4 • Bookings: 020 7401 9919 • Exhibition/theatre tour: May–Sep: 9am–noon daily; Oct–Apr: 10am–5pm daily • Admission charge*

10 Imperial War Museum

It is well worth the effort to visit this museum, which documents the social effects of war as much as the technology involved in fighting it, with displays on food rationing, censorship, air-raid precautions and morale-boosting strategies. Concerned mainly with conflicts in the 20th century to the present, it has changing exhibitions and an excellent shop that will appeal to those with a nostalgia for wartime London *(see p45)*. ✪ *Lambeth Road SE1 • Map F5 • Open 10am–6pm daily • Admission charge (free after 4:30pm)*

A Day By the River

Morning

🕐 Start at Waterloo with breakfast and a self-guided tour of the Marriott Hotel, based in the splendid former headquarters of the Greater London Council. Cross Westminster Bridge to visit **Westminster Abbey** *(see pp32–3)* and nearby St. Margaret's Church.

Continue along Abingdon Street to Lambeth Bridge and re-cross the river. Before visiting **Lambeth Palace** *(see p70)* have a coffee at the delightful little café at Lambeth Pier. Walk along the Albert Embankment for a stunning view of the **Houses of Parliament** *(see p81)* across the river.

For lunch, you might like to try the Japanese restaurant YO! Sushi or the innovative **fish!** *(see p87)*. Both are in Belvedere Road, behind the London Eye.

Afternoon

Walk along the embankment to the **South Bank Complex**, browsing the second-hand bookstalls outside the National Film Theatre. Continue past the craft shops of **Gabriel's Wharf** *(see p85)* to the **Oxo Tower's** *(see p84)* designer galleries just beyond and take the lift to the tower's viewing platform for a great view of the city.

Afterwards, head along the embankment to **Tate Modern** *(see pp18–19)* – a wonderful place to spend the rest of the afternoon. Have tea with more views in the **Café: Level 7** *(see p77)*. Further downriver, the **Anchor** pub *(see p86)* is a good place to relax and have dinner.

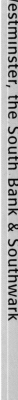

Around Town – Westminster, the South Bank & Southwark

Left **County Hall building** Right **Oxo Tower**

🔟 The Best of the Rest

1 Clink Exhibition
London's first prison now houses a small exhibition devoted to crime and punishment. ◈ *1 Clink Street SE1 • Map G4 • Open 10am–6pm daily • Admission charge*

2 London Aquarium
See sharks and rays swim among recreated reef and ocean environments at one of Europe's largest aquariums *(see p68)*. ◈ *County Hall SE1 • Map N6 • Open 10am–6pm daily • Admission charge*

3 Dalí Universe
A permanent exhibition of 500 works by the great Spanish surrealist Salvador Dalí (1904–89). ◈ *County Hall SE1 • Map N6 • Open 10am–5:30pm daily • Admission charge*

4 BFI London IMAX
Giant-screen theater that shows exciting movies set in the natural world. ◈ *South Bank SE1 • Map N4 • Open daily (screening times vary) • Admission charge*

5 Namco Station
Popular with children, this center has arcade games, bumper cars and a bowling alley. ◈ *County Hall SE1 • Map N6 • Open 10am–midnight*

6 Florence Nightingale Museum
Fascinating museum devoted to the life and work of 19th-century nurse, Florence Nightingale. ◈ *2 Lambeth Palace Road SE1 • Map N6 • Open 10am–5pm Mon–Fri, 11:30am–4:30pm Sat & Sun • Admission charge*

7 Golden Hinde
A replica of the ship in which Sir Francis Drake circumnavigated the world from 1577 to 1580. ◈ *St. Mary Overie Dock SE1 • Map G4 • Open 9am–sunset daily • Admission charge*

8 The Long View of London
A day in the life of London Bridge in just eight minutes, plus a variety of displays about London and the City. ◈ *Montague Close SE1 • Map G4 • Open 10am–6pm Mon–Sat, 11am–5pm Sun • Admission charge*

9 Rose Theatre Exhibition
A sound-and-light show tells the history of this Shakespearian theatre, the first to be built in Southwark, in 1587. ◈ *56 Park Street SE1 • Map G4 • Open 10am–5pm daily • Admission charge*

10 Oxo Tower
For great city views, take a lift to the small free public viewing gallery next to the restaurant at the top *(see p77)*. Check out the designer shops and galleries on the first and second floors. ◈ *Bargehouse Street SE1 • Map P4 • Open daily*

Left **Gabriel's Wharf**, Centre **Signs, South Bank centre** Right **Llewellyn Alexander art gallery**

🔟 Shopping

1 Parliamentary Bookshop
Buy the day's political reading, plus parliamentary-related prints and other souvenirs. ◎ *1 Parliament SW1 • Map L6*

2 Lower Marsh
Once London's longest street market, stalls sell inexpensive music, clothes, hardware and food. Open mornings Mon–Fri. ◎ *Lower Marsh SE1 • Map P6*

3 Llewellyn Alexander
This art gallery has changing, quality exhibitions, notably in the summer. ◎ *124 The Cut SE1 • Map Q5 • Open 10am–7:30pm Mon–Sat • Free*

4 South Bank
Free concerts are held at both the Royal Festival Hall and the Royal National Theatre. Both have shops selling books and music and there are secondhand books stalls under Waterloo Bridge. ◎ *South Bank SE1 • Map N4*

5 Gabriel's Wharf
Shops in riverside Gabriel's wharf display hand-painted glassware, fashion, interiors, jewellery and ceramics. ◎ *56 Upper Ground SE1 • Map P4*

6 Bankside Gallery
The gallery for the Royal Watercolour Society and Royal Society of Painter-Printmakers has work for sale, as well as a shop. ◎ *48 Hopton Street SE1 • Map R4 • Open 10am–8pm Tue, 10am–5pm Wed–Fri, 1–5pm Sun • Admission charge*

7 Oxo Tower Wharf
Two floors are given over to designers of fashion, jewelry and interiors and "the.gallery@ oxo" paintings, photography and ceramics. ◎ *Bargehouse Street SE1 • Map P4 • Open daily*

8 The Furniture Union
Have a browse through the latest in British interior design in trendy Bankside Lofts opposite Tate Modern. ◎ *Bankside Lofts, 65a Hopton Street SE1 • Map R4*

9 Vinopolis
Wines can be tried out on a tour of this exhibition of viticulture, and the shop stocks over a thousand varieties. ◎ *1 Bank End SE1 • Map G4 • Open 11am–6pm Mon–Fri, 11am–8pm Sat, 11am–6pm Sun • Admission charge*

10 Borough Market
Good food from all over the country comes to this traditional covered market near Southwark Cathedral. Try some cheeses, breads, chocolate and local beer. ◎ *8 Southwark Street SE1 • Map R4 • Open noon–6pm Fri, 9am–4pm Sat*

For more on shopping **See p170**

Left **Pub, The Anchor** Right **Young Vic theatre Café**

TOP 10 Pubs and Cafés

1 Westminster Arms and Storey's Wine Bar
Parliament has its own busy bars and canteens, but you might see a politician in the Big Ben Bar at this nearby pub, or in the basement wine bar next door. ✎ *9 Storeys Gate SW1 • Map L6*

2 Footstool
In the basement of St. John's, Smith Square, this is a good spot for a lunchtime snack. ✎ *St John's, Smith Square SW1 • Map E5*

3 Fire Station
This cavernous former fire station is a popular bar and restaurant. Close to Waterloo Station. ✎ *150 Waterloo Road SE1 • Map P5*

4 Young Vic Café
The Konditor & Cook bar-restaurant at the Young Vic theatre is open all day and acts as the theatre bar during performances. It offers an innovative menu and the chance of spotting a star. ✎ *66 The Cut SE1 • Map Q5*

5 The Anchor at Bankside
Snug, old English pub with tables outside in summer. The dining room upstairs serves traditional English food. ✎ *34 Park Street SE1 • Map Q4*

6 Vinopolis Wine Wharf
The bar of this modern temple to viticulture has a vast wine list plus 20 varieties of champagne served by the glass. ✎ *Stoney Street SE1 • Map G4*

7 Globe Café at Shakespeare's Globe
Wonderfully located café on the first floor of this handsomely restored Shakespearian theatre building, with a fine view of St. Paul's *(see p83)*. ✎ *New Globe Walk SE1 • Map R4*

8 Market Porter
A popular, historic market pub. Open for traders and all-night ravers from 6–8:30 am. ✎ *9 Stoney Street SE1 • Map G4*

9 Borough Café
One of the few remaining workmen's cafés in central London, where friendly waitresses serve hearty "fry-ups" and industrial-strength cups of tea. ✎ *11 Park Street SE1 • Map G4*

10 George Inn
London's only surviving galleried coaching inn is a maze of plain, wood-paneled rooms and upstairs bars. Bar meals are served at lunchtime – à la carte menu in the evenings. Courtyard tables are pleasant in summer. ✎ *57 Borough High St SE1 • Map G4*

Turkish restaurant, Tas

Price Categories

For a three-course meal for one with half a bottle of wine (or equivalent meal), taxes and extra charges.

£	under £15
££	£15–£25
£££	£25–£35
££££	£35–£50
£££££	over £50

🔟 Restaurants

1 The Cinnamon Club
Innovative Indian cuisine served in comfortable, clublike premises. ⊗ *The Old Westminster Library, Great Smith Street SW1 • Map E5 • 020 7517 9898 • ££££*

2 Atrium
This light, airy restaurant serves such modern European dishes as risotto and Thai noodles. There is also a tempting selection of desserts. A good place to spot political faces. ⊗ *4 Millbank SW1 • Map E6 • 020 7233 0032 • ££££*

3 People's Palace
Spacious restaurant with linen-draped tables and picture windows overlooking the Thames. Modern European food and attentive service. ⊗ *Level 3 Royal Festival Hall SE1 • Map N4 • 020 7928 9999 • lunch and pre-concert menus• £££*

4 Chez Gerard
Between Waterloo Station and the London Eye, this is one of a chain of French restaurants whose simple steak and fries are unbeatable. ⊗ *The White House 9 Belvedere Road SE1 • Map N5 • 020 7202 8470 • £££*

5 Livebait
Opposite the Young Vic theatre, this is one of a chain of modern fish restaurants. If you can't decide on a main course, go for variety with two starters. ⊗ *43 The Cut SE1 • Map P5 • 020 7928 7211 • Lunch and pre- and post-theatre menus • £££*

6 Tas
Two branches of an exciting, modern, yet inexpensive Turkish restaurant. ⊗ *33 The Cut SE1. Map P5. 020 7928 2111 • 72 Borough High St SE1. Map G4. 020 7403 7277 • ££*

7 Gourmet Pizza Company
A range of pizza toppings is offered at this wonderful riverside shack. ⊗ *Gabriel's Wharf SE1 • Map P4 • 020 7928 3188 • £*

8 Oxo Tower Restaurant Bar and Brasserie
Delicious modern dishes are served in the restaurant. The bar has live jazz *(see p77)*. ⊗ *Oxo Tower Wharf SE1 • Map G4 • 020 7803 3888 • ££££ • Brasserie: ££*

9 Cantina Vinopolis
Huge, vaulted dining room serving excellent French-Italian food. ⊗ *1 Bank End SE1 • Map P4 • 020 7940 8333 • £££*

🔟 fish!
Innovative fish dishes served in modern, stylish restaurants. ⊗ *Cathedral St SE1. Map G4 • 3b Belvedere Rd SE1. Map N5 • 020 7234 3333 • £££*

Left **Fountain, Trafalgar Square** Center **Old Compton Street** Right **Leicester Square statue**

Soho and the West End

LONDON'S WEST END *is where everyone heads for a night out.* Clubbers from outside London catch the last trains into the capital and head for its bars and music venues, knowing they won't leave till dawn. Here are the great theatres of Shaftesbury Avenue and Charing Cross Road, the star-struck movie theaters of Leicester Square and, at its heart, Soho, abuzz with activity as the night wears on. But it's not all for the night owl – Trafalgar Square has the National Gallery, the National Portrait Gallery and free lunchtime concerts at St. Martin-in-the-Fields.

🔟 Sights

1. National Gallery
2. National Portrait Gallery
3. Trafalgar Square
4. Piccadilly Circus
5. Chinatown
6. Soho Square
7. Old Compton Street
8. Berwick Street Market
9. London Trocadero
10. Rock Circus

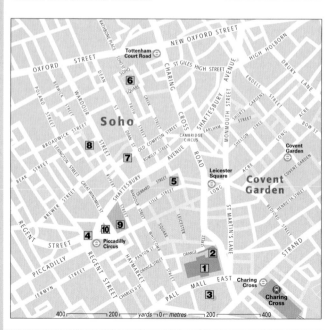

Statue of Eros, Piccadilly Circus

National Gallery
See pp12–13.

National Portrait Gallery
See pp14–15.

Trafalgar Square
Trafalgar Square – once the royal mews – is a hub of the West End and a venue for public rallies and events. From the top of a 165-ft (50-m) column, Admiral Lord Nelson, who famously defeated the French at the Battle of Trafalgar in 1805, looks down Whitehall towards the Houses of Parliament. The column is guarded at its base by four huge lions – the work of Edwin Landseer. On the north side of the square is the National Gallery *(see pp12–13)* and the church of St.-Martin-in-the-Fields *(see p46)* while, to the southwest, Admiralty Arch leads to Buckingham Palace. ⊗ *WC2* • *Map L4*

Piccadilly Circus
Designed by John Nash as a junction in Regent Street, the Circus is the endpoint of the street called Piccadilly. Its Eros statue – erected as a memorial to the Earl of Shaftesbury – is a familiar London landmark and a popular meeting place. Piccadilly Circus is also renowned for its neon advertising displays, which mark the entrance to the city's entertainment district. On the south side of the Circus is the Criterion Theatre, next to Lillywhite's – a leading London sporting-goods store. ⊗ *W1* • *Map K3*

Chinatown
Ornate oriental archways in Gerrard Street mark the entrance to Chinatown, an area of London that has, since the 1950s, been the focus of the capital's Chinese residents. Here you can shop at Chinese supermarkets, gift shops and martial arts suppliers and, on Sundays, browse the street stalls selling exotic vegetables. The Chinese New Year, celebrated in late January or early February, is a particular highlight. Chinatown abounds with excellent-value restaurants. ⊗ *Streets around Gerrard Street, W1* • *Map L3*

Left **Admiralty Arch** Right **Chinese dragon, Chinatown**

6 Soho Square

This pleasant square, spiked with palms, is popular at lunchtime, after work and at weekends, when there's always a friendly atmosphere, especially in summer. With the most fashionable address in London, many of the square's buildings are now occupied by movie companies. On the north side is a church built for French Protestants under a charter granted by Edward VI in 1550. The redbrick St. Patrick's, on the east side, sometimes has music recitals. On the corner of Greek Street is the House of St. Barnabas in Soho, a charitable foundation in an 18th-century building which is occasionally open to visitors. ◈ Map K2

7 Old Compton Street

The main street in Soho is a lively thoroughfare both day and night. It is also the center of London's sex scene, and now the site of popular gay pubs, the Compton and the Admiral Duncan. Soho's vibrant streetlife spills into Frith, Greek and Wardour streets, where pubs, clubs, restaurants and cafés have pavement tables, often warmed by gas heaters in winter. Some, like Bar Italia in

Mock-Tudor shed, Soho Square

Nelson's Column

The centerpiece of Trafalgar Square, this huge column is topped by a statue of Horatio, Viscount Nelson (1758–1805). Britain's great naval hero was fatally shot at his hour of greatest triumph, the drubbing of the French and Spanish fleets off Cape Trafalgar, southern Spain. His lasting affair with vivacious Emma Hamilton added to his romantic image.

Frith Street, are open 24 hours, and even the Alpha One fish-and-chip shop at 43 Old Compton Street is open until one or two in the morning. Everywhere fills up when the evening's performance at the Prince Edward Theatre ends. A delicious breakfast is to be had at Patisserie Valerie, and such long-standing shops as the Italian delicatessen I Camisi, and the Vintage House (700 whiskies in stock), give the area its village feel. Body tattooists are at work here, and fetish shops show that the sex industry still flourishes. ◈ Map L2

8 Berwick Street Market

There has been a market here since the 18th century, and the daily fruit and vegetable stalls remain cheap, cheerful and thoroughly Cockney. Half the

Left **Old Compton Street** Right **Berwick Street Market**

Bar Italia, Frith Street

time, traders talk in old money ("ten bob" is 50p) and round things up to a "nicker" or a "quid" (£1). It opens around 9am six days a week. ◈ *Map K2*

9 London Trocadero

Take the escalator to the top of Funland and make your way down through this electronic jungle of video games and virtual-reality rides. There are bumper cars, a racetrack simulator and a bowling alley. Themed restaurants, bars, shops and cinemas fill up the space, as well as an HMV record store. The Planet Hollywood restaurant is next door. ◈ *Piccadilly Circus W1 • Map K3 • 10am–1am daily*

10 Rock Circus

Strictly for pop and rock fans who want to come face to face with waxwork effigies of their rock and roll idols, Rock Circus is run by Madame Tussauds *(see p129)*. See the Sex Pistols, posed on London's trendy Carnaby Street; join Madonna on a video shoot; see Bob Marley in his recording studio; and go to an aftershow party with the Spice Girls. ◈ *1 Piccadilly Circus W1 • Map K3 • Open 10am–5:30pm daily (11am–5:30pm Mon, Tue) • Admission charge*

A Walk Around the West End

Morning

🕐 Start the day in **Trafalgar Square** *(see p89)* at 10am when the fountains are switched on. You could spend a day at the **National Gallery** *(see pp12–13)*, but limit yourself to an hour, perhaps just visiting the Sainsbury Wing.

☕ For coffee, head next door to the Portrait Restaurant at the **National Portrait Gallery** *(see pp14–15)*. It has fine views over Trafalgar Square.

Head up Charing Cross Road to Leicester Square. Note the statues of Shakespeare and Charlie Chaplin in the middle of the square. Continue towards the bright lights of **Piccadilly Circus** *(see p89)* and the famous statue of Eros, and then walk up Shaftesbury Avenue, centre of the city's theatre district. Turn off here into bustling **Chinatown** *(see p89)*, with its colorful shops and restaurants.

🍴 Lunch in Chinatown is obligatory. Enjoy the bustle of the Golden Dragon on Gerrard Street, or the calm of the excellent Joy King Lau in Leicester Street, just off Lisle Street.

Afternoon

Give the afternoon over to colourful and lively **Soho**. Eat a peach right off the stall in **Berwick Street Market**, then stroll up Wardour Street, home of the movie industry. Reward yourself with tea and a slice of cake at **Patisserie Valerie** *(see p94)* in **Old Compton Street**.

Left **Façade, Algerian Coffee House** Right **Coffee makers, Algerian Coffee House**

10 Shopping

1 Ann Summers
When in Soho, you have to do something naughty. Ann Summers sex shops have been around so long they seem quite tame – but their products really are rather risqué. ◈ 79 Wardour Street W1 • Map K3

2 Merc
A Carnaby Street classic, fans may still buy clothes cut from original 1960s patterns here. ◈ 10 Carnaby Street W1 • Map J3

3 Foyles
In a street of bookshops, this grandmother of all bookshops is something of an institution. A vast range of subject matter is covered. ◈ 113–19 Charing Cross Road WC2 • Map L2

4 Tower Records
This large record store is open until midnight every day except Sunday, when it closes at 6pm. ◈ 1 Piccadilly Circus W1 • Map K3

5 Milroy's Whisky
A West End whisky specialist, Milroy's has a small bar where single malts can be sampled. ◈ 3 Greek Street W1 • Map L2

6 Contemporary Ceramics
The best of British ceramics, made by members of the Craftsmen Potters Association, are on sale here. Prices are reasonable and the work is bright, original and inspiring. ◈ 7 Marshall Street W1 • Map K2

7 Anything Left-Handed
Scissors, clocks, books, boomerangs – this store shows what a right-handed world we live in. All left-handed people should find something here. ◈ 57 Brewer Street W1 • Map K3

8 Fratelli Camisa
One of London's best-known delicatessens, famous for its fresh pasta, this is like stepping into a 1950s Italian grocery store. ◈ 61 Old Compton Street W1 • Map K3

9 Algerian Coffee House
Opened in 1887, this is one of the oldest shops in Soho. It exudes a wonderful aroma of the many kinds of coffee it sells. Speciality teas and herbal infusions can also be bought here. ◈ 52 Old Compton Street W1 • Map K3

10 The Witch Ball
Beautiful, antique theatre posters and prints are sold here. The street is lined with antiquarian print and book shops. ◈ 2 Cecil Court WC2 • Map L3

For more on shopping **See p170**

Left **Japanese restaurant, YO! Sushi** Center **Café Latino poster** Right **Café Latino façade**

Late Night Venues

1 Ronnie Scott's
London's premier jazz venue *(see p58).* 47 Frith Street W1 • Map L2 • 020 7439 0749

2 Atlantic Bar and Grill
Trendy cocktail bar and restaurant serving modern European cuisine. Open until 3am Mon–Sat. 20 Glasshouse Street W1 • Map K3

3 Café Boheme
Sandwiches, salads and light meat and fish dishes are served round-the-clock on Fridays and Saturdays, and until 3am Sunday to Thursday. 13 Old Compton Street W1 • Map L2

4 Cork and Bottle
A range of champagnes and wines are available at this basement bar near Leicester Square. Open until midnight, Monday to Saturday. 46 Cranbourn Street WC2 • Map L3

5 Old Compton Café
Invariably packed in the evenings, this inviting bar stays open around the clock. Hot dishes and sandwiches are on hand to keep people on their feet. 34 Old Compton Street W1 • Map L2

6 Break for the Border
Tex-Mex food and western music to put you in the mood. Downstairs, the Borderline nightclub is open until 3am Thursday to Saturday *(see p59).* Goslett Yard WC2 • Map L2

7 Café Latino
Open until 1am, this lively venue, on three floors, attracts cocktail drinkers as well as lovers of Spanish and Latin American dishes. When the basement gets steamy, cool off in an upstairs room. 25 Frith Street W1 • Map L2

8 Jazz After Dark
Things don't get going here much before 9pm, and the blues and soul go on until 2am Mon–Thu, 3am Fri–Sat. Cajun chicken and moussaka are on the menu. 9 Greek Street, W1 • Map L2

9 YO! Below
Tabletop taps deliver beer in the comfortable basement of this high-tech Japanese restaurant, which serves until 1am. Try a flavored sake with your sushi. 52 Poland Street W1 • Map K2

10 Pizza Express
One of a chain of 80 outlets in London, this one is open until midnight, with regular jazz nights. 10 Dean Street W1 • Map K2

For more live music venues **See pp58–9**

Left **Coach and Horses pub** Right **Patisserie Valerie**

🔟 Pubs and Cafés

1 Patisserie Valerie
A classic Soho café with a wide range of delicious cakes and pastries: the fresh croissants make it a good place for breakfast. Its Frenchness extends to the smoky atmosphere, but there is a no-smoking area downstairs. ⊗ *44 Old Compton St W1 • Map L3*

2 Maison Bertaux
This little corner of Paris in the heart of Soho attracts a faithful clientele, who love its delicious coffee and heavenly cakes. ⊗ *36 Greek St W1 • Map L3*

3 French House
A small, one-bar establishment where conversation flows freely among strangers, this Soho pub was once the haunt of the artist Francis Bacon (1909–92). ⊗ *49 Dean Street W1 • Map L3*

4 Bar Italia
Sit at the bar or out on the heated pavement and enjoy the best Italian coffee in London. A huge screen at the back of the bar shows Italian soccer matches. Open 24 hours. ⊗ *22 Frith Street W1 • Map L2 •*

5 The Coach and Horses
This pub has long attracted the artistic and the disreputable, including the late, infamously drunken columnist, Jeffrey Barnard. His antics featured in the highly successful stage play, *Jeffrey Barnard is Unwell.* ⊗ *29 Greek Street W1 • Map L2*

6 The Admiral Duncan
A small, lively bar in Old Compton Street – one of dozens in the area with a gay clientele. ⊗ *54 Old Compton St W1 • Map L3*

7 EAT
One of an excellent chain of sandwich bars with a selection of sandwiches, soups, sushi and salads. ⊗ *16A Soho Square W1 • Map L2*

8 Le Beatroot
A small, bright vegetarian restaurant serving delicious salads and hot dishes, packed in boxes. ⊗ *92 Berwick St W1 • Map K3*

9 The Cork and Bottle
A 1970s basement wine bar with vintage music, bistro food and a fine selection of wines *(see p93).* ⊗ *44–6 Cranbourn St WC2 • Map L3*

🔟 The Dog and Duck
Small, friendly pub with Victorian tiled walls and a choice of British beers *(see p62).* ⊗ *18 Bateman St W1 • Map L2*

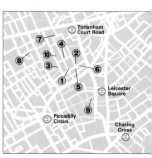

For more pubs **See pp 62–3**

Price Categories		
For a three-course	**£**	under £15
meal for one with half	**££**	£15–£25
a bottle of wine (or	**£££**	£25–£35
equivalent meal), taxes	**££££**	£35–£50
and extra charges.	**£££££**	over £50

Left **Sugar Club restaurant** Right **Tokyo Diner**

TOP 10 Restaurants

1 Tokyo Diner
Inexpensive Japanese diner near Leicester Square, serving Japanese curry, *donburi* and noodles. ✪ *Newport Place WC2 • Map L3 • 020 7287 8777 • No disabled access • £*

2 The Lindsay House
A clublike restaurant based in a fine Georgian town house; ingredients are the best of British and the desserts are delicious. ✪ *21 Romilly St W1 • Map L3 • 020 7439 0450 • No disabled access • £££*

3 Incognito
Solid French food, such as fried goose liver, is leavened by the touch of one of London's best chefs, Nico Ladenis.
✪ *117 Shaftesbury Ave WC2 • Map L3 • 020 7836 8866 • Lunch and pre-theatre menus • ££££*

4 Harbour City
Specialities at this mid-range Cantonese restaurant include aromatic duck and dim sum: just say how much you want to spend and they will make it to order.
✪ *46 Gerrard St W1 • Map L3 • 020 7439 7859 • ££*

5 Criterion Brasserie
This is a fabulous place to sit and dine, especially at lunchtime when the inexpensive menu of mainly French food seems a treat among the gold, wood and marble furnishings. ✪ *224 Piccadilly W1 • Map K3 • 020 7930 0488 • Lunch and pre-theatre menus • £££*

6 L'Odéon
Delicious French cuisine in this large first-floor restaurant. ✪ *65 Regent St W1 • Map K3 • 020 7287 1400 • Lunch and pre-theatre menus • ££££*

7 J Sheekey
A taste of London elegance. Fish is on the menu, from oysters to lobsters. ✪ *28–32 St Martin's Court WC2 • Map L3 • 020 7240 2565 • ££££*

8 Itsu
An oriental conveyor-belt restaurant with imaginative dishes passing before your eyes. ✪ *103 Wardour St • Map K3 • 020 7479 4794 • ££*

9 Busaba Ethai
Recently opened, trendy Thai restaurant. ✪ *110 Wardour St W1 • Map K2 • 020 7255 8686 • ££*

10 The Sugar Club
Minimal modern décor and postmodern cooking in this fashionable restaurant *(see p76).* ✪ *21 Warwick Street W1 • Map K3 • 020 7437 7776 • No disabled facilities • ££££*

Unless otherwise stated, all restaurants accept credit cards and serve vegetarian options

Left **Covent Garden piazza and central market** Right **Somerset House**

Covent Garden

ONE OF LONDON'S LIVELIEST AREAS, *Covent Garden* is a popular destination for Londoners and tourists alike. At its heart is the capital's first planned square, laid out in the 17th century by Inigo Jones and recently completed by the addition of the imperious, pearly-white Royal Opera House. In spite of such grandeur, there is still a local feel to the surrounding streets and lanes, especially around Neal's Yard and Endell Street. To the south of Covent Garden is another recently developed institution, Somerset House, which contains the Courtauld Gallery and two other major galleries. To get the full impact of the imposing riverside setting, enter from the Embankment side.

🔟 Sights

1. The Piazza and Central Market
2. Royal Opera House
3. Courtauld Institute
4. Somerset House
5. Photographers' Gallery
6. Theatre Museum
7. London Transport Museum
8. Neal's Yard
9. St. Paul's Church
10. Theatre Royal, Drury Lane

Clowns in Covent Garden

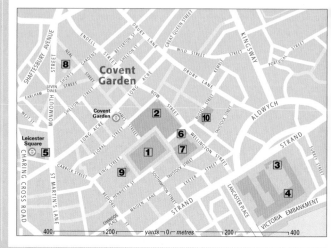

Preceeding pages *Phantom of the Opera,* Her Majesty's Theatre

Shops and cafés in the former market area

The Piazza and Central Market

For 300 years, Covent Garden was a fruit, vegetable and flower market – immortalized by Lerner and Loewe's hit musical *My Fair Lady*. In 1980 the Victorian halls, with their lovely iron and glass roofs, were transformed into a vibrant, modern-day market place, surrounded by cafés and bars and enlivened by regular street entertainment. ✆ WC2 • Map M3

Royal Opera House

London's impressive premier music venue is home to both the Royal Opera and Royal Ballet Companies. The present Neo-Classical theatre was designed in 1858 by E.M. Barry and incorporated a portico frieze recovered from the previous building, which had been destroyed by fire. The Opera House has recently spread its wings into the lovely Floral Hall, once part of Covent Garden market and now housing a champagne bar. ✆ *Bow Street WC2* • *Map M2* • *Open to visitors 10am–3:30pm* • *See p56 for performance details*

Courtauld Institute

Founded in 1932 for the study of the history of European art, the Courtauld is part of Britain's oldest institute for teaching the history of art. Located in the North Block of Somerset House *(below)* the gallery rooms are particularly strong on Impressionist paintings. Each Tuesday at 1:15pm there is a free talk on one of the paintings in the exhibition. ✆ *Strand WC2* • *Map N3* • *Open 10am–6pm Mon–Sat, noon–6pm Sun* • *Admission charge*

Somerset House

Once a grand riverside palace, and later home to the Navy Board, Somerset House is now partly occupied by the Civil Service. A large amount of the building, though, is open to the public. Aside from the Courtauld Institute *(above)* it houses the Gilbert Collection of decorative art and the Hermitage Rooms, which display a collection of art from the Hermitage Museum in St. Petersburg, Russia. ✆ *Strand WC2* • *Map N3* • *Open 10am–6pm Mon–Sat, noon–6pm Sun* • *Admission charge*

Left **Street entertainment in Covent Garden** Right **Royal Opera production of *Platee***

5 Photographers' Gallery

The main galleries of this major photographic showcase are at No. 8, where there is also a bookshop. At No. 5, a black-tiled building where the artist Sir Joshua Reynolds once lived, there is a small exhibition area, a café and a sale room offering vintage, modern and contemporary photographic work. ◈ 5 & 8 Gt. Newport Street WC2 • Map L3 • Open 11am–6pm Mon–Sat, noon–6pm Sun • Free

Theatre Museum, Covent Garden

6 Theatre Museum

Right in the heart of theatreland, this museum thrives on regular exhibitions and events, including costume workshops and makeup demonstrations. The galleries chart the development of British theater from Shakespeare's day. Buy a ticket for a combined tour of the museum and the Theatre Royal (see p49). ◈ Russell Street WC1 • Map M3 • Open 10am–6pm Tue–Sun • Admission charge

Covent Garden Architect

Inigo Jones (1573–1652) designed Covent Garden as London's first planned square. The low roofs and classical portico of St. Paul's Church were influenced by the Italian architect Andrea Palladio (1518–80). As set designer for royal masques, Jones was responsible for introducing the proscenium arch and moveable scenery to the London stage.

7 London Transport Museum

Some of the most innovative British designers have worked for London Transport, and their posters and furnishings are on display here. See vehicles that have served the city for two centuries. The bookshop is great for souvenirs: model buses, trains, taxis and the distinctive London Underground symbol on anything that will sell (see p49). ◈ The Piazza WC2 • Map M3 • Open 10am–6pm Sat–Thu, 11am–6pm Fri • Admission charge

8 Neal's Yard

This delightful enclave is full of color, with painted lofts and shop fronts, flower-filled window boxes and oil-drums and cascades of plants tumbling down the old brick walls. This is alternative London, with organic foods and such alternative therapies as Chinese medicines, walk-in back rubs, acupuncture and self-esteem training. Try the wholesome

Left **London Transport Museum** Right **Theatre Royal, Haymarket**

Neal's Yard, Covent Garden

bread and cakes at Neal's Yard Bakery and be amazed by the variety of British cheeses on offer in nearby Neal's Yard Dairy. ◈ *Neal Street WC2 • Map M2*

9 St. Paul's Church
Inigo Jones built this church (known as the actors' church) with the main portico facing east, onto the Piazza, and the altar at the west end. Clerics objected to this unorthodox arrangement, so the altar was moved. The entrance is via the west portico while the grand east door is essentially a fake. ◈ *Bedford Street WC2 • Map M3*

10 Theatre Royal, Drury Lane
Drury Lane is synonymous with the London stage and this glorious theater explains why. It has a splendid entrance, with magnificent stairways leading to the circle seats. The auditorium is large enough to put on the biggest musical extravaganzas, including *South Pacific*, *My Fair Lady*, *Hello Dolly* and *Miss Saigon*. The first theater on this site was built in 1663 for Charles II whose mistress Nell Gwynne trod the boards. ◈ *Catherine Street WC2 • Map M2 • Guided tours*

A Walk around Covent Garden

Morning

Take the tube to Leicester Square and have a coffee at the Arts Theatre café before taking in the latest exhibition at the Photographer's Gallery next door.

Head up Monmouth Street to Seven Dials, a lofty sundial where seven streets converge. Check out the market stalls and shops in Earlham Street then continue up Monmouth Street to the small entrance to **Neal's Yard** with its fine cheese and bread shops. Buy soap at Neal's Yard apothecary. Visit **Covent Garden Piazza** *(see p99)* for some pre-lunch entertainment from the street entertainers outside Inigo Jones' elegant **St. Paul's Church**. Take a look inside before lunch in the **Royal Opera House's** *(see p99)* Amphitheatre Restaurant, with its wonderful views.

Afternoon

Leave the Piazza via Russell Street, past the **Theatre Museum**, down Wellington Street to the Strand. Cross the road and turn left to the recently refurbished **Somerset House**, home of the **Courtauld Institute** *(see p99)*. Start with their collection of Impressionist and Post-Impressionist paintings. Pause to relax by the Courtyard fountains or at the River Terrace Café before checking out the Gilbert Collection's decorative arts objects. If you want to add a little glamour to the day cross back over the Strand for tea in the splendid Palm Court restaurant of the **Waldorf Hotel** *(see p177)*.

Left **Street entertainment, Covent Garden** Right **Globe atop London Coliseum**

ᵀᴼᴾ10 The Best of the Rest

1 Free Entertainment
Every day from 8am–10pm there are street entertainers in the Piazza, while opera singers and classical musicians perform in the Central Market areas. ◈ *WC1 • Map M3*

2 The Sanctuary
A totally hedonistic day can be spent in this women-only spa with pools, jacuzzis, saunas and solarium. ◈ *12 Floral Street WC2 • Map M3 • Open 9:30am–6pm Sun–Tue, 9:30am–10pm Wed–Fri, 10am–8pm Sat • Admission charge*

3 Africa Centre
As well as a lively program of African and Caribbean music, the center has a restaurant, bar and shop selling ethnic goods. ◈ *38 King Street WC2 • Map M3*

4 Victoria Embankment Gardens
In summer, outdoor concerts are held in these attractive gardens by the river. ◈ *WC2 • Map M4*

5 Savoy Hotel
Enjoy a traditional afternoon tea in the Thames Foyer of this grand old London hotel *(see p70)*. ◈ *Strand WC2 • Map M3*

6 London Coliseum
Built in 1904, the home of the English National Opera has retained its Edwardian flavor, with gilded cherubs and scarlet curtains in the foyer *(see p56)*. ◈ *St. Martin's Lane WC2 • Map L3*

7 River Entertainment
Two ships moored near the Embankment are open to the public: *RS Hispaniola* offers jazz piano, bellydancers and magicians with dinner, while the *Queen Mary* has bars on its sunny decks. ◈ *Embankment WC2 • Map M4*

8 Oasis Sports Centre
Famous for its heated outdoor pool, there is also an indoor pool, gym and sunbeds at this central sports center. ◈ *32 Endell St WC2 • Map M2 • Admission charge*

9 Players Theatre
Seating just 240, this tiny Victorian Theatre beneath the arches at Charing Cross station recreates Victorian music hall shows at 8.15pm Tue–Sun. ◈ *The Arches, Villiers Street WC2 • Map M4 • Admission charge*

10 Bush House
Home of the BBC World Service, Bush House has an imposing portico on its north side. In the Bush House arcade the BBC World Service Shop sells tapes, videos and books. ◈ *Strand WC2 • Map N3*

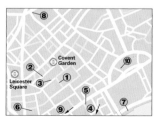

Left **Knutz joke shop** Right **Specialist travel book shop, Stanford's**

TOP10 Shopping

1 Neal Street East
This oriental emporium is a venerable Covent Garden institution, and sells a great range of goods from tea to kimonos.
◈ *5 Neal Street WC2 • Map M2*

2 Paul Smith
Leading British clothes designer Paul Smith's trendy minimalist window displays adorn three adjacent shops, for men, women and children.
◈ *40–44 Floral Street WC2 • Map M3*

3 Dr. Martens Store
The name is familiar but you will be surprised at the varieties that these boots and shoes come in. Well worth a browse.
◈ *1–4 King Street WC2 • Map M3*

4 Stanford's
With an extensive range of travel guides, literature and maps, this shop is a traveler's paradise. The basement is devoted to the British Isles and sailing. ◈ *12–14 Long Acre WC2 • Map M3*

5 Ellis Brigham
All the outdoor gear you could ever want plus lots of useful gadgets and gizmos. ◈ *32 Southampton Street WC2 • Map M3*

6 Theatre Shop
Here you can pick up a CD of a musical you've just seen and, in the basement, buy the song sheets and books so you can sing along at home. ◈ *St. Martin's Lane • Map L3*

7 Penhaligon's
In business since 1870, this traditional perfumery carries a glorious range of old-fashioned English scents and soaps for men and women. Perfect for gifts.
◈ *41 Wellington Street WC2 • Map M3*

8 Knutz
Zany, rude, fun and childish, here you'll find a great choice of jokes and costumes. A shop for parties and for unusual souvenirs.
◈ *1 Russell Street WC2 • Map M2*

9 The Tea House
Twenty teas – from Moroccan Minty to Mango & Maracuja – are on sale at this speciality shop in Neal Street. There are also novelty teapots and books on how to master the very English art of tea-making.
◈ *15a Neal Street WC2 • Map M2*

10 Thomas Neal Centre
This upmarket designer shopping mall has a good range of fashionable boutiques arranged over two floors. On the lower floor there is a pleasant café and restaurant.
◈ *Earlham Street WC2 • Map L2*

⬅ *For more on shopping See p170*

Left **World food café sign** Right **Freedom Brewing Company's long bar**

Pubs & Cafés

1 Royal Opera House Café
Take the escalator up to the café in the Amphitheatre Bar for coffees, cakes and drinks.
⊗ *Covent Garden WC2 • Map M2*

2 World Food Café, Neal's Yard Dining Room
Have a pot of tea or a coffee, an Indian mango ice cream or a vegetarian snack in this pretty corner of Covent Garden.
⊗ *14 Neal's Yard WC2 • Map M2*

3 Freuds
This small basement attracts a designer crowd in the evenings. Huge choice of coffees (some with liqueurs), cocktails and bottled beers. ⊗ *198 Shaftesbury Avenue W1 • Map L2*

4 Freedom Brewing Company
Four special ales are brewed on the premises here: wheat beer, pale ale, Soho red and a light summer lager. Reasonably priced dishes to mop it up. ⊗ *41 Earlham Street WC2 • Map M2*

5 The Lamb and Flag
This traditional pub, serving cask bitter, is one of the oldest in the West End *(see p62)*. Delicious roasts are served upstairs at weekday lunchtimes.
⊗ *33 Rose Street WC2 • Map M3*

6 Paul
The best patisserie in Covent Garden has authentic French fruit tarts, croissants, breads and gateaux, as well as filled baguettes and real French coffee.
⊗ *30 Bedford Street WC2 • Map M3*

7 Gordon's Wine Bar
An ancient dive where wine, port and Madeira are served from the barrel in schooners or beakers.
⊗ *47 Villiers Street WC2 • Map M4*

8 Corney and Barrow
A classy ground-floor wine bar with a champagne bar in the basement and a restaurant upstairs. Open till 2am Thu–Sat.
⊗ *116 St. Martin's Lane WC2 • Map L3*

9 Soupworks
One of a small takeaway chain serving a daily selection of freshly-made soups. Drinks include Indian yogurt lassis.
⊗ *29 Monmouth Street WC2 • Map L2*

10 Monmouth Coffee House
One of the best places in town to buy and sample really good coffee, including organically produced brews. The tantalizing aroma drifts up to the wooden bench tables in the café at the back of the premises. ⊗ *27 Monmouth Street WC2 • Map L2*

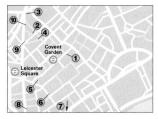

For more pubs See pp62–3

Price Categories

For a three course meal for one with half a bottle of wine (or equivalent meal), taxes and extra charges.

£	under £15
££	£15–£25
£££	£25–£35
££££	£35–£50
£££££	over £50

Left **The Ivy** Right **View of Covent Garden from Chez Gerard**

🔟 Restaurants

1 The Ivy
Mere mortals need to reserve six weeks ahead for the West End's most star-struck restaurant, but it's worth waiting for the immaculate brasserie-style food and smart atmosphere. ✪ *1 West St WC2 • Map L2 • 020 7836 4751 • ££££*

2 Belgo Centraal
Mussels with mayonnaise and frites, washed down with one of a 100 different beers, are the mainstay here, with waiters dressed as monks serving at the long refectory tables. Try the set-price £5 lunches. ✪ *50 Earlham St WC2 • Map L2 • 020 7813 2233 • £*

3 Mon Plaisir
One of the oldest French restaurants in London. Daily specials keep the menu fresh. ✪ *21 Monmouth St WC2 • Map L2 • 020 7836 7243 • Set lunch and pre-theatre menus • ££££*

4 Rock and Sole Plaice
This is simply the best place in Central London for traditional British fish and chips. ✪ *47 Endell St WC2 • Map M2 • 0207836 3785 • £*

5 Chez Gerard
This branch of a popular chain of French restaurants has a glass roof and spectacular setting overlooking Covent Garden market. Robust, unfussy French food at its best. The café is open 11am–5pm. ✪ *Covent Garden Central Market WC2 • Map M2 • 020 7379 0666 • No disabled access • pre-theatre menus • ££*

6 Prospect Grill
Sophisticated American grill serving delicious fish, meats and desserts. ✪ *4–6 Garrick St WC2 • Map L3 • 020 7379 0412 • No disabled access • £££*

7 Orso
A popular, atmospheric, mid-priced Italian restaurant. ✪ *27 Wellington St WC2 • Map N3 • 020 7240 5269 • ££££*

8 Joe Allen
Modern European cuisine plus American classics in this friendly, New York-style restaurant. ✪ *13 Exeter St WC2 • Map M3 • 020 7836 0651 • ££££*

9 Rules
London's oldest restaurant has been famed since 1798 for its "porter, pies and oysters" (see p77). ✪ *35 Maiden Lane WC2 • Map M3 • 020 7836 5314 • No disabled access • ££££*

🔟 The Admiralty
French country cooking in elegant surroundings. ✪ *Somerset House, The Strand WC2 • Map N3 • 020 7845 4646 • £££££*

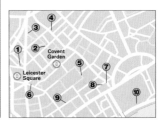

Left **Museum Street** Right **Fitzroy Square**

Bloomsbury and Fitzrovia

LITERARY, LEGAL AND SCHOLARLY, *this is the brainy quarter of London.* Dominated by two towering institutions, the British Museum and London University, and bolstered by the Inns of Court, it could hardly be otherwise. It is an area of elegant squares and Georgian façades, of libraries, bookshops and publishing houses. Most famously, the Bloomsbury Group, known for novelist Virginia Woolf (see p72) lived here during the early decades of the 20th century. Fitzrovia's reputation as a raffish place was enhanced by the characters who drank at the Fitzroy Tavern, such as the Welsh poet Dylan Thomas (1914–53) and the painter Augustus John (1878–1961).

🔟 Sights

1. British Museum
2. British Library
3. Sir John Soane's Museum
4. Dickens House Museum
5. University College London
6. Percival David Foundation of Chinese Art
7. Telecom Tower
8. Pollock's Toy Museum and Shop
9. St. George's Church
10. St. Pancras Station

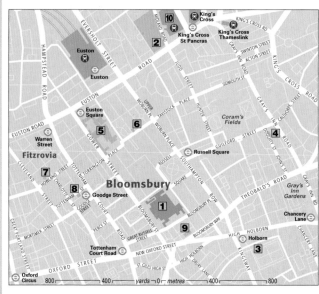

Sir John Soane's Museum

British Museum
1 See pp8–11.

British Library
2 Now housed in a spectacular new building in St. Pancras, the British Library holds copies of everything published in Britain, as well as many historical publications from around the world. Members have free access to these, while non-members can enjoy the magnificent space and the regular exhibitions put on here. A dazzling, permanent display in the John Ritblatt Gallery includes the earliest map of Britain (1250), a Gutenberg Bible (1455), Shakespeare's first folio (1623), Handel's *Messiah* (1741) and many breathtaking illuminated manuscripts. The glass walls in the core of the building reveal the huge leather volumes from the King's Library, donated by George III. There are regular talks and events, a café, restaurant and, of course, a well-stocked bookshop. ◉ *96 Euston Road NW1 • Map L1 • Open 9:30am– 6pm Mon, Wed, Thu, Fri, 9.30–8pm Tue, 9.30am– 5pm Sat, 11am–5pm Sun & public hols • Exhibition galleries free. Pass required for Reading Room*

Sir John Soane's Museum
3 A particular pleasure of this unique museum is watching visitors' faces as they turn a corner and encounter yet another unexpected gem. Sir John Soane, one of Britain's leading 19th-century architects, crammed three adjoining houses with antiques and treasures, displayed in the most ingenious ways. The basement crypt, designed to resemble a Roman catacomb, is particularly original. *The Rake's Progress* (1753), a series of eight paintings by Hogarth, is another highlight.

The houses are on the northern side of Lincoln's Inn Fields, the heart of legal London, where gowned and bewigged lawyers roam. Lincoln's Inn, on the east side of the square, is one of the best preserved Inns of Court in London, part of it dating from the 15th century. ◉ *13 Lincoln's Inn Fields WC2 • Map L1 • Open 10am–5pm Tue–Sat, 6–9pm first Tue of month • Free*

Left **Illuminated manuscript, British Library** Right **Sir John Soane's Museum**

For more on London's literary figures See pp72–3

4 Dickens House Museum

Home to Charles Dickens from 1837–39, during which time he completed some of his best work (including *Oliver Twist*, *Nicholas Nickleby* and *Pickwick Papers*), this four-story terraced house offers a fascinating glimpse into the life and times of the great Victorian author and social reformer. Some rooms have been laid out exactly as they were in Dickens' time. Nearby Doughty Mews provides another step back to Victorian times. ◈ *48 Doughty Street WC1 • Map F2 • Open 10am–5pm Mon–Sat • Admission charge*

5 University College London

Founded in 1836, UCL is the oldest college of London University and owns several fine academic collections. In the Petrie Museum is one of the largest collections of Egyptian archaeology in the world. Etchings, engravings and early English Mezzotints from the college's art collection are exhibited in the Strang Print Room. Check out performances at the college's Bloomsbury Theatre in Gordon Street. ◈ *Gower Street WC1 • Map K1 • Petrie Museum: open 1–5pm Tue–Fri, 10am–1pm Sat • Free • Bloomsbury Theatre • Map E2 • 020 7388 8822*

Bloomsbury Connections

Many Bloomsbury streets and squares are named after members of the Russell family – the Dukes of Bedford. The first duke features in Shakespeare's play *Henry V*. In 1800, the fifth Duke sold the family mansion in Bedford Place and retired to the country. The current Duke has turned the family seat into a huge tourist attraction *(see p167)*.

6 Percival David Foundation of Chinese Art

Comprising around 1,700 pieces from the 10th–18th centuries, this is regarded as the finest collection of Chinese porcelain outside China. The collection was given to the University of London's School of Oriental and African Studies in 1950 by the scholar Sir Percival David. ◈ *55 Gordon Square WC1 • Map E2 • Open 10:30am–5pm Mon–Fri • Free*

Telecom Tower

7 British Telecom Tower

At 620 ft (190 m), this was the tallest building in London when it opened in 1965. Sadly, the revolving restaurant on top has been closed, for security reasons, but the Tower Tavern in Cleveland Street has a good large-scale diagram explaining the tower's constituent parts (as well as hand-pulled beer). ◈ *Map J1*

Left **Façade, St Pancras Station** Right **Carved figures, St Pancras Parish Church**

For more London museums See pp48–49

Pearly dolls, Pollock's Toy Museum

8 Pollock's Toy Museum and Shop

This delightful child-sized museum is a treasure-trove of historic toys. The shop below is crammed with old-fashioned playthings including Victorian toy theatre sheets, originally published by Benjamin Pollock. ✆ *1 Scala Street W1 • Map K1 • Open 10am–5pm Mon–Sat • Admission charge*

9 St. George's Church

This church was described in a 19th-century guide book as "the most pretentious, ugliest edifice in the metropolis". The steeple is topped with a statue of King George I posing as St. George. ✆ *Bloomsbury Way WC1 • Map M1 • Open 9:30am– 5:30pm Mon–Fri and for services*

10 St. Pancras Station

One of the glories of Victorian Gothic architecture, this railway terminus was designed in 1874 by Sir George Gilbert Scott, who also designed the Albert Memorial *(see p119)*. Most of the frontage is in fact the former Midland Grand Hotel, which is due to be refurbished as part of the current Channel Tunnel railway terminus project. ✆ *Euston Road NW1 • Map E1*

Bloomsbury & Fitzrovia on Foot

Morning

🕙 Arrive at the **British Museum** *(see pp8–11)* at 10am (opening time) so that you can enjoy the new Great Court in peace. View Norman Foster's glass dome while having coffee at the café here. Stroll past the great Assyrian bas-reliefs on your way out.

🚶 Browse the antiquarian book and print shops, such as **Jarndyce** *(see p110)*, along Great Russell and Museum streets. Turn left up Little Russell Street, noticing the fine Hawksmoor church of St. George's. Loop around Bloomsbury Square and check out the list of Bloomsbury group literary figures posted here. Head west to Bedford Square with its elegant Georgian houses. Cross Tottenham Court Road and carry on to Charlotte Street.

Afternoon

See the photos of literary figures such as Dylan Thomas in the basement bar of **Fitzroy Tavern** *(see p111)* at No.16 Charlotte Street, while enjoing a pre-lunch drink. If you fancy something more substantial than bar food, try a curry from **Rasa Samudra** *(see p111)* at No. 5.

After lunch amble gently back to Tottenham Court Road for some shopping. **Heals** *(see p110)* and Habitat sell a wide range of furniture and household items, many at the cutting edge of British design. In the joint basement of these two shops, the **Table Café** *(see p111)* serves good tea.

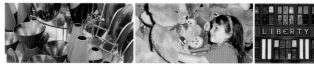

Left **Stylish vases at Heals** Center **Choosing a teddy at Hamleys** Right **Liberty**

🔟 Shopping

1 Liberty
One of London's most appealing department stores, Liberty sells cutting-edge contemporary design in clothing, jewelry and household items. Opened in 1875, to specialise in goods and silks from the Empire, the shop remains famous for its "Liberty Print" fabric *(see p64)*. 🔄 *210–220 Regent Street W1 • Map J2*

2 Hamleys
London's largest toy shop sells everything from dolls to computer games. Worth a visit just to see their fabulous window displays *(see p64)*. 🔄 *188–196 Regent Street W1 • Map J2*

3 Heals
London's leading furniture store is a showcase for the best of British design. There is a pleasant café at the back of the 3rd floor. 🔄 *196 Tottenham Court Road W1 • Map E2*

4 Virgin Megastore
This vast store has four floors of CDs, videos, computer games and magazines. Open till 9pm Mon–Sat. 🔄 *14–16 Oxford Street W1 • Map L4*

5 British Museum Shop
Find exquisite crafts and jewellery in this museum shop. Everything from a pair of earrings modeled on those of ancient Egypt or a replica Roman bust to contemporary crafts. 🔄 *22 Bloomsbury Street WC1 • Map L1*

6 Hi-Fi Experience
One of the best stereo and home theater stores in a street full of electronic equipment shops. 🔄 *227 Tottenham Court Road W1 • Map L1*

7 Jessops Classic Photographica
Enter this shop from Pied Bull's Yard, a camera collector's haven, and browse among old Leicas and Hasselblads. 🔄 *67 Great Russell Street WC1 • Map L1*

8 Cornelissen & Son
The most appealing art shop in town has wood paneling and rows of glass jars full of pigments. 🔄 *105 Great Russell Street WC1 • Map M1*

9 Jarndyce
The handsome antiquarian bookshop is best for 18th- and 19th-century British literature. 🔄 *46 Great Russell Street WC1 • Map L1*

10 Falkiner Fine Papers
Write a letter home on these fine handmade papers. The shop is also a specialist on bookbinding. 🔄 *76 Southampton Row • Map M1*

For more on shopping **See p170**

Price Categories

For a three-course	**£** under £15
meal for one with half	**££** £15–£25
a bottle of wine (or	**£££** £25–£35
equivalent meal), taxes	**££££** £35–£50
and extra charges.	**£££££** over £50

Left **R K Stanleys** Right **Mash**

🔟 Eating and Drinking

1 Rasa Samudra
Exquisite dishes from the Kerala region of southern India, including fish and vegetarian curries. A cookbook on display helps explain dishes you have never heard of. ◈ *5 Charlotte Street W1 • Map K1 • 020 7637 0222 • Disabled, with advance booking • £££*

2 Wagamama
This classic no-frills noodle bar attracts everyone from students to businessmen, who all eat at long, bench tables. ◈ *4a Streatham Street WC1 • Map L1 • 020 7323 9223 • No disabled access • £*

3 Bam-Bou
Set in a lovely four-story Georgian townhouse, this is a traditional Vietnamese restaurant. ◈ *1 Percy Street W1 • Map K1 • 020 7323 9130 • No disabled access • ££££*

4 Pied à Terre
Brilliant modern French cuisine is always to be found in this award-winning restaurant with a list of 750 wines. ◈ *34 Charlotte Street W1 • Map K1 • 020 7636 1178 • £££*

5 Fitzroy Tavern
The pub that gave its name to the area (Fitzrovia) has a large central bar that attracts a lively after-work crowd. Good Samuel Smith beer is reasonably priced. ◈ *16 Charlotte Street W1 • Map K1*

6 Table Cafe
Stop here for an informal Italian lunch in the basement of Habitat and Heals *(see p110)*. ◈ *196 Tottenham Court Road W1 • Map E2 • 020 7636 8330 • £*

7 Villandry Foodstore
Attached to an excellent food shop, the restaurant has a simple French-based menu that changes twice a day. ◈ *170 Great Portland Street W1 • Map J1 • 020 7631 3131 • ££££*

8 Mash
Fashionable eaterie that specialises in house-brewed beer and wood-barbecued food. ◈ *19–21 Great Portland Street W1 • Map J1 • 020 7637 5555 • £££*

9 Carluccio's Caffe
A touch of authentic Italy in this quiet square behind Oxford Street. Eat handmade pasta at pavement tables. ◈ *8 Market Place W1 • Map J2 • 020 7636 2228 • ££*

10 R K Stanleys
Sausages and beer are the things to have in this trendy restaurant. ◈ *6 Little Portland Street W1 • Map J1 • 020 7462 0099 • £££*

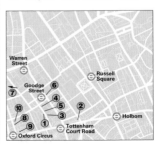

Left **Buckingham Palace** Right **Royal Opera Arcade**

Mayfair and St. James's

THIS IS WHERE *royalty shop and the rest of us go to gaze.* Many of the wonderful small shops around here were established to serve the royal court at St. James's Palace. Piccadilly – named after the fancy collars called "picadils" sold at a shop in the street in the 18th century – divides St. James's to the south from Mayfair to the north, where top shops continue up Bond Street, Cork Street and Savile Row to Oxford Street. Home to the Royal Academy of Arts since 1868, Mayfair has long been one of the best addresses in town. Today most of London's top-flight art galleries are here.

🔟 Sights

1. Buckingham Palace
2. St. James's Park
3. Royal Academy of Arts
4. St. James's Palace
5. Bond Street
6. Shepherd Market
7. Apsley House
8. Berkeley Square
9. Burlington Arcade
10. Faraday Museum

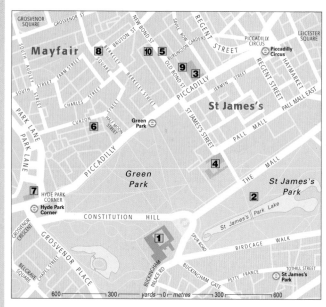

Victoria Memorial, Buckingham Palace

1 Buckingham Palace
See pp26–7.

2 St. James's Park
This is undoubtedly London's most elegant park, with dazzling flower beds, exotic wildfowl on the lake (watch the pelicans being fed at 3pm), a good café with outdoor seating and music on the bandstand in summer. The bridge over the lake has a good view to the west of Buckingham Palace and, to the east, of the former Colonial Office where just 125 civil servants once governed the British Empire that covered one fifth of the world *(see p28)*. ◊ *SW1 • Map K5–L5 • Open 5am–midnight daily*

3 Royal Academy of Arts
Major visiting art exhibitions are staged at Burlington House, home of Britain's most prestigious fine arts institution. The building is one of Piccadilly's few surviving 17th-century mansions – you can see the former garden front on the way up to the Sackler Galleries. Near the entrance to the galleries is Michelangelo's *Madonna and Child* (1505) – part of the Royal Academy's permanent collection and one of only four Michelangelo sculptures outside Italy. In the Academy's popular, annual summer exhibition, new works by both established and unknown artists are displayed *(see p51)*. ◊ *Burlington House, Piccadilly W1 • Map J4 • Open 10am–6pm daily (10pm Fri) • Admission charge*

4 St. James's Palace
Built by Henry VIII, on the site of the former hospital of St. James, the palace is the official residence of Prince Charles. The red brick Tudor gatehouse is a familiar landmark *(see p54)*. ◊ *The Mall SW1 • Map K5 • Closed to public*

Left **St. James's Park** Right **Gatehouse, St. James's Palace**

For more on royal London **See pp54–5**

5 Bond Street

London's most exclusive shopping street, Bond Street (known as New Bond Street to the north and Old Bond Street to the south) has long been the place for high society to promenade: many of its establishments have been here for over 100 years. The street is home to top fashion houses, elegant galleries such as Agnews and the Fine Art Society, Sotheby's auction rooms and jewelers such as Tiffany and Asprey. Where Old and New Bond Street meet, there is a delightful sculpture of wartime leaders Franklin D. Roosevelt and Winston Churchill – well worth a photograph. ◈ *Map J3–J4*

6 Shepherd Market

The market was named after Edward Shepherd who built a two-story house here in around 1735. Today, this pedestrianized area in the heart of Mayfair is a good place to visit on a summer evening for a drink or meal. Ye Grapes, dating from 1882, is the principal pub, while local restaurants include L 'Artiste Musclé, Le Boudin Bleu and The Village Bistro. During the 17th century, an annual May Fair was held here, giving the area its name. ◈ *Map D4*

Americans in Mayfair

America's connection with Mayfair dates from World War II when General Eisenhower stayed in a house on Grosvenor Square. In 1960 the Embassy building opened on land leased from the Grosvenor Estate, who refused to sell the freehold unless 12,000 acres of their estate in Florida, confiscated after the War of Independence, was returned.

7 Apsley House

The home of the Duke of Wellington *(see p53)*, Apsley House is still partly occupied by the family. Designed by Robert Adam in the 1770s, the mansion is given over to paintings, and memorabilia of the great military leader. Paintings include several fine works by Diego Velázquez, including *The Waterseller of Seville*. Antonio Canova's nude statue of Napoleon has special poignancy. ◈ *Hyde Park Corner W1 • Map D5 • Open 11am–5pm Tue–Sun • Admission charge*

Interior, Apsley House

8 Berkeley Square

This pocket of green in the middle of Mayfair was planted in 1789 and its 30 huge plane trees may be the oldest in London. In 1774 Clive of India, hero of the

Left **Shepherd Market** Right **Berkeley Square**

Beadle, Burlington Arcade

British Empire in India, committed suicide at No. 45. Memorial benches in the square bear moving inscriptions, many from Americans who were stationed in Mayfair during World War II. The main UK Bentley and Rolls-Royce dealer's showroom is on the east side of the square. ✎ *Map D4*

9 Burlington Arcade

This arcade of bijou shops was built in 1819 for Lord George Cavendish of Burlington House *(see Royal Academy of Arts p113)* to prevent people from throwing rubbish into his garden. The arcade is patrolled by uniformed beadles who make sure that no unseemly behavior, such as whistling, takes place. ✎ *Piccadilly W1 • Map J4*

10 Faraday Museum

Michael Faraday (1791–1867), a pioneer of electro-technology, experimented in the laboratories of the Royal Institution, where he was Professor of Chemistry from 1833–67. These Neo-classical laboratory buildings now house a museum. ✎ *The Royal Institution, 21 Albemarle Street W1 • Map J3 • Open 10am–5:30pm Mon–Fri • Admission charge*

Exploring St. James's

Morning

🕐 Starting from St. James's Park Underground, walk up through Queen Anne's Gate, noting the lovely 18th-century houses. Pass through the alley in the corner into Birdcage Walk then into **St. James's Park** *(see p113)*. Get a coffee from the kiosk by the lake and watch the pelicans before heading up to **Buckingham Palace** *(see p26)* for the Changing of the Guard at 11am. After the ceremony, head up The Mall, past **St. James's Palace** *(see p113)* and into St. James's Street. Turn right into Jermyn Street, and check out such traditional shops as cheese-seller, Paxton and Whitfield, and perfumery, Floris. Walk through Wren's St. James's Church near the end of the street, leaving by the north exit where a craft market is held. Head west down Piccadilly to Fortnum's.

Afternoon

Fortnum & Mason *(see p63)* is the perfect place to buy tea, as a souvenir, and to have lunch, in the Fountain restaurant, where the dieter's choice is caviar and half a bottle of champagne.

Cross Piccadilly to the **Royal Academy of Arts** *(see p113)* and spend an hour on their permanent collection, including Michelangelo's sculpture, *Madonna and Child*. Window shop along Burlington Arcade and then the galleries of **Cork Street** *(see p116)*. Turn left into Bond Street, heading for **Brown's** *(see p177)* stylish hotel in Albemarle Street, where you can relax over a lavish English tea.

Left **Sotheby's auction house** Right **Designer dresses, Browns**

🔟 Shopping

1 Fortnum and Mason
Famous for its food hall and restaurants, this elegant department store still has male staff who wear tailcoats. Try the extravagant ice creams in the Fountain restaurant *(see p64)*. ◉ *181 Piccadilly W1 • Map J4*

2 Asprey and Garrard
The British royal family have bought their jewels here for more than a century. Other gift items to be found here include pens and silver picture frames. ◉ *165 New Bond Street W1 • Map J3*

3 Charbonnel et Walker
One of the best chocolate shops in town selling a tempting array of handmade chocolates. Fill one of the pretty boxes, which come in a range of sizes, with your own choice of chocolates. ◉ *1 The Royal Arcade, 28 Old Bond Street W1 • Map J4*

4 Gieves and Hawkes
Purveyors of fine, handmade suits and shirts to the gentry since 1785, this shop is one of the best-known in a street of expert tailors. Off-the-rack clothes are also available. ◉ *1 Savile Row W1 • Map J3*

5 Browns
London's most famous designer clothing store stocks pieces by Jill Sander, Dries van Noten and John Galliano among many others. ◉ *23–7 South Molton Street W1 • Map D3*

6 Mulberry
Come here for the complete country-house look, including clothing, household items and gorgeous leather goods. ◉ *41–2 New Bond Street W1 • Map J3*

7 Cork Street Galleries
Cork Street is famous for its art galleries. You can buy works by the best artists here, from Picasso and Rothko to Damien Hirst and Tracey Emin. ◉ *Map J3*

8 Sotheby's
View everything from pop star memorabilia to Old Master paintings at this fine arts auction house founded in 1744. ◉ *34–5 New Bond Street W1 • Map J3*

9 Fenwick
An upmarket, pleasantly small department store. ◉ *63 New Bond Street W1 • Map J3*

10 Waterstone's
What is possibly Europe's largest bookshop occupies a large building on Piccadilly *(see page 65)*. ◉ *203– 206 Piccadilly • Map K4*

Price Categories

For a three-course meal for one with half a bottle of wine (or equivalent meal), taxes and extra charges.

£	under £15
££	£15–£25
£££	£25–£35
££££	£35–£50
£££££	over £50

Quaglino's dining room

🔟 Eating and Drinking

1 Nobu
An original menu combines Japanese food with South American accents. The seven-course chef's menu *(omakase)* is a good introduction. Reservations essential. ◈ *19 Old Park Lane W1* • *Map D4* • *020 7447 4747* • *££££*

2 Momo
Brilliantly-decorated in a kasbah style, this modern, North African restaurant serves *tajines* and couscous. The Mo Tea Room and Bazaar next door serves tea and snacks. ◈ *25 Heddon Street W1* • *Map J3* • *020 7434 4040* • *££££*

3 The Avenue
Join the smart set in this vast, lively restaurant. Food is European and caters to the British preference for large portions. ◈ *7–9 St James's Street SW1* • *020 7321 2111* • *££££*

4 Quaglino's
Chic restaurant with an elegant, swooping staircase to the upstairs bar. Brasserie-style food is served until late (12pm), attracting a post-theatre crowd. ◈ *16 Bury Street SW1* • *Map J4* • *020 7930 6767* • *££££*

5 The Square
Wonderful French food is on offer at this sophisticated modern restaurant. Only set-course meals are served, lunchtime costs less than dinner: 2- and 3-course meals are £20 and £25. ◈ *6–10 Bruton Street W1* • *Map J3* • *020 7495 7100* • *£££££*

6 China House
Authentic Chinese food at bargain prices is served in a lofty 1919 bank building. ◈ *160 Piccadilly W1* • *Map J4* • *020 7499 6996* • *£*

7 Nicole's
Located in the Nicole Farhi fashion shop, this café is a popular lunch stop. ◈ *158 New Bond Street W1* • *Map J3* • *020 7499 8408* • *££*

8 Alloro
This Mayfair restaurant has an airy first-floor dining room, and good Italian food. ◈ *19–20 Dover St W1* • *Map J4* • *020 7495 4768* • *££££*

9 Phillip Owens at the ICA Café
Good food at reasonable prices is on offer at this delightful arts center restaurant. ◈ *The Mall SW1* • *Map L4* • *020 7930 8619* • *£££*

10 Red Lion
This traditional pub serves real ale and bar snacks. A restaurant at the rear has good English food. ◈ *Waverton Street W1* • *Map D4* • *020 7499 1307* • *£££*

Left **Tiles, Holland House** Center **Kensington Palace Gardens** Right **Natural History Museum**

Kensington and Knightsbridge

THIS IS WHERE *London's gentry lives. Nannies push baby carriages around Kensington Gardens, uniformed children line up in Hans Crescent and the social "in-crowd" gossip in the Fifth-Floor Café at Harvey Nichols. Whatever time of year, nobody is without a tan. Harrods is the light beacon of the area; the solid rocks are the great museums established in South Kensington by Prince Albert, whose name is never far away. Kensington is the Royal Borough where Lady Diana roamed. She lived in Kensington Palace, the choicest of royal residences, and shopped in Beauchamp Place. Foreign royalty have homes here, too. Such mansions need the finest furnishings and some of London's best antique shops are in Kensington Church Street and Portobello Road, the most fun place to be on Saturday mornings.*

Sights

1. Natural History Museum
2. Science Museum
3. Victoria and Albert Museum
4. Kensington Palace
5. Albert Memorial
6. Harrods
7. Albert Hall
8. Portobello Road
9. Holland Park
10. Leighton House

Decorative relief, Natural History Museum

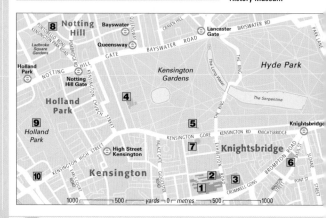

Tippoo's Tiger, Victoria and Albert Museum

1 Natural History Museum
The whole world of animals and minerals is vividly explained (see pp22–3).

2 Science Museum
Traces the history of scientific and technical innovation (see pp24–5).

3 Victoria and Albert Museum
A cornucopia of treasures is housed in this enchanting museum named after the devoted royal couple. There are fine and applied arts from all over the world, from ancient China to contemporary Britain. Highlights include extraordinary plaster copies of statues, and monuments and artifacts from the Italian Renaissance. Displays are arranged over six floors of galleries. The new British Galleries show domestic interiors from 1500 to 1900. Pick up a plan at the entrance and realise you won't see it all. Don't miss the Morris, Gamble and Poynter Rooms *(see p48)*. ✆ Cromwell Road SW7 • Map B5–C5 • Open 10am–5:50pm daily (10pm Wed) • Free

4 Kensington Palace
This is a delightful royal residence on a domestic scale, still in use by members of the royal family: Diana, Princess of Wales lived here and Princess Margaret, the Queen's sister, still occupies a large part of the building. The first-floor state apartments built for King William III and Queen Mary are open to the public, and the audio guide (free; you must pick one up because there is no literature or labeling in the rooms) evokes 17th–18th-century court life. Rooms on the ground floor have a collection of royal costumes, including some of Diana's *(see p54)*. ✆ Kensington Palace Gardens W8 • Map A4 • Open Mar–Oct: 10am–5pm daily; Nov–Feb: 10am–4pm daily • Admission charge

5 Albert Memorial
This edifice to Queen Victoria's beloved consort, Prince Albert, glowing from a recent restoration, is a fitting tribute to the man who played a large part in establishing the South Kensington museums. Opposite the Royal Albert Hall, the memorial was designed by Sir George Gilbert Scott and completed in 1876. At its four corners are tableaux representing the Empire, which was at its height in Victoria's reign. ✆ Kensington Gardens SW7 • Map B4

Left **Earth Galleries, Natural History Museum** Right **Albert Memorial**

For more London museums **See pp48–9**

6 Harrods

No backpacks, no torn jeans… Harrods' doormen ensure even the people in the store are in the best possible taste. This world-famous emporium began life in 1849 as a small, impeccable grocer's, and the present terracotta building was built in 1905. It is most striking at night, when it is illuminated by 11,500 lights. It has more than 150 departments and on no account should you miss the wonderfully tiled and decorated food halls. Pick up a floor plan as you go in. An Egyptian theme decorates the central well, at the bottom of which is a shrine to Diana, Princess of Wales, and Dodi Al Fayed (see p64). ◈
Knightsbridge SW1 • Map C4

7 Royal Albert Hall

When Queen Victoria laid the foundation stone for The Hall of Arts and Sciences, to everyone's astonishment she put the words *Royal Albert* before its name, and today it is usually just referred to as the Albert Hall. It is a huge, nearly circular building, modeled on Roman amphitheaters, and seats 7,000. Circuses, boxing matches and all manner of musical entertainments are held here, notably the Sir Henry Wood Promenade Concerts (see p57). ◈ *Kensington Gore SW7 • Map B5 • Open for performances*

Statue of Prince Albert, outside Albert Hall

Prince Albert

Queen Victoria and her first cousin Prince Albert of Saxe-Coburg-Gotha were both 20 when they married in 1840. A Victorian in every sense, his interest in the arts and sciences led to the founding of the great institutions of South Kensington. He died at the age of 41, and the Queen mourned him for the rest of her life. They had nine children.

8 Portobello Road

Running through the center of the decidedly fashionable Notting Hill, Portobello Road, with its extensive selection of antique shops, is a great place to spend some time. It is especially good on Saturday when the market is in full swing. This starts just beyond Westbourne Grove, with fruit and vegetables, bread, sausages, cheeses, then music, clothes and bric-à-brac. Beyond the railway bridge it becomes a flea market. Sit upstairs in the Café Grove (No. 253a) and watch it all go by, or quench your thirst in Fluid's juice bar (13 Elgin Crescent). Ethnic food is otherwise what goes down best, and the West Indian flavor spills over into the vibrant music and colorful clothes stalls (see p65). ◈ *Map A3–A4*

Left **Portobello Road Market** Right **Royal Albert Hall**

Café, Holland Park

9 Holland Park

There is a great deal of charm about Holland Park, where enclosed gardens are laid out like rooms in an open-air house. At its center is Holland House, a beautiful Jacobean mansion, which was destroyed in a bombing raid in 1941. What remains is used as a youth hostel and the backdrop for summer concerts. Peacocks roam in the woods and in the gardens, including the Dutch Garden, where dahlias were first planted in England. ⦿ Abbotsbury Road W14 • Map A4–A5

10 Leighton House

All the themes of the Victorian Aesthetic movement can be found in Leighton House. It was designed by Lord Leighton (see p52) and his friend George Aitchison in1866. Its high point is the fabulous Arab Hall, with a fountain and stained-glass cupola. Other friends contributed friezes and mosaics, but many features are original, notably the Islamic tiles, collected by Leighton and his friends on their travels. ⦿ 12 Holland Park Road W14 • Map A5 • Open 11am–5:30pm Wed–Mon • Free

Kensington on Foot

Morning

🕐 Start at South Kensington Underground station, and follow the signs to the **Victoria & Albert Museum**, (see p119). Spend a delightful hour in the dress galleries and see the Raphael cartoons: all on the ground floor. Follow Old Brompton Road to the **Brompton Oratory** (see p47), where you should take a look at its sumptuous Italianate interior, with 12 marble Apostles. Cross the road for a coffee and a pastry at Patisserie Valerie.

Turn right into Beauchamp Place, where window shopping takes in creations by such English designers as Bruce Oldfield and Caroline Charles. Continue down into Pont Street, and turn left up Sloane Street. Check out Hermés, Chanel and Dolce e Gabbana before turning left along Knightsbridge to Harrods.

Harrods has a choice of 21 bars and restaurants. The food hall's Deli and the Oyster Bar are best. Save dessert for the 4th-floor ice-cream parlor.

Afternoon

Just five minutes north of Harrods, **Hyde Park** (see p28), offers a peaceful walk along the south bank of the Serpentine. Heading for **Kensington Palace** (see p119) you pass the famous statue of J.M. Barry's Peter Pan and the Round Pond, where model-makers sail their boats. West of here, the palace's costume exhibit includes many of Princess Diana's dresses. Next door, **The Orangery Tea Rooms** (see p124) provide a restorative cup of tea.

Around Town – Kensington & Knightsbridge

Left **Riding, Hyde Park** Center **Serpentine Gallery** Right **Holland Park Orangery**

🔟 The Best of the Rest

1 Royal College of Music
The UK's leading music college stages musical events throughout the year. It also houses a Museum of Musical Instruments. ◈ *Prince Consort Road SW7 • Map B5 • Museum Open 2–4:30pm Wed (term-time only) • Admission charge*

2 Holland Park Concerts
The open-air theatre in Holland Park hosts an annual summer season of opera, theatre and dance, while art exhibitions are held regularly in the Ice House and the Orangery *(see p121)*. ◈ *Abbotsbury Road W14 • Map A4–A5 • Admission charge*

3 Serpentine Gallery
In the southeast corner of Kensington Gardens, this gallery houses temporary exhibitions of contemporary paintings and sculpture. ◈ *Kensington Gardens W2 • Map B4 • Open 10am–6pm daily • Free*

4 Christie's
Visiting the salerooms here is like going to a small museum. Their experts will value items brought in by the public. ◈ *85 Old Brompton Road SW7 • Map B5 • Open 9am–5pm Mon–Fri (7pm Mon)*

5 Electric Cinema
London's oldest purpose-built movie theater, it remains one of the prettiest. Recently reopened after refurbishment, with luxury seats, a bar and restaurant. ◈ *Portobello Road W11 • Map A3–A4*

6 Leisure Box
Go ice skating and tenpin bowling here – but try to avoid the after-school crowd. ◈ *17 Queensway W2 • Map A3 • Bowling 10am–11pm daily, Skating 10am–10:45pm daily (10pm Sun) • Admission charge*

7 V&A Late View
On Wednesdays the ground-floor galleries at the Victoria and Albert Museum are open until 10pm, with talks and live music *(see p119)*. ◈ *Cromwell Road SW7 • Map B5–C5 • Free*

8 Park Café
Alongside the Serpentine Lido, the Park Café has lakeside tables. Jazz and poetry sessions take place on summer evenings. ◈ *Hyde Park W2 • Map C4*

9 Speakers' Corner
This corner of Hyde Park attracts assorted public speakers, especially on Sundays. ◈ *Hyde Park W2 • Map C3*

10 Hyde Park Stables
Ride around Hyde Park or take lessons – this is the best place for horse riding in London. ◈ *63 Bathurst Mews W2 • Map B3*

Left **Harvey Nichols** Right **Harvey Nichols mannequin**

🔟 Shopping

1 Harrods
London's most famous store has 300 departments full of the finest goods that money can buy. Specialities include food, fashion, china, glass and kitchenware *(see p64 and p120)*. ◈ 87–135 Brompton Rd SW1 • Map C5

2 Harvey Nichols
Another top London store. Fashion houses occupy five floors, with many British designers represented. There are also home departments, a fine restaurant and a food hall *(see p64)*. ◈ 109–125 Knightsbridge SW1 • Map C4

3 Scotch House
This tranquil shop sells well-made women's and men's woollen clothes. Check out your clan and tartan in the Tartan Room. ◈ 2 Brompton Road SW1 • Map C5

4 Nicole Farhi
Sophisticated urban clothing from one of the UK's leading designers is available is this cool, minimalist shop. ◈ 193 Sloane St SW1 • Map C5

5 Monte's Cigar Store
A club as well as a cigar store: the club restaurant is now open to the public. ◈ 164 Sloane Street SW1 • Map C5

6 Barker's
Based in the 1930s building that once housed two of London's major department stores are various fashion outlets including Monsoon, Jigsaw, Hobbs and Karen Millen. ◈ 63 Kensington High Street W8 • Map A4

7 The Lacquer Chest
Offering an enticing mix of Victoriana, including porcelain, china and Oriental ware. This is one of many antique shops in Kensington Church Street. ◈ 75 Kensington Church Street W8 • Map A4

8 The Tanning Shop
Open seven days a week, this beauty treatment and tanning center (one of a chain), is the place to top up your suntan. ◈ 4 Campden Hill Road W8 • Map A4

9 Art 4 Fun
Creative café, popular with children, where you can decorate your own ceramic, glass, fabric or wooden items. They provide all the equipment as well as coffee, tea and snacks. ◈ 196 Kensington Park Road W11 • Map A4

10 The Travel Bookshop
Excellent specialist bookshop selling both new and old books. The shop achieved fame in the film *Notting Hill*. ◈ 13 Blenheim Crescent W11 • Tube Ladbroke Grove

Left **Fifth floor café, Harvey Nichols** Right **Churchill Arms pub**

TOP 10 Pubs and Cafés

1 Beach Blanket Babylon
Famous for its wildly-gothic interior, this bar serves coffee and snacks during the day, and becomes a swanky cocktail lounge in the evenings. A good place to mingle with the fashionable Notting Hill crowd. ◎ 45 Ledbury Road W11 • Map A3

2 Churchill Arms
Filled with intriguing bric-à-brac and Churchill memorabilia, this is a large, friendly Victorian pub. Inexpensive Thai food is served in the conservatory at lunchtime and for dinner until 9:30pm. ◎ 119 Kensington Church Street W8 • Map A4

3 The Orangery Tea Rooms
Open for tea, coffee and lunch, this delightful café is located in a pretty conservatory overlooking Kensington Gardens (see p121). ◎ Kensington Palace W8 • Map A4

4 Portobello Gold
This trendy bar, used by local antique dealers, has a suitably alternative atmosphere and an upstairs internet bar. There is also a conservatory restaurant. ◎ 95–97 Portobello Road W11 • Map A3

5 Le Metro
This smart wine bar makes a convenient rest stop for tired shoppers. Located just behind Harrods, Le Metro serves tea, coffee and a short menu of light meals, both for lunch and dinner. ◎ 28 Basil Street SW3 • Map C5

6 Paxton's Head
A popular watering hole for both locals and visitors, this old pub caters for all tastes, with cocktails and flavored vodkas as well as real ales. ◎ 153 Knightsbridge SW1 • Map C4

7 Harrod's Ice-cream Parlour
Freshly-made in Harrod's kitchens, the ice cream in this fourth-floor café is arranged into mouthwatering, elaborate sundaes, including such old-fashioned treats as banana splits. ◎ Knightsbridge SW1 • Map C5

8 Fifth Floor Café
Open all day for breakfast, lunch, tea and dinner. ◎ Harvey Nichols, 67 Brompton Rd SW3 • Map C4

9 Market Bar
This atmospheric pub is popular with locals. ◎ 240A Portobello Road W11• Map A3

10 Portobello Stalls
Along the market there are stalls offering ethnic food of every kind. The area also has a good choice of cafes around Portobello Green. ◎ Portobello Road W11 • Tube Westbourne Park

Façade, Kensington Place

Price Categories

For a three-course	**£** under £15
meal for one with half	**££** £15–£25
a bottle of wine (or	**£££** £25–£35
equivalent meal), taxes	**££££** £35–£50
and extra charges.	**£££££** over £50

🔟 Restaurants

1 Clarke's
The menu consists of whatever chef Sally Clarke decides to cook for the evening meal. Whatever it is it will be excellent. ◎ *124 Kensington High Street W8* • *Map A5* • *020 7221 9225* • *££££*

2 Belvedere
The restaurant's romantic setting in Holland Park is enhanced by its good French cooking. From the patio in summer, you may hear distant opera from the park's open-air theatre. ◎ *Holland Park W8* • *Map A4* • *020 7602 1238* • *£££*

3 Kensington Place
Renowned chef Rowley Leigh presides over this trendy eaterie dominated by its huge windows. ◎ *201 Kensington Church Street W8* • *Map A4* • *020 7727 3184* • *£££*

4 Pharmacy
Kensington's trendiest restaurant was designed by the artist Damien Hirst, and feels as if you are dining in one of his installations. There is a bar, and the restaurant serves eclectic dishes. Book in advance. ◎ *150 Notting Hill Gate W11* • *Map A4* • *020 7221 2442* • *Disabled access to bar only* • *££££*

5 Bistro 190
Set in a large Victorian house, this traditional bistro is open from 7am to midnight. The more formal restaurant downstairs offers modern European cooking. ◎ *190 Queensgate SW7* • *Map A3* • *020 7581 5666* • *£££*

6 Royal China
A tempting variety of dim sum, including delicious *char siu* buns, are the main attraction here. ◎ *13 Queensway W2* • *Map A3* • *020 7221 2535* • *££*

7 Magic Wok
The menu offers an exciting range of Cantonese dishes. ◎ *100 Queensway W2* • *Map A3* • *020 7792 9767* • *No disabled access* • *££*

8 Wódka
Vodka comes in carafes at this leading East European restaurant. Try the smoked salmon and caviar blinis. ◎ *12 St Albans Grove W8* • *Map B5* • *020 7937 6513* • *No disabled access* • *££££*

9 Isola
An ultra-trendy interior of chrome and red leather provides the setting for top-notch Italian cooking. ◎ *145 Knightsbridge SW1* • *Map C4* • *020 7838 1044* • *££££*

10 Monte's
Scottish scallops, Cornish crabs and game are served in this club restaurant open at lunch to non-members. ◎ *164 Sloane Street SW1* • *Map D5* • *020 7235 0555* • *££££*

Note: Unless otherwise stated, all restaurants accept credit cards and serve vegetarian meals

Left **Madame Tussaud's** Right **Regent's Park**

Regent's Park and Marylebone

NORTH OF OXFORD STREET *and south of the park are the grand mansion blocks of Marylebone. Once a medieval village surrounded by fields and a pleasure garden, now it is a fashionable and elegant inner city area. In the 19th century, doctors started using these spacious houses to see wealthy clients. The medical connection continues today in the discreet Harley Street consulting rooms of private medical specialists. Madame Tussaud's and the Planetarium in Marylebone Road may be less fashionable, but the queues outside testify to their popularity. Behind Marylebone Road, encircled by John Nash's magnificent terraces, is Regent's Park where the residents' tranquillity is ruffled only by the muezzin calling from the London Central Mosque and the bellowing of elephants in London Zoo.*

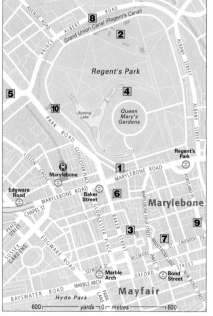

John Nash's Cumberland Terrace dating from 1828

🔟 Sights

1. **Madame Tussaud's**
2. **London Zoo**
3. **Wallace Collection**
4. **Regent's Park**
5. **Marylebone Cricket Club Museum**
6. **Sherlock Holmes Museum**
7. **Wigmore Hall**
8. **Regent's Canal**
9. **BBC Broadcasting House**
10. **London Central Mosque**

Preceding pages **Notting Hill Carnival**

Lord Snowdon's aviary, London Zoo

Madame Tussaud's

1 Madame Tussaud's museum of waxwork models of the famous has been one of London's major attractions for a century. Arrive early in the day or book ahead by phone or web to get a timed ticket. Next door, the Planetarium has a 30-minute show about the night sky. You can buy a combined ticket for both *(see p68)*. ❂ *Marylebone Road NW1 • Map C2 • Open May–Sep: 10am–5:30pm; Oct–Jun: 10am–5:30pm Mon–Fri, 9:30–5:30 Sat & Sun • Admission charge*

London Zoo

2 Lying on the northern side of Regent's Park, London Zoo is home to 600 different animal species. The zoo is heavily into conservation and you can see the breeding programs of endangered animals, such as the giant weta and Knysna seahorse. A map is provided and their booklet is full of fascinating animal lore *(see p68)*. ❂ *Regent's Park NW1 • Map C1 • Open Mar–Oct: 10am–5:30pm; Nov–Feb: 10am–4pm • Admission charge*

Wallace Collection

3 "The finest collection of art ever assembled by one family," is the claim of the Wallace Collection, and it is hard to disagree. Sir Richard Wallace, who left this collection to the nation in 1897, was not only outrageously rich but a man of great taste. As well as 25 galleries of fine Sèvres porcelain, there is a substantial collection of master works by English, French and Dutch artists, including Frans Hals' *The Laughing Cavalier (see p50)*. ❂ *Manchester Square W1 • Map D3 • Open 10am–5pm Mon–Sat, 2–5pm Sun • Free*

Regent's Park

4 The best part of Regent's Park lies within the Inner Circle. Here are Queen Mary's Gardens, with beds and bowers of roses, the Open Air Theatre with its summer Shakespeare productions and the popular Park Café – one of half a dozen cafés in the park. Rowing boats, tennis courts and deck chairs can be rented and in summer musical performances take place on the bandstand *(see p29)*. ❂ *NW1 • Map C1–D2 • Open 5am–dusk daily*

Left **Shirley Bassey, Madame Tussaud's** Right **Boating lake, Regent's Park**

5 Marylebone Cricket Club Museum

This is the place to unravel the mysteries of England's greatest gift to the world of sports. Founded in 1787, the MCC is the governing body of the game, and its home ground, Lord's, is one of two London venues for Test matches. The museum can only be seen as part of a guided tour of the ground. ✪ St. John's Wood NW8 • Map B2 • Tours Apr–Oct: 10am, noon, 2pm

Lord's Cricket Ground

6 Sherlock Holmes Museum

Take a camera when you visit here so you can have your picture taken sitting by the fire in the great detective's front room, wearing a deerstalker hat and smoking a pipe. This museum is great fun, brilliantly reconstructed with some excellent touches. A Victorian policeman stands guard outside, uniformed maids let you in and, upstairs, wax dummies (including the villainous Moriarty) re-enact moments from Holmes's most famous cases (see p52). ✪ 221b Baker Street NW1 • Map C2 • Open 9:30am–6:30pm daily

Regency London

Regent's Park was named after the Prince Regent (the future George IV) who employed John Nash in 1812 to lay out the park on the royal estate of Marylebone Farm. Nash was given a free hand and the result is a harmonious delight. Encircling the park are sumptuous Neoclassical terraces, including Cumberland Terrace, intended to be the Prince Regent's residence.

7 Wigmore Hall

Concerts in the Wigmore Hall have a middle-European quality to them, particularly the Sunday morning Coffee Concerts. Nobody is here to be seen – they are only here for the music, which they know and love. The accoustically wonderful hall was built in 1907 by the Bechstein piano company, which had showrooms next door. ✪ 36 Wigmore Street W1 • Map D3

8 Regent's Canal

John Nash wanted the canal to go through the center of his new Regent's Park, but objections from neighbors, who were concerned about smelly canal boats and foul-mouthed crews, resulted in it being sited on the northern side of the park. In 1874, a cargo of explosives demolished the North Gate bridge beside London Zoo (see p168). ✪ Map C1

Left **Residential narrow boats, Regent's Canal** Right **BBC Broadcasting House**

London Central Mosque

9 BBC Broadcasting House

Synonymous with the BBC, Broadcasting House has sailed majestically down Portland Place like a great liner since it was built in 1932. The expansion in radio and, later, television, meant that additional, larger premises were soon required, and now most broadcasting is done from other studios. New plans, however, aim to redevelop Broadcasting House as a new, modern centre for BBC Radio, the BBC World Service and BBC News. ✈ *Broadcasting House, Portland Place W1 • Map J1 • Closed to public*

10 London Central Mosque

Five times a day the muezzin calls the faithful to prayer from the minaret of the London Central Mosque. Built in 1978, with a distinctive copper dome, it acts as a community and cultural center for followers of Islam. It is a hospitable place: step inside and see the sky-blue domed ceiling and its shimmering chandelier. Prayer mats cover the floor for the faithful who turn towards Mecca to pray. ✈ *146 Park Road NW8 • Map C2*

Exploring Marylebone

Morning

🕐 Before setting out for the day, reserve a ticket for **Madame Tussaud's** *(see p68)* for the afternoon. Start at Bond Street Underground, exiting on Oxford Street. Opposite is St. Christopher Place, a narrow lane with charming shops, which opens into an attractive pedestrian square. Stop for a coffee break at one of Sofra's pavement tables.

Continue into Marylebone Lane, a pleasant side street of small shops, which leads to Marylebone High Street and its wide choice of designer shops, including **The Conran Shop** *(see p132)*. Stop awhile in the peaceful memorial garden of St. Marylebone Parish Church, planted with various exotic trees. Methodist minister and hymn-writer Charles Wesley (1707–88) has a memorial here.

Afternoon

🍽 For lunch, the **Orrery** *(see p133)*, beside The Conran Shop, is recommended. For a lighter snack, try Patisserie Valerie at 105 Marylebone High Street.

After lunch, bypass the legendary lines outside **Madame Tussaud's** and, brandishing your ticket, spend an hour and a half checking out celebrity wax figures and the Planetarium.

Cross Marylebone Road to Baker Street, for tea and a sandwich at **Reubens** *(see p133)*, before heading for the charming **Sherlock Holmes Museum** at No. 221b, a faithful reconstruction of the fictional detective's home.

Left **Selfridges columned façade** Center **John Lewis department store** Right **Selfridges window**

TOP 10 Shopping

1 Daunt's
All kinds of travel books, including fiction, are arranged along oak galleries in this atmospheric Edwardian travel bookshop. There is also a coffee shop. ✇ 83–84 Marylebone High Street W1 • Map D3

2 Button Queen
A dazzling array of buttons, from antique silver to Art Deco pearl, are available in this charming shop. ✇ 19 Marylebone Lane W1 • Map D3

3 The Conran Shop
Conran sells the best of both modern British and historic European design, such as a classic Mies Van der Rohe reclining chair. ✇ 55 Marylebone High Street, W1 • Map D3

4 Divertimenti
This innovative London kitchen store has a huge variety of cooking implements, utensils and tableware. Open Sunday afternoons. ✇ 45–7 Wigmore Street W1 • Map D3

5 London Beatles Store
Every kind of souvenir commemorating Britain's most famous band is on sale here. The Elvis Presley shop is next door. ✇ 230 Baker Street NW1 • Map C3

6 Talking Bookshop
A wide selection of audio and video books, including most English classic works. Most are read by famous actors. ✇ 11 Wigmore Street W1 • Map C3

7 John Lewis
This sophisticated department store prides itself on being "never knowingly undersold". If you can prove another shop sells the same item for less, you pay the lower price. It has a thoughtful gifts department on the ground floor, and the staff are both helpful and knowledgeable. ✇ 278–306 Oxford Street W1 • Map D3

8 Selfridges
Opened in 1909, this store has a handsome neoclassical façade adorned with imposing columns and a huge clock. A London institution, Selfridges is still popular for women's fashion. ✇ 400 Oxford Street W1 • Map D3

9 Marks & Spencer
This flagship British brand is known for its underwear and food. ✇ 458 Oxford Street W1 • Map D3

10 Debenhams
A middle-of-the-road department store that sells everything from tools to toys. ✇ 334–348 Oxford Street W1 • Map D3

Price Categories

For a three course meal for one with half a bottle of wine (or equivalent meal), taxes and extra charges.

£	under £15
££	£15–£25
£££	£25–£35
££££	£35–£50
£££££	over £50

Left **Ibla restaurant** Right **Ibla's decorative sign**

🔟 Eating and Drinking

1 Café Bagatelle
Located in the courtyard of the Wallace Collection, this wonderful restaurant serves delicious lunches. Choose from big salads, wild mushroom risotto and pistachio and chocolate crème brulée with shortbread *(see p50)*. ❧ *Hertford House, Manchester Square W1 • Map D3 • 020 7935 0687 • £££*

2 Original Tagines
A distinctive Moroccan wine list complements the hearty tagines and couscous, including vegetarian versions, offered here. ❧ *7A Dorset Street W1 • Map C3 • 020 7935 1545 • ££*

3 Ibla
This smart Italian restaurant has stylish decor and an excellent selection of Italian wines. There is a choice of set-price menus. ❧ *89 Marylebone High Street W1 • Map D3 • 020 7224 3799 • ££££*

4 Reubens
One of London's best kosher restaurants offering such comfort food as chopped liver and salt beef. ❧ *79 Baker Street W1 • Map C3 • 020 7486 0035 • £££*

5 Mandalay
A Burmese café where the food is a pleasing mix of Chinese, Indian and Thai. Mandalay is friendly, inexpensive and non-smoking. ❧ *444 Edgware Road W2 • 020 7258 3696 • Map B2 • £*

6 Patogh
Kebabs are a speciality of this Iranian restaurant that attracts a cheerful crowd. It is unlicensed, but you can take your own beer or wine. ❧ *8 Crawford Place W1 • Map C3 • 020 7262 4015 • £*

7 Giraffe
This bright restaurant serves light meals with an international flavor, everything from Thai to Mexican. ❧ *6–8 Blandford Street W1 • Map C3 • 020 7935 2333 • £££*

8 Orrery
This is a lovely restaurant, serving French-inspired cooking. ❧ *55 Marylebone High Street W1 • Map D3 • 020 7616 8000 • £££££*

9 O'Conor Don
Genuine Irish pub serving stews and oysters alongside their Guinness, and a good choice of whiskeys. ❧ *88 Marylebone Lane W1 • Map D3 • 020 7935 9311 • ££*

10 ITS
A stylish pizza and pasta restaurant at the back of Oxford Street. ❧ *60 Wigmore Street W1 • Map D3 • 020 7224 3484 • ££*

> **Note:** Unless otherwise stated, all restaurants accept credit cards and serve vegetarian meals

Left **Fish weathervane at Old Billingsgate Market** Right **Old Billingsgate Market**

The City

THE ANCIENT SQUARE MILE OF LONDON, *defined roughly by the walls of the Roman city, is a curious mixture of streets and lanes with medieval names, state-of-the-art finance houses and no fewer than 38 churches, many of them, including St. Paul's Cathedral, designed by Sir Christopher Wren. Don't miss the City's old markets: Smithfield still operates as a meat market, Leadenhall is in many ways more attractive than Covent Garden, while the former fish market of Billingsgate offers a great view of the once busy Pool of London.*

🔟 Sights

1. Tower of London
2. St. Paul's Cathedral
3. Tower Bridge
4. Barbican Centre
5. Museum of London
6. Guildhall
7. Guildhall Art Gallery
8. Bank of England Museum
9. Monument
10. St. Katharine's Dock

Stone dragon in Smithfield market

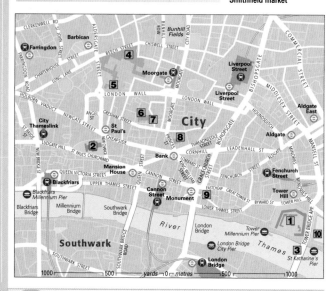

Tower Bridge and the Pool of London

1 Tower of London
See pp36–9.

2 St. Paul's Cathedral
See pp40–43.

3 Tower Bridge
When the Pool of London was the gateway to the city's larder, this flamboyant bridge (see p71) was constantly being raised and lowered for sail and steam ships bringing their cargoes from all corners of the Empire. Pedestrians who needed to cross the river when the bridge was open had to climb up the 300 steps of the towers to the walkway overhead. Today, visitors on the 90-minute Tower Bridge Experience tour still have views from the 135-ft (40-m) high walkways. The entrance is beneath the north pier, where a "journey through time" begins. It ends with a hands-on experience in the massive engine room, and exits via a shop on the south bank of the river. ⊗ *SE1 • Map H4 • Open 9:30–6pm • Admission charge*

4 Barbican Centre
The cultural jewel of the City, owned, funded and managed by the Corporation of London, the Barbican is a modern building of some complexity. Music, dance, theatre, film and art all take place here, with top visiting performers and artists. Opened in 1982, the arts complex is part of a major development covering 20 acres and flanked by 42-story blocks of flats. Access from the Barbican tube station is along a marked route above ground level, passing the Museum of London (see p136) and looking down on the church of St. Giles Cripplegate. This church, dating from 1550, is a lone survivor of World War II bombs (see p56). ⊗ *Silk Street EC2 • Map R1*

Left **Barbican Centre** Right **Tower of London**

5 Museum of London

An essential visit for anyone interested in the history of London. The city of the past is evoked through reconstructed streets, shops and domestic interiors and visits are organized to historic London buildings. There is a café and an extensive bookshop (see p48). ⊗ London Wall EC2 • Map R1 • Open 10am–5:50pm Mon– Sat, 12–5:50pm Sun • Admission charge

Roman wall painting, Museum of London

6 Guildhall

For around 900 years the Guildhall has been the administrative center of the City of London. City ceremonials are held in its magnificent 15th-century Great Hall, which is hung with banners of the main livery companies. In the Guildhall Library are rotating displays of wonderful historic manuscripts and an intriguing collection of watches and clocks, from the Worshipful Company of Clockmakers – some from 1600. ⊗ Guildhall Yard, Gresham Street EC2 • Map G3 • Open 9am–5pm (Winter:10am–5pm) Mon–Sat • Free

Dick Whittington

A stained-glass window in St. Michael, Paternoster Royal, depicts Dick Whittington (and his cat) – hero of a well-known London rags-to-riches fairy-tale. In fact, Richard Whittington, who was Lord Mayor of London four times between 1397 and 1420, was a wealthy merchant and the City's first major benefactor. He pioneered public lavatories, building them to overhang the Thames.

7 Guildhall Art Gallery

On the east side of Guildhall Yard is the Guildhall Art Gallery, two floors of paintings of varying quality and enormous interest. Many are associated with the City, and there are a number of highly romantic 19th-century paintings, including pre-Raphaelite works. With the aid of a computerized cataloging system, it is possible to view all the Guildhall's 31,000 prints and paintings. ⊗ Gresham Street EC2 • Map G3 • Open 10am–5pm Mon–Sat, noon–4pm Sun • Admission charge

8 Bank of England Museum

Liveried doormen greet visitors to this excellent museum, housed in a marvellous building designed by Sir John Soane (see p107). A variety of material is on display, including 45 bars of gold bullion at the center of the 1930s rotunda. There is a map of the

Yacht haven, St Katharine's Dock

Façade, Guildhall

City's financial institutions and an electronic trading desk similar to those used by dealers today. ◈ *Bartholomew Lane EC4 • Map G3 • Open 10am–5pm Mon–Fri • Free*

9 Monument
This 202-ft (62-m) monument by Sir Christopher Wren is the world's tallest free-standing stone column. Its height is equal to the distance from the baker's shop in Pudding Lane where the Great Fire of London began in 1666 – the event that it marks. Inside, 311 stairs spiral up to a viewing platform; when you return to the entrance, you will receive a certificate to say that you have made the climb. ◈ *Monument Street EC3 • Map H4 • Open 10am–5:40pm daily • Admission charge*

10 St. Katharine's Dock
Near Tower Bridge and the Tower of London, this is the place to come and relax, to watch the rich on their yachts and the working sailors on the Thames barges. There are several cafés, the Dickens Inn, with outside tables, and the Aquarium restaurant for a serious meal *(see p71)*. ◈ *E1 • Map H4*

The City on Foot

Morning

Start the day with a brisk trot up the 311 steps of the Monument and see how the surrounding narrow streets all slope down towards the Thames. Descend and carry on down Fish Street Hill across Lower Thames Street to the historic church of **St. Magnus the Martyr** *(see p138)*, where a model of the former London Bridge shows the city's great landmark as it was until the 18th century.

Return up Fish Street Hill and Philpot Lane, to Lime Street where you will see the glass elevator of Richard Rogers' 1986 Lloyd's of London building whiz up and down. Enter the ornate, 1881 Leadenhall Market building, which houses a selection of trendy shops, restaurants and bars. Have a delicious lunch at Luc's Brasserie in the market.

Afternoon

After lunch, see the City's historic financial buildings along Cornhill. Notice the Royal Exchange building's grand Corinthian portico and hear its carillon of bells at 3pm. Opposite is the Mansion House, the official residence of the Lord Mayor of London. To the north, across Thread-needle Street, is the Bank of England. Continue into Lothbury and along Gresham Street to Guild-hall, where you should look at the medieval Great Hall.

Head up Wood Street to the **Barbican** *(see p135)* for tea and cakes by the lake at the Waterside Café. Check the programe for the evening's events and maybe take in a show.

Left **Organ at St. Katherine Cree** Right **Carved capital in St. Paul's Cathedral**

🔟 City Churches to Visit

1 St. Paul's Cathedral
(See pp40–43).

2 St. Bartholomew-the-Great
London's oldest church, St. Bartholomew, was built in the 12th century. Several Norman architectural details may be seen *(see pp 46).* 🅢 *West Smithfield EC1 • Map R1 • Open 8:30am–5pm (4pm in winter) Tue–Fri, 10:30am–1:30pm Sat, 2:30–6pm Sun • Free*

3 St. Mary-le-Bow
Located in Cheapside, St. Mary-le-Bow was rebuilt by Wren following its destruction in the Great Fire of London in 1666. 🅢 *Cheapside EC2 • Map G3 • Open 6:30am–6pm Mon–Thu, 6:30am–4pm Fri • Free*

4 St. Sepulchre-without-Newgate
The largest church in the city, St. Sepulchre is famous for its peal of 12 bells. Lunchtime concerts are held on Tue and Wed. 🅢 *Holborn Viaduct EC1 • Map Q1 • Open noon–2pm Tue–Thu, 11am–3pm Wed • Free*

5 St. Katherine Cree
One of eight churches to survive the Great Fire, it dates from about 1630. Purcell and Handel both played on its organ. 🅢 *Leadenhall Street EC3 • Map H3 • Open 10:30am–4:30pm Mon–Fri • Free*

6 St. Magnus the Martyr
Designed by Wren in the 1670s, the church retains his elegant pulpit. Lunchtime recitals

are held on Tuesdays throughout the year. 🅢 *Lower Thames Street EC3 • Map H4 • Open 10am–3pm Tue–Fri, 10:15am–2pm Sun • Free*

7 All Hallows by the Tower
Take a 40-minute audio tour of the church, which dates from Saxon times. 🅢 *Byward Street EC3 • Map H3 • Open 9am–5:45pm Mon–Fri, 10am–5pm Sat & Sun • Free*

8 St. Stephen Walbrook
The Lord Mayor's parish church is considered to be Wren's finest. 🅢 *Walbrook EC4 • Map G3 • Open 10am–4pm Mon–Thu, 10am–3pm Fri • Free*

9 Anne and St. Agnes
This Lutheran church has its own choir, the St. Anne's Singers. Lunchtime concerts are held on Mon, and Fri. 🅢 *Gresham Street EC2 • Map R2 • Open 10am–4pm Mon–Fri, services on Sun • Free*

10 St. Lawrence Jewry
Beautiful stained glass windows of historic figures are the highlight here. 🅢 *Guildhall EC2 • Map R2 • Open 7:30am–2pm daily • Free*

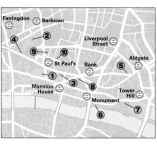

Price Categories

For a three-course meal for one with half a bottle of wine (or equivalent meal), taxes and extra charges.

£	under £15
££	£15–£25
£££	£25–£35
££££	£35–£50
£££££	over £50

Terminus restaurant at Liverpool Street station

Eating and Drinking

1 St. John
A delight for serious meat eaters, St. John is an award-wining restaurant. ◎ *26 St John Street EC1 • Map F2 • 020 7251 0848 • Difficult access but disabled facilities inside • £££*

2 Top Floor at Smiths Smiths of Smithfield
Another carnivores' delight, this large warehouse restaurant serves daily meat-market specials. ◎ *66–7 Charterhouse Street EC1 • Map Q1 • 020 7236 6666 • £££*

3 Club Gascon
Top-notch cuisine from south-west France. Pick three or four "taster" dishes, such as squid or cassoulet, from four themed sections, or there is a five-course gourmet "tasting" menu, including wines. ◎ *57 West Smithfield EC1 • Map R1 • 020 7796 0600 • ££££*

4 Sweetings
Full of character, this is a haven for fish lovers. Timeless starters, such as potted shrimp, are followed by simple but well-prepared plaice, haddock and Dover sole. Leave space for the yummy English "puds": bread-and-butter pudding and jam roly-poly. ◎ *39 Queen Victoria Street EC4 • Map R2 • 020 7248 3062 • No credit cards • £££*

5 Moshi Moshi Sushi
Fun conveyor-belt sushi bar in Liverpool Street Station. ◎ *Unit 24, Liverpool Street Station EC2 • Map H3 • 020 7247 3227 • £*

6 Terminus
Contemporary, but hearty dishes, from lamb to hamburger, are served in this lively city eaterie. ◎ *40 Liverpool Street EC2 • Map H3 • 020 7618 7400 • £££*

7 Noto Ramen House
The best Japanese noodles in the City. With just 32 seats, it is mostly a take-out place. No alcohol. ◎ *7 Bread Street EC4 • Map G3 • 020 7329 8056 • No credit cards • £*

8 The Place Below
Popular lunchtime vegetarian canteen in the crypt of St. Mary-le-Bow church. ◎ *Cheapside EC2 • Map G3 • 020 7329 0789 • £*

9 Searcy's
The Barbican Arts complex has a good restaurant with views out over St. Giles. ◎ *Level 2, Barbican EC2 • Map R1 • 020 7588 3008 • ££££*

10 Jamaica Wine House
A lovely pub dating from 1682 serving a good choice of wines, as well as beer and bar food. ◎ *St. Michael's Alley EC3 • Map H3*

Note: Unless otherwise stated, all restaurants accept credit cards and serve vegetarian meals. Many City restaurants close at weekends.

139

Left **View over London from Hampstead Heath** Right **Camden Lock Market**

Heading North

BEYOND REGENT'S PARK AND THE RAILWAY TERMINI *of Euston, King's Cross and St. Pancras, North London drifts up into areas that were once distant villages where the rich built their country mansions to escape the city. Many of these houses remain and several are open for the public to wander around and imagine a bygone age. Parts of their extensive grounds now make up the wild and lofty expanse of Hampstead Heath. Some of the "villages", such as Hampstead and Highgate, are still distinct from the urban sprawl that surrounds them. Home to the wealthy, cultured and famous, their attractive streets are full of well-preserved architecture as well as dozens of inviting pubs and restaurants. Other parts of North London have different flavors, however – from bustling Camden, with its canal-side market, lively pubs and clubs, to fashionable Islington, with its clothes and antique shops, good restaurants, smart cafés and bars.*

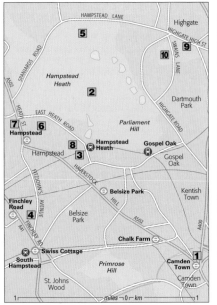

Site of the well on Well Walk, Hampstead

Sights

1	Camden Markets
2	Hampstead Heath and Parliament Hill
3	Keats House
4	Freud Museum
5	Kenwood House
6	Burgh House
7	Fenton House
8	2 Willow Road
9	Lauderdale House
10	Highgate Cemetery

Hampstead Heath

1 Camden Markets

The most exciting North London markets are open every weekend, and linked by the busy and colourful Camden High Street. Camden Market, near the tube station, is packed with stalls selling clothes, shoes and jewelry. Further up the road, by the canal, Camden Lock Market focuses on crafts and ethnic goods. Stalls in the warehouses of Stables Market have great food on sale. Open weekends only between 8am and 6pm (see p65). ◐ Camden High Street & Chalk Farm Road NW1 • Tube Camden Town

2 Hampstead Heath and Parliament Hill

A welcome retreat from the city, this large, open area is one of the best places in London for walking. Covering 800 acres of countryside, it contains ancient woodlands and ponds for swimming and fishing. The high point of Parliament Hill has great city views and is a popular place for kite-flying (see p74). ◐ Heath Information Centre, Staff Yard, Highgate Road NW5 • Tube Hampstead • 020 7482 7073

3 Keats House

Keats Grove, off Downshire Hill, is one of the loveliest areas of Hampstead. The house where the poet John Keats wrote much of his work is a pretty white villa, containing a collection of his manuscripts and letters, as well as some personal possessions. Poetry readings and talks are given on Wednesday evenings (see p52). ◐ Keats Grove NW3 • Train to Hampstead Heath • Open noon–5pm Tue–Sun • Admission charge

4 Freud Museum

This was the home of Anna Freud, daughter of Sigmund Freud and a pioneer in child psychology. The house contains the famous couch on which patients of her father, the founder of psychoanalysis, related their dreams. This was brought here when he fled Nazi-occupied Vienna. There is also a large collection of his works (see p52). ◐ 20 Maresfield Gardens NW3 • Tube Swiss Cottage • Open noon–5pm Wed–Sun • Admission charge

Regent's Canal, Camden Lock

5 Kenwood House

This magnificent mansion, filled with Old Masters, is set in an idyllic lakeside estate on the edge of Hampstead Heath. Vermeer's *The Guitar Player* and a self-portrait by Rembrandt are among the star attractions. Concerts are held by the lake in summer – audiences sit in the grassy bowl, with picnic hampers to sustain them *(see p51)*. ◎ *Hampstead Lane NW3 • Tube Highgate • Open 1 Apr–30 Sep: 10am–6pm daily; Oct: 10am–5pm daily; 1 Nov–31 Mar: 10am–4pm daily • Free*

6 Burgh House

Built in 1703, Burgh House houses Hampstead Museum, which has a good selection of local books and a map of the famous people who have lived in the area. The paneled music room is used for art exhibitions, concerts and meetings, and there is a pleasant café, the Buttery, with garden tables. ◎ *New End Square NW3 • Tube Hampstead • Open noon–5pm Wed–Sun • Free*

7 Fenton House

This splendid 1693 mansion is the oldest in Hampstead. Its exceptionally fine collection of Oriental and European porcelain, furniture and needlework was

Hampstead Wells

Hampstead's heyday began in the early 18th century, when a spring in Well Walk was recognized as having medicinal properties. This brought Londoners flocking to take the waters in the Pump Room within the Great Room in Well Walk, which also housed an Assembly Room for dances and concerts. The spa gradually fell into disrepute, but Hampstead retained its fashionable status.

bequeathed to the National Trust with the house in 1952. A formal walled garden contains an orchard and rose garden. ◎ *Windmill Hill NW3 • Tube Hampstead • Open 31 Mar–4 Nov: 2–5pm Wed–Sun • Admission charge*

8 2 Willow Road

Designed in 1939 by the architect Ernö Goldfinger for himself and his wife, the artist Ursula Blackwell, this is one of the most important examples of modern architecture in the UK. A film helps put the life and times of the couple in context. Goldfinger designed all the furniture and collected some fine works by Henry Moore, Max Ernst and Marcel Duchamp. ◎ *2 Willow Road NW3 • Train to Hampstead Heath • Open 31 Mar–1 Nov: 12:15–4pm Thu–Sat (tours only) • Admission charge*

Left **Staircase, Burgh House** Right **Fenton House**

Memorial, Highgate Cemetery

9 Lauderdale House

Dating from the late 16th century, Lauderdale House was once associated with Charles II and his mistress Nell Gwynne. It now houses a popular arts and cultural center, with regular concerts, exhibitions and Sunday craft and antique fairs. ❧ *Highgate Hill N6 • Tube Highgate • Open 11am–4pm Tue–Fri, 1:30–5pm Sat, noon–5pm alternate Sundays (times may vary in summer).*

10 Highgate Cemetery

On the opposite side of the Heath to Hampstead, Highgate grew up as a healthy, countrified place for nobility who built large mansions here. Many of the famous people who lived in the area are buried in Highgate Cemetery. Soon after it had been consecrated in 1839, its Victorian architecture and fine views over the capital made it a popular outing for Londoners. Karl Marx and the novelist George Eliot are buried in the less glamorous East Cemetery (see p75). ❧ *Swain's Lane N6 • Tube Archway • 020 8340 1834 • East Cemetery: Open 10am–5pm Mon–Fri, 11am–5pm Sat–Sun (closes at 4pm in winter). Closed for funerals (phone to check). Admission charge • West Cemetery: tours Apr–Oct. Admission charge*

Exploring the North

Morning

🕐 Starting at Hampstead tube station, head left down pretty Flask Walk (The Flask pub once sold spa water) to the local museum in **Burgh House** for some background on the area. Then spend some time exploring the many attractive back streets, which are lined with expensive Georgian houses and mansions. Visit Well Walk, fashionable in the days of the Hampstead spa (a fountain in Well Passage on the left still remains), and Elm Row, where D.H. Lawrence lived at No. 1.

☕ Stop for a coffee at one of the many cafés along Hampstead High Street and then make your way to **Keats House** (see p141), spending half an hour looking around. Afterwards, a stroll across Hampstead Heath to **Kenwood House** will prepare you for lunch.

Afternoon

🍴 The Brew House Café at Kenwood serves excellent light meals and has a fine position beside the house, overlooking the lake. After lunch, a visit to the house will take an hour or so.

🕐 Leave the Heath by the nearby East Lodge and catch a No. 210 bus back towards Hampstead. The bus passes the **Spaniards Inn** (see p63) and White-stone Pond – the highest point on the Heath. Alight at the pond and walk to the tube station, taking a train to Camden Town. Get lost for the rest of the afternoon in lively **Camden Lock Market** (see p141), ending 🍴 the day with a drink and some food at **Sauce Bar Organic Diner** (see p145).

Left **Camden Passage antique shop** Right **Crafts Council façade**

Best of the Rest

1 Sadler's Wells
London's premier venue for contemporary dance perfomances *(see p57)*. Ⓢ *Rosebery Avenue EC1 • Map F2 • 020 7863 8000 • www.sadlers-wells.com*

2 Camden Mall and Camden Passage
More than 35 dealers sell everything from furniture to books at North London's most exciting antiques market. Open Tue–Sat. Ⓢ *Camden Passage N1 • Map F1*

3 Almeida Theatre
This tiny theatre attracts the best actors and directors from the UK and the US. Currently based in King's Cross, the Almeida will return to Islington in 2002. Ⓢ *Omega Place, Caledonian Road N1 (until late 2002 then Cross St N1) • Tube King's Cross • 020 7359 4404 • www.almeida.co.uk*

4 Alexandra Palace
Located in a beautiful park, this reconstructed 1873 exhibition centre offers a range of amusements, including regular antique fairs. Tours of the 1920s BBC studios may be booked. Ⓢ *Tube Wood Green • BBC tours: 020 8365 2121*

5 King's Head Theatre Pub
Delightful Victorian pub with a theatre located in an upper room. Delicious vegetarian food is available in the downstairs bar. Ⓢ *115 Upper Street N1 • Map F1 • 020 7226 1916*

6 Camden Arts Centre
Known for its fascinating contemporary art exhibitions and excellent art book shop. Ⓢ *Arkwright Road NW3 • Train or Tube to Finchley Road • 020 7435 2643*

7 Crafts Council
Exhibitions of the finest products of British design are held regularly here. The resource center offers books, videos and a database of images to visitors. Ⓢ *44a Pentonville Road N1 • Map F1 • Open 11am–6pm Tue–Sat, 2–6pm Sun • Free*

8 Hampstead Theatre
This important fringe theatre is a venue for ambitious new writing, and has hosted plays by such innovative British artists as Harold Pinter. Ⓢ *Avenue Road NW3 • Tube Swiss Cottage • 020 7722 9301*

9 UK Golf Driving Range
Central London's only full length driving range with 24 floodlit bays, a shop and a café. Ⓢ *Outer Circle, Regent's Park NW1 • Tube Camden Town • 020 7837 1616*

10 Raceway
This is one of London's best-kept secrets – a 817-yd (750-m) go-cart track. Only groups of ten or more people, 18 years and up may book, may book. A trip costs £70.50 per person for 20 minutes practice followed by two 25-minute races with trophies for the winners. Ⓢ *Central Warehouse, York Way N1 • Map E1 • 020 7833 1000*

For more London theatres See pp56–7

Price Categories

For a three-course	**£**	under £15
meal for one with half	**££**	£15–£25
a bottle of wine (or	**£££**	£25–£35
equivalent meal), taxes	**££££**	£35–£50
and extra charges.	**£££££**	over £50

Left **Sauce Bar Organic Diner** Right **Mango Room**

🔟 Eating and Drinking

1 Granita
A favorite restaurant among Islington locals, with dishes mixing ingredients from around the world to produce an eclectic and regularly changing menu. ◈ *127 Upper Street N1 • Map F1 • 020 7226 3222 • £££*

2 The White Onion
Perfect for a romantic evening, this mid-price French restaurant provides meals that are a notch up from bistro cooking. ◈ *297 Upper Street N1 • Map F1 • 020 7359 3533 • £££*

3 Tartuf
This friendly restaurant serves well-cooked specialities from French Alsace, including *choucroute*, (pickled cabbage served with meat) and *galettes* (pancakes). The bargain, 2-course "lunch express" costs £4.80 (£5.50 at weekends). ◈ *88 Upper St NW1 • Map F1 • 020 7288 0954 • £*

4 Metrogusto
This Italian restaurant offers authentic pasta dishes, as well as such oddities as the surprisingly appetising parmesan cheese ice cream. Excellent house wines. ◈ *14 Theberton Street N1 • Map F1 • 020 7226 9400 • £££*

5 Mango Room
Distinctive Caribbean food is served in this bright restaurant. Try the "Camden curried goat". ◈ *10 Kentish Town Road NW1 • Tube Camden Town • 020 7482 5065 • £££*

6 Sauce Bar Organic Diner
All the drinks, fries, burgers and ketchup here are organic, and absolutely delicious. ◈ *214 Camden High Street NW1 • Tube Camden Town • 020 7482 0777 • £*

7 The New End
Hampstead's best-loved restaurant, the New End has a reasonably-priced menu offering fish, meat and vegetarian dishes in equal proportions. ◈ *102 Heath Street NW3 • Tube Hampstead • 020 7431 4423 • ££*

8 Louis Patisserie
This wonderful old tea room is part of Hampstead folklore. Sink into a comfortable sofa and sample some of the tempting cakes on display in the window. ◈ *32 Heath Street NW3 • Tube Hampstead • 020 7435 9908 • £*

9 The Flask
Dating from 1700, this pub has a country atmosphere and good cask beer. It serves home-made pub food, lunchtime and evenings between 6 and 8:30pm. ◈ *14 Flask Walk NW3 • Tube Hampstead • 020 7435 4580 • £*

10 Spaniards Inn
Opposite the toll house on Hampstead Heath, this is one of London's most famous old pubs. Traditional English pub food is mingled with more exotic choices such as *calamari* (squid). ◈ *Spaniards Road NW3 • 020 8731 6571 • Tube Hampstead, Golders Green • £*

> **Note:** *Unless otherwise stated, all restaurants accept credit cards and serve vegetarian meals*

145

Left **Old Royal Naval College, Greenwich** Right **Deer in Richmond Park**

South and West

THE PALACES THAT ONCE GRACED LONDON'S *river to the south and west of the city center were built in places that remain popular today, from Hampton Court and Richmond in the west, downriver to Greenwich. There, on a deep meander in the Thames, a vast Tudor palace was the dramatic first sight of the city for anyone arriving by ship. That palace has been replaced by Wren's handsome Royal Naval College, a stunning riverside building that is the high point of this World Heritage Site and the start of the many delights of Greenwich Park. These include the Old Royal Observatory, home of world time. Richmond's palace has also disappeared, but opposite the Park lies Kew Palace in the grounds of the incomparable Royal Botanic Gardens. Chiswick House, Ham House and Syon House are the best of a number of palatial mansions near Richmond, while culture is catered for in the Dulwich Picture Gallery and the Horniman Museum.*

🔟 Sights

1. Hampton Court
2. Greenwich
3. Royal Botanic Gardens, Kew
4. Richmond
5. Dulwich Picture Gallery
6. Chiswick House
7. Horniman Museum and Gardens
8. Syon House and Park
9. Ham House
10. Wimbledon Tennis Museum

Carving over entrance to remains of Richmond Palace

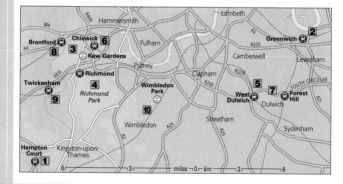

Palm House, Kew Gardens

1 Hampton Court

Visiting this historic, royal Tudor palace and its extensive grounds is a popular day out from London. As well as family trails and special exhibitions, tours of six separate areas with costumed or audio guides are available. Events held here throughout the year include a week-long music festival in June, which regularly attracts big-name performers. In July, the grounds are filled by the world's largest flower show, organized by the Royal Horticultural Society. A frequent train service from Waterloo takes about half an hour but for a delightfully leisurely trip, catch a boat from Westminster Pier, which takes about four hours *(see pp54–5)*. ⊗ *East Molesey, Surrey • Train Hampton Court • Open Apr–Oct: 9:30am–6pm Tue–Sun, 10:15am–6pm Mon; Nov–Mar: 9:30am–4:30pm Tue–Sun, 10:15am–4.30pm Mon • Admission charge*

2 Greenwich

The World Heritage Site of Greenwich includes Sir Christopher Wren's Old Royal Naval College, Greenwich Park *(see p29)* and the Old Royal Observatory where the Prime Meridian, Longitude 0°, was established. In the fine park are the Queen's House *(see p55)* and National Maritime Museum *(see p48)*. Greenwich has several excellent restaurants and marine-related shops as well as a market selling arts, crafts and antiques. The old tea clipper, the *Cutty Sark (see p71)* and the first solo round-the-world yacht, *Gipsy Moth IV*, are nearby. ⊗ *Greenwich SE10 • Train to Greenwich; DLR Cutty Sark, Greenwich; Tube North Greenwich • Old Royal Observatory: Open 10am–5pm daily • Admission charge*

3 Royal Botanic Gardens, Kew

Within the lovely riverside grounds of this former royal garden is the world's largest plant collection, with around 30,000 specimens. Kew Palace and Queen Charlotte's Cottage *(see p54)* were used as residences by George III, whose mother, Princess Augusta, laid the first garden here. Take a Kew Explorer Bus tour of the gardens – you can get on and off it any time. ⊗ *Richmond, Surrey • Train & tube Kew Gardens • Open 9:30–dusk daily • Admission charge*

Left **Gipsy Moth IV** Centre **Clock at Royal Observatory** Right **Queen Charlotte's Cottage**

For more on royal London **See pp54–5**

4 Richmond

This attractive, wealthy riverside suburb, with its quaint shops and pubs and pretty lanes, is particularly worth a visit for its attractive riverside walks *(see p74)* and its vast royal park *(see p29)*. There is also a spacious Green, where cricket is played in summer, which is overlooked by the lovely restored Richmond Theatre and the early 18th-century Maids of Honour Row, which stands next to the last vestiges of an enormous Tudor Palace. For some history visit the local Museum, in the Old Town Hall, where the Tourist Information office is based. ◈ *Richmond, Surrey • Train to Richmond • Museum of Richmond: open 11am–5pm Tue–Sat, 1–4pm Sun (May–Sep), admission charge*

Restored façade of Richmond Theatre

5 Dulwich Picture Gallery

This wonderful gallery *(see p51)* is well worth the journey from Central London. Apart from the stunning collection, there are regular exhibitions, Thursday lunchtime lectures and friends events, usually including music, food and wine, to which anyone is welcome. ◈ *College Road SE21 • Train to North or West Dulwich • Open 10am–5pm Tue–Fri, 11am–5pm Sat–Sun • Admission charge (free on Fri)*

Greenwich Palace

The ruins of this enormous royal riverside palace lie beneath the Old Naval College green. Built in 1462, many of the Tudor monarchs lived here, including Henry VI, Henry VII and Henry VIII. Abandoned under the Commonwealth in 1652, it was eventually demolished for Wren's present buildings.

6 Chiswick House

This piece of Italy in London is a high spot of English 18th-century architecture. The square villa, with its dome and portico, was built for Lord Burlington, with beautifully painted interiors by William Kent. Temples, statues and a lake complete the Italianate gardens. ◈ *Burlington Lane, Chiswick W4 • Tube Turnham Green • Open summer: 10am–6pm daily; winter: 10am–4pm Wed–Sun • Admission charge*

7 Horniman Museum

A distinctive museum, this started as the collection of the Victorian tea trader Frederick Horniman. There are three permanent exhibitions: African Worlds, Natural History and Living Waters Aquarium. The shop and cafe look out on to a 16-acre garden. ◈ *London Road, Forest Hill SE23 • Train to Forest Hill • Open 10:30am–5:30pm Mon–Sat, 2–5:30pm Sun • Admission charge*

Left **Richmond alley** Right **Chiswick House**

Ham House

8 Syon House and Park

This sumptuous Neoclassical villa is home to the Duke of Northumberland. It has fine Robert Adam interiors and a 40-acre garden landscaped by Capability Brown and dominated by a splendid conservatory. The park contains a butterfly house and aquatic center. ◈ *Brentford, Middlesex • Train to Kew Bridge • Open Apr–Oct: 11am–5pm Wed, Thu & Sun (gardens open 10am–5:30pm daily) • Admission charge*

9 Ham House

This outstanding 17th-century house and garden was at the center of court intrigue during Charles II's reign. Its interiors are rich and well furnished and there is an excellent picture collection. The menu in the Orangery is inspired by 17th-century dishes. ◈ *Richmond, Surrey • Train to Richmond • Open Easter to Oct: 1–5pm Sat–Wed (garden 10:30am–6pm) • Admission charge*

10 Wimbledon Tennis Museum

With a view of the famous Centre Court, the museum tells the story of tennis, from its gentle, amateur beginnings to its exciting professional status today. The first tennis championship were held in Wimbledon in 1877. ◈ *Church Road, Wimbledon SW19 • Tube Southfields • Open 10:30am–5pm daily (except during Jun–Jul championship) • Admission charge*

A Day Exploring Maritime Greenwich

Morning

🕐 Start the day from Westminster Pier, because the best way to arrive at **Greenwich** *(see p147)* is by boat. The journey takes 50–60 minutes (£6 single, £7.50 return), and there are terrific river sights on the way *(see pp70–71)*. The old tea clipper **Cutty Sark** *(see p71)* is visible on arrival and worth an immediate visit. Afterwards step into the nearby Greenwich Gateway visitor center to get your bearings.

Behind the visitor center is Greenwich Market, which is liveliest on weekends. Grab a coffee here, and then explore the surrounding streets, full of antique and marine shops. Turn into Wren's Old Royal Naval College, walk around the Grand Square, and then down to the river. Take a break for some lunch and a pint at the old Nelson Tavern on the far side of the Naval College overlooking the river.

Afternoon

After lunch, make your way back up to the **National Maritime Museum** *(see p48)* and buy a combined ticket for this and the Old Royal Observatory *(see p147)*, which is on the hill behind. Spend a couple of hours exploring the fascinating museum, the largest of its kind in the world, then make your way to the Observatory. This is the home of world time, and stands on the Prime Meridian. You can be photographed with one foot in the eastern hemisphere and one in the west. Return to Central London by boat, or by rail from Greenwich.

Left **Battersea Park** Right **Brixton Market**

🔟 Best of the Rest

1 Brixton Market
This colorful market lies at the heart of London's Caribbean community. The atmosphere is lively, with music stalls pumping out a variety of sounds, and the scent of aromatic ethnic foods. Look for secondhand vinyl, fresh produce and bargain fabrics. Open 8am–5pm Mon–Sat. ✆ *Electric Avenue to Brixton Station Road SW9 • Tube Brixton*

2 Battersea Arts Centre
One of the main fringe theatre venues in the capital, with a huge program of activities. ✆ *Lavender Hill SW11 • Train to Clapham Junction • 020 7223 2223*

3 Battersea Park
Entertainments in this large park include a boating lake, a children's zoo, sports facilities, and a gallery. There is also a woodland walk, nature reserve and therapy garden. ✆ *Battersea Park SW11 • Train to Battersea Park • Open 7:30am–10pm daily*

4 The Bush
This off-West End theatre is one of London's premier show-cases for new writers. ✆ *Shepherd's Bush Green W12 • Tube Shepherd's Bush • 020 7610 4224*

5 Merton Abbey Mills
An arts and crafts village on the River Wandle, with an old watermill, pub, restaurant, shops and weekend craft market. Arts festival in the summer. ✆ *Merantum Way SW19 • Tube Colliers Wood*

6 Wetland Centre
In this major bird sanctuary by the Thames, there are different recreated habitats to explore, as well as a Discovery Centre *(see p75)*. ✆ *Barnes SW13 • Train to Barnes • Open 9:30am–6pm daily (winter: 9:30am–5pm) • Admission charge*

7 Wimbledon Common
Start with a visit to the wind-mill, and then try not to get lost roaming the 1,100 acres. The Crooked Billet and the Hand in Hand on the south side are pubs to head for. ✆ *Wimbledon Common SW19 • Train to Wimbledon*

8 Wimbledon Stadium
Have a night at this dog track, where you can urge on your favorites from the stands or one of the restaurants. ✆ *Plough Lane SW17 • Tube Wimbledon Park • Races 7:30–10pm Tue, Fri, Sat • Admission charge*

9 Firepower
An exciting new museum at the historic home of the Royal Artillery, there are hundreds of exhibits as well as a spectacular multimedia display. ✆ *Royal Arsenal, Woolwich SE18 • Train to Woolwich Arsenal • Open 10am–5pm daily • Admission charge*

10 Museum of Rugby
At Twickenham Stadium, the national home of rugby. A Mecca for rugby fans, a visit includes a tour of the stadium. ✆ *Rugby Road, Twickenham, Middlesex • Train to Twickenham • Open 10am–5pm Tue–Sat, 2–5pm Sun • Admission charge*

Price Categories

For a three-course		
meal for one with half	**£**	under £15
a bottle of wine (or	**££**	£15–£25
equivalent meal), taxes	**£££**	£25–£35
and extra charges.	**££££**	£35–£50
	£££££	over £50

River Café

Eating and Drinking

1 The River Café
The "best Italian restaurant outside Italy" is the long-standing reputation of this imaginative Fulham restaurant, housed in a converted warehouse with a river terrace. ◊ *Thames Wharf, Rainville Road W6 • Tube Hammersmith • 020 7381 8824 • £££££*

2 Putney Bridge
A brilliant view of the river from this smart, innovative glass restaurant makes it a good spot year-round, and the modish French menu is excellent. ◊ *The Embankment SW15 • Tube Putney Bridge • 020 8780 1811 • £££££*

3 Canyon
American dining by the river towpath, with hearty American portions. Good for weekend roasts and brunch. ◊ *Riverside, Richmond, Surrey • Tube/train to Richmond • 020 8948 2944 • £££*

4 The Glasshouse
The food is exciting, modern European at this relaxed restaurant. ◊ *14 Station Parade, Kew, Surrey • Tube Kew Gardens • 020 8940 6777 • No disabled access • £££*

5 The Gate
Probably the best vegetarian restaurant in London, The Gate is worth hunting out. The gourmet menu changes regularly, and the meals are hearty and inventive. Closed Sundays. ◊ *51 Queen Caroline Street W6 • Tube Hammersmith • 020 8748 6932 • No disabled access • ££*

6 The Atlas
A popular, friendly "gastro-pub" serving excellent Mediterranean-style food and wine. Real ales and an attractive garden. ◊ *16 Seagrave Road, Fulham SW6 • Tube West Brompton • 020 7385 9129 • £££*

7 Monsieur Max
This fabulous French restaurant is unhurried, unpretentious and oozing Gallic goodness. The menu changes daily. ◊ *133 High Street, Hampton, Surrey • Train to Fulwell • 020 8979 5546 • ££££*

8 Bush Bar and Grill
A thoroughly modern venue in an old-fashioned part of town. Great cocktails at the stylish bar, simple but good Anglo-French food in the restaurant. ◊ *45A Goldhawk Road W12 • Tube Goldhawk Road • 020 8746 2111 • ££*

9 Tandoori Kebab Centre
This is one of the best Asian restaurants in the area, specializing in *balti* dishes, fried in searingly hot saucepans, and *tandoori* dishes, cooked in clay ovens. ◊ *161–163 The Broadway, Southall, Middlesex • Train to Southall • 020 8571 5738 • £*

10 The Dove
With the smallest bar in Britain, a warm fire, good local beer, a riverside terrace and no children, this is as close to a perfect pub as you can get. Good bar food is served lunchtime and evening. ◊ *19 Upper Mall W6 • Tube Hammersmith*

Note: *Unless otherwise stated, all restaurants accept credit cards and serve vegetarian meals*

Left **Columbia Road Market** Right **Bengali sweet factory**

Heading East

THE EAST END IS *booming. Always a vibrant, working-class area and home to London's dockworkers, the area has also prided itself on providing a refuge for successive generations of immigrants, from French silk weavers to Jews and Bangladeshi garment workers. Since the 1980s, the East End, where the murderous Jack the Ripper roamed, has undergone a radical transformation. Today, the media and finance worlds occupy stylish Dockland developments, galleries and restaurants have sprouted in Hoxton and a host of Sunday markets, including trendy Spitalfields, draw newcomers who marvel at the area's unspoilt 18th- and 19th-century architecture.*

 Sights

1. Canary Wharf
2. Museum In Docklands
3. Hoxton
4. Whitechapel Art Gallery
5. National Museum of Childhood
6. Spitalfields
7. The Thames Barrier
8. Brick Lane
9. Columbia Road Market
10. Geffrye Museum

Fifty-story-high Canada Tower at Canary Wharf

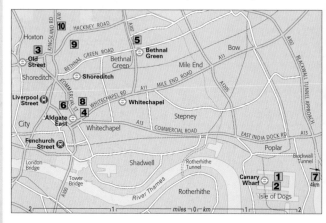

Vaulted glass roof, Canary Wharf station

1 Canary Wharf
The centerpiece of the Docklands development is Canary Wharf and the 800-ft (240-m) - high, 50-story Canada Tower designed by US architect, Cesar Pelli. Although the tower is not open to the public, parts of the complex are open to visitors, including the mall, where there are shops, restaurants and bars. The star of area's exciting architecture is the magnificent Canary Wharf station, designed by Norman Foster. ◈ Tube & DLR Canary Wharf

2 Museum In Docklands
This museum tells the story of London's Docklands. Displays of shipbuilding equipment and photographs illustrate the late-19th- and early-20th century, when the docks were at their peak, handling more ships than any

other country. There is a complete 1920s salon from the *Queen Mary* passenger liner, complete with elegant Art Deco fittings, and a recreation of a 1930s loading dock. ◈ No 1 Warehouse E14 • Tube & DLR Canary Wharf • (Due to open in Spring 2002) Open 10am–6pm daily

3 Hoxton
If you want to see the latest in British contemporary art, then this is the place to come. Hoxton Square is home to the White Cube gallery, where such established modern artists as Damien Hirst, Sarah Lucas and Tracey Emin, first made their names. The Lux Centre is also a gallery and shows art-house films. Acrobats and aerial performers put on shows at Circus Space on the north side of Hoxton Market. Popular cafés and restaurants include the Hoxton Kitchen and Bar and the Real Greek *(see p157)*. ◈ Tube Old Street

4 Whitechapel Art Gallery
This excellent gallery has a reputation for showing cutting-edge contemporary art from around the world. The Whitechapel has launched the careers of David Hockney, Gilbert and George and Anthony Caro. Behind the Art Nouveau façade there is also a great bookshop and café. ◈ Whitechapel High Street E1 • Map H3 • Open 11am–5pm Tue–Sun (Wed 8pm) • Free

Left **Diving equipment, Museum In Docklands** Right **Whitechapel Art Gallery's 1901 entrance**

5 Bethnal Green Museum of Childhood

Everyone will find something to delight them here: from dolls and teddy bears to train sets and games through the ages. Each weekend there is a soft-play zone for under-fives and art classes for older kids. There are regular activities themed to complement current exhibitions. ® *Cambridge Heath Road E2 • Tube Bethnal Green • Open 10am–5:50pm daily • Free*

6 Spitalfields

Streets such as Fournier Street, lined with 18th-century Huguenot silk weavers' houses, are a reminder that this area, just north of the City, has provided a refuge for immigrant populations for centuries. London's oldest market, Old Spitalfields Market still has stalls selling food, as well as several cafés and shops dotted around its edge. But Sunday is the day when the market draws hundreds, eager to find a bargain among the fashion, vintage clothing, and crafts stalls here. Opposite the market is one of Europe's great Baroque churches. Christ Church (1716) was designed by Wren's pupil, architect Nicholas Hawksmoor (1661–1736). ® *Commercial Street E1 • ® Map H2*

Christ Church Spitalfields

The Huguenots in London

Driven from France in 1685, the Huguenots were Protestants fleeing religious persecution by Catholics. They were mostly silk weavers, whose masters and merchants built the beautiful Georgian houses around Fournier, Princelet and Elder streets. Spitalfields silk was famous for its fine quality, but by the mid-19th century the industry had declined.

7 Thames Flood Barrier

Rising like a series of shark fins from the river, this piece of engineering is an impressive sight *(see p71).* ® *Unity Way SE18 • Train to Charlton • Open 10am–5pm daily • Admission charge*

8 Brick Lane

Once the centre of London's Jewish population, this street is now the heart of London's Bangladeshi community. Head here for inexpensive, authentic Indian cooking at restaurants such as Preem and Shampan, where a three-course meal can be had for as little as £6. Some of the best bagels in the city are made at the Brick Lane Bagel Bake at No. 159 – a famous dawn haunt for late-night revelers. There are gorgeous saree shops and, on Sundays, there is a lively flea market. ® *Brick Lane • Tube Aldgate East*

Left **Brick Lane Music Hall** Right **Dining room, Geffrye Museum**

Columbia Road Market

9 Columbia Road Market

Londoners head east on Sunday mornings for the bustling street markets. In addition to Petticoat Lane in Middlesex Street, with its bargain clothes, and household items and Brick Lane's bric-à-brac, there is the teeming plant and flower market in Columbia Road. Ten minutes' walk from the north end of Brick Lane, Columbia Road is a delightful cornucopia of all things horticultural at bargain prices.

⊗ Columbia Road E2 • Tube Old Street
• Petticoat Lane • Tube Aldgate East

10 Geffrye Museum

Devoted to the evolution of family life and interior design, this fascinating museum has a series of rooms decorated in distinct period style. Originally a 1715 almshouse, the building has been transformed and you can wander through an oak-paneled 17th-century drawing room, a 1930s flat or a contemporary loft apartment. Stroll through a series of period gardens between April and October.

⊗ Kingsland Road E2 • Map H2 • Open 10am–5pm Tue–Sat, noon–5pm Sun

A Day Around the East End

Morning

🕐 Start at **Old Spitalfields Market**, close to Liverpool Street station, where organic food stalls hold sway during the week, and many more, selling clothes and collectibles, fill the floor on Sundays. Cafés and stalls sell delicious coffee and breakfasts both in and around the market.

Emerging from the market on its southeast corner, cross into Fournier Street, where the gallery at No. 5 retains the original panelling of the 18th-century silk weavers' houses. Stroll Princelet and Elder streets, just off Fournier, for a real taste of historic London.

Head into **Brick Lane** to browse among the saree and Bangladeshi gift shops. Stop for lunch at one of the many authentic curry houses that line the street.

Afternoon

After lunch turn right into Whitechapel Road. Notice the distinctive Art Nouveau façade of the **Whitechapel Art Gallery** (see p153) and pop into the gallery's stunning three-floor exhibition space to take in a contemporary art show. Have a cup of tea in the museum café and stop by the bookshop to buy a £1 souvenir artwork from its vending machine.

Finally, take a ride on the Docklands Light Railway (from Tower Gateway, a short walk from Whitechapel), for views of East London. Emerge at Canary Wharf to see London's latest architecture around Cabot Square, and finish with a drink at **Via Fosse** (see p157) on West India Quay.

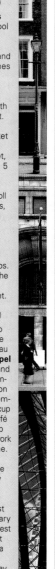

Left **Decorative panel, Brick Lane Music Hall** Right **Sailing, Docklands Watersports Centre**

Best of the Rest

1 Theatre Royal Stratford East

A local theatre with an international reputation – established by the pioneering director Joan Littlewood in 1953 – where exciting new work can still be seen. Next door is a new arts centre with a gallery and cinema. ◎ *Gerry Raffles Square E15 • DLR Stratford East • 020 8534 0310*

2 Victoria Park

One of East London's largest and most pleasant parks, there are two lakes, where model boats are sailed at weekends, ornamental gardens, a children's zoo, tennis courts and a bowling green. ◎ *Bow E9 • Tube Bethnal Green*

3 18 Folgate Street

This 18th-century silk-weaver's home *(see p154)* is kept perfectly in period. Open on the first Sunday and Monday of each month, this "still-life drama" was created by artist Dennis Severs. Each room appears as if the inhabitants have only just left it – dinner is half eaten and cooking smells emanate from the kitchen. ◎ *18 Folgate Street E1 • Map H2 • Open 2–5pm 1st Sun of month, noon–2pm & eve 1st Mon • 020 7247 4013 • Admission charge*

4 Sutton House

This Tudor merchant's house dates from 1535 and is the oldest in the East End. Open Wed, Sun, Bank Holiday Mondays. ◎ *2–4 Homerton High Street E9 • Tube Bethnal Green, then 253 bus • 020 8986 2264*

5 London Arena

Docklands' major concert venue and indoor sports arena is also home to the the London Knights ice-hockey team, which has league games at weekends from September to March. ◎ *Limeharbour E14 • DLR Crossharbour • 020 7538 1212*

6 Cabot Hall

A performance venue in Docklands with free lunchtime concerts. ◎ *Canary Wharf E14 • DLR Canary Wharf • 020 7418 2780*

7 Docklands Sailing & Watersports Centre

Sailing, rowing and canoeing facilities are available here. ◎ *Millwall Dock, Westferry Road E14 • DLR Crossharbour • 020 7537 2626*

8 Mudchute Farm

Britain's largest city farm ha a collection of livestock, plus a riding school. ◎ *Pier Street E14 • Open 9am–5pm daily • DLR Crossharbour • 020 7515 5901*

9 ExCel

An impressive new development beside the Royal Victoria Docks with shops, cafés and a vast exhibition space. ◎ *Victoria Dock Road E16 • DLR Custom House.*

10 Mile End Park

For skateboarders, BMX riders and rollerbladers, this new park also has a go-cart track. ◎ *Mile End Road E3 • Tube Mile End • 020 7264 4660 (Environment Trust)*

Price Categories

For a three-course meal for one with half a bottle of wine (or equivalent meal), taxes and extra charges.

£	under £15
££	£15–£25
£££	£25–£35
££££	£35–£50
£££££	over £50

ity bar and restaurant, Cantaloupe

10 Eating and Drinking

1 The Real Greek
Award-winning restaurant serving Greek food like you've never tasted before – the best in London. Start with *mezedes*, small portions of tasty appetizers. The wine list offers excellent Greek wines. ◈ *15 Hoxton Market N1 • Map H2 • 020 7739 8212 • ££££*

2 Hoxton Kitchen and Bar
Popular hang-out in arty Hoxton, serving coffees and drinks all day long. The lunchtime menu offers light meals such as barbecued chicken baguettes, artichoke quiches and pasta dishes. ◈ *2 Hoxton Square N1 • Map H2 • 020 7613 0709 • £*

3 Shoreditch Electricity Showrooms
The old showrooms are now a large open bar with a neon-lit restaurant in the back where modern European dishes are served. Dancing in the basement Fri–Sat and some weekdays. ◈ *39A Hoxton Square N1 • Map H2 • 020 7739 6934 • £££*

4 Great Eastern Dining Room
Stylish Italian restaurant attracting a youthful crowd. The menu features such favorites as olive-oil mashed potatoes and duck breasts with pomegranates. ◈ *54 Great Eastern St EC2 • Map H2 • 020 7613 4545 • £££*

5 Cargo
Imaginatively set in three railway arches, this large space is devoted to music, drink and food until 1am. There is live music every night in the back-room club. ◈ *Kingsland Viaduct, 83 Rivington Street EC2 • Map H2 • 020 7739 3440 • £*

6 Home
This basement bar, fitted out with domestic furniture, has a good-value restaurant upstairs. ◈ *100–106 Leonard Street EC2 • Map H2 • 020 7684 8618 • ££*

7 Cantaloupe
A large warehouse bar where art students meet city workers. Fries and other snacks are served at the bar and a restaurant area serves up Mediterranean food. ◈ *35–42 Charlotte Road EC2 • Map H1 • 020 7613 4411 • ££*

8 Via Fosse
Occupying three floors of an old coffee warehouse, this bar is a good stopping-off place on any visit to Docklands. ◈ *West India Quay E14 • DLR West India Quay • 020 7515 8549*

9 Café Spice Namaste
One of a chain of Indian restaurants focusing on Goan and regional cooking. ◈ *16 Prescot Street E1 • Tube Tower Hill • 020 7488 9242 • £££*

10 Prospect of Whitby
East London's finest pub dates from 1520, and has old beams and barrels, a pewter bar and great river views. ◈ *37 Wapping Wall E1 • Tube Wapping • 020 7481 1095*

Note: *Unless otherwise stated, all restaurants accept credit cards and serve vegetarian meals*

STREETSMART

LONDON'S TOP 10

Umbrellas on a wet London day

TOP 10 Planning Your Trip

1 What to Pack
Be prepared for all weathers, and be sure to bring a waterproof jacket and umbrella, even in summer. In winter, you will need a warm coat and sweater. Formal dress is rarely obligatory, but people do dress up for the opera as well as for some theatrical shows and smart restaurants. If you are coming in summer bring sunscreen as London sun can be strong.

2 Currency
For security, bring a cash card or traveler's checks. Check that your cash withdrawal card is acceptable in the UK – most ask the some British currency to pay for fares and immediate needs on arrival. There is no restriction on how much currency you can bring in or take out of the country (see Banking p165).

3 Passports and Visas
A valid passport is needed to enter the UK. Visitors from the EU, Commonwealth countries and the US do not need a visa. Always check with the British Embassy in your country. Contact your London-based embassy if you need to extend your stay beyond six months.

4 Customs Regulations
Apart from firearms, plants and perishable foods, there are few limits on what

may be brought into the UK for personal use. If you need regular medicine, bring adequate supplies and/or a prescription with you.

5 Insurance
Take out an insurance policy that covers loss of baggage, theft and health. Although emergency treatment is usually free from the National Health Service, and there are reciprocal arrangements with other EU countries, special care, drugs and repatriation are costly.

6 Driver's License
If you are planning to drive in the UK and you are an EU citizen, be sure to bring your license as well as registration and insurance documents. Also inform your insurance company of the trip. Other foreign nationals require an international driver's license.

7 Time Difference
Don't forget to set your watch to Greenwich Mean Time for the UK, which is one hour behind Continental European Time and five hours ahead of US Eastern Seaboard Time. From March to September clocks go forward an hour ("summer time").

8 Electrical Appliances
Throughout the UK, the electricity supply is 240 volts AC, and plugs are of a three-square-pin type,

so buy an adaptor and/or transformer before you travel. Most hotels have two-pin sockets in their bathrooms for shavers.

9 Children's Needs
Planning ahead when traveling with young children can make a trip more enjoyable. Avoid traveling by public transport during peak hours (see p169). Book tickets for shows and musems in advance, and make sure you bring a fold-up stroller for tired children.

10 Membership Cards
Bring any membership cards for driving or heritage organizations with links to the UK, such as the AA or National Trust, that offer discounted entry into many attractions. A student ISIC card (see p171) is also useful.

Embassies

Australian High Commission
Australia House, Strand WC2 • Map M3 • 020 7379 4334

Canadian High Commission
Macdonald House, 1 Grosvenor Square W1 • Map D3 • 020 7258 6600

United States Embassy
24 Grosvenor Square W1 • Map D3 • 020 7499 9000

Left **Eurostar train** Right **Aeroplane, Heathrow Airport**

Arriving in London

1 Heathrow Airport
London's main airport is 24 km (15 miles) west of central London. The Heathrow Express train to Paddington is the quickest way into the center, and takes only 15 minutes. Trains run from 5am until about 11:30pm daily. Taxis take about an hour, depending on the traffic, and are very expensive. Cheaper options include the tube (Piccadilly line) or Airbus, both of which take you into the center. ✪ *Heathrow information: 0870 000 0123*

2 Gatwick Airport
London's second airport is 31 miles (50 km) south of the centre, on the Surrey-Sussex border. The Gatwick Express train runs every 15 minutes into Victoria Station, taking around 30 minutes. There are also train connections on City Thameslink trains to London Bridge. The Airbus is a little cheaper and takes an hour longer, but their low-cost return ticket is an option. ✪ *Gatwick information: 0870 0002 468*

3 Stansted Airport
This fast-growing airport is 35 miles (56 km) to the northeast of London. From here, the half-hourly Stansted Express to Liverpool Street station takes 45 minutes. The Airbus service to Victoria takes about 90 minutes. ✪ *Stansted information: 0870 000 0303*

4 Luton Airport
This quieter airport is some 31 miles (50 km) north of London. A bus takes passengers from the airport to Luton station, from where Thameslink trains to King's Cross and the city take around 35 minutes. A Green Line coach service to Victoria takes 90 minutes. ✪ *Luton information: 01582 405 100*

5 London City Airport
Situated in Docklands, 9 miles (14 km) from the city centre, this relatively new airport is best served by the Shuttlebus from Liverpool Street station. A taxi to the center of London takes around 35 minutes, depending on traffic. ✪ *London City information: 020 7646 0000*

6 Other Airports
England's other main airports are Birmingham, Liverpool, Manchester, Newcastle and East Midlands. All have direct road, rail and bus connections to and from London.

7 Victoria Coach Station
Both national and international buses arrive and depart from here, London's main bus station. The terminal is a 10-minute walk from Victoria railway station. ✪ *Victoria Coach Station, 164 Buckingham Palace Rd SW1 • Map D5 • Reservations: 020 7730 3499*

8 London Waterloo International
This is the London terminus for the Channel Tunnel rail service, which has been run by Eurostar since it opened in 1995. The train takes 3 hours from Paris Nord and just 2 hours 40 minutes from Bruxelles Midi. ✪ *London Waterloo International SE1 • Map N5 • Eurostar enquiries and reservations: 0870 160 6600*

9 Channel Crossings
Eurotunnel operates a drive-on-drive-off train service between Calais, in northern France, and Folkestone, in the south of England (35 minutes). Ferries from Calais to Dover, the shortest Channel crossing, take around 90 minutes. The drive to London on the M20 motorway takes around one and a half hours, depending on traffic conditions.

10 Other Sea Links
Car ferries sail from northern France to other Channel ports in the south of England, as well as from Bilbao and Santander in northern Spain to Portsmouth or Plymouth. Hoverspeed operates a fast catamaran service from Dieppe to Newhaven (summer only). Passenger and car-ferry services also run to other ports around the country from the Netherlands, Scandinavia and Ireland.

Streetsmart

Left **Taxis** Center **Bus line** Right **Walking**

Getting Around

1 The Underground

London's underground train network, or "tube", is the fastest way to get around town, but trains are crowded during rush-hour. Lines are color-coded and easy to follow on the map on the back cover of this book. Trains run from around 5:30am to midnight, with fares based on the six zones into which the network is divided. Zone 1 covers Central London. ✆ Transport for London: 020 7222 1234 • www.londontransport.co.uk

2 London Buses

Slower than the tube but a cheaper way to travel, buses are also a good way of seeing the city as you go. To travel in the city between midnight and 6am, you will need a night bus. All night buses may be picked up outside the National Gallery in Trafalgar Square.

3 Docklands Light Railway (DLR)

The automated over-land railway serving Docklands is a fairly recent addition to the transport system. It is linked to the Underground network at Bank, Tower Gateway (near Tower Hill) and other points. One arm heads south, under the river, to Greenwich and Lewisham. Outside rush hour, it is a pleasant way of seeing this regenerated area of the East End.

4 Travel Passes

One-day and weekend Travelcards are economical if you are going to make more than two trips by public transport in a day. They can be bought at tube stations and at many newsagents and grocer shops. Valid on the Underground, buses and the DLR, on weekdays they are only valid after 9:30am. Weekly and monthly Travelcards are also available: for these, you will need to produce a passport-sized photo for a Photocard.

5 Rail Travel

Suburban and intercity travel is served through the 10 main London termini. Rail travel is expensive and the fare structures complicated. Planning ahead for long journeys is advisable and may save money. ✆ National Rail Enquiries: 08457 484950

6 Taxis

London's black cabs can be hailed anywhere; their "For Hire" sign is lit up when they are free. You can also find them at railway stations, airports and taxi ranks. A 10 per-cent tip is customary. Black cabs can be ordered in advance from Radio Taxis and Dial-a-Cab. ✆ Dial-a-Cab: 020 7253 5000 • Radio Taxis: 020 7272 0272

7 Minicabs

Minicabs are best obtained by telephone or by visiting a firm's office. Avoid picking one up on the street, or from one of the shady offices in Soho, as they are likely to be uninsured, ignorant of the city and unsafe drivers. "Lady Cabs" have only women drivers. ✆ Lady Cabs: 020 7254 3501

8 Car Rental

Car hire is not cheap in the United Kingdom and the rates are similar among the larger companies. Europcar and Thrifty are most likely to offer deals. Drivers must show a valid license and be aged 21 or even 24. ✆ Europcar: 0870 607 5005 • Thrifty: 01494 751600

9 Cycle Rental

You need a strong nerve to cycle in London's busy traffic, but it can be a great way to see the city. Lock up bikes as theft is common. There is a choice of bicycle rental companies in London. ✆ Bikepark: 020 7430 0083 • On Your Bike: 020 7378 6669

10 London on Foot

Walking is a rewarding option in London. The center of the capital is not large, and you will be surprised at how short the distance usually is between two points that seem quite far apart when traveled by tube. Traffic drives on the left in the UK, so take care when crossing the road, and watch for light signals.

Left **Britain Visitor Centre sign** Right **Britain Visitor Centre interior**

TOP 10 Sources of Information

1 London Tourist Board

The London Tourist Board has a range of services for visitors to the capital, including a useful accommodation booking scheme. Their information line gives a number of options. ✪ *London Tourist Board Information Line: 0906 866 3344 • www.londontown.com*

2 Tourist Information Centers

Offering advice on anything and everything from day trips and guided tours to accommodation, you will find these offices at Heathrow airport, Euston, King's Cross, Liverpool Street and Victoria stations and Oxford Circus, Piccadilly and St. James's Park Underground stations. They stock a wide range of free leaflets on current events and attractions.

3 Accommodation

The London Tourist Board operates a free accommodation booking program (unless you give less than six weeks' notice, in which case they will charge a small fee). You can book by credit card over the phone, or in person at centres in Victoria and Liverpool Street stations, and at Heathrow. Visit *www.Top 10London.dk.com* for useful accommodation links. ✪ *London Tourist Board: 020 7932 2020 • book@ london touristboard.co.uk*

4 Restaurant Services

This organization, which has been in business for 20 years, will find you a restaurant and reserve a table for you if you call, fax or e-mail your requirements to them. They have a comprehensive database and will try to meet your needs. There is no charge. ✪ *020 8888 8080 • www.restraguide.co.uk*

5 Television

Apart from satellite and cable television, there are five terrestrial channels in the UK: two run as public service channels by the BBC (BBC1 and BBC2), and the three commercial channels (ITV, Channel 4 and Channel 5). Ceefax and Teletext are text programs on these channels, giving travel and weather updates.

6 Radio

London radio stations bring constant news and travel updates for the capital. They include BBC London Live (94.9FM), Capital FM (95.8FM), News Direct (97.3FM) and LBC (1152 MW).

7 Publications

For current events in London, see the daily papers, particularly the *Evening Standard* (the capital's evening paper) and *Time Out*, a weekly listings magazine. The Thursday edition of the *Standard* also includes a free listings magazine, *Hot Tickets*, for the week ahead. Their website *www.thisislondon.co.uk* is also useful. The Tourist Board publishes two useful booklets: *Where To Stay* and *What To Do*.

8 Weather

London's weather is as unpredictable as elsewhere in the country, but if you want to check ahead phone Weathercall for an up-to-the minute forecast. There are also regular weather forecasts for the capital and other regions on radio and television. ✪ *Weathercall: 0906 850 0401*

9 Britain Visitor Centre

Here you will find a vast amount of information on London and the rest of the country, with advice on accommodation, travel, attractions and activities. As well as the Visitor Centre in Regent Street, there is a good website which covers the same type of information. ✪ *1 Regent Street W1 • Map J2 • www.visit britain.com*

10 London Lesbian & Gay Switchboard

This 24-hour information line provides information, support and a referral service for lesbians and gay men. They can give advice on pubs, clubs and bars for gay visitors to the capital. ✪ *020 7837 7324 • www.llgs.org.uk*

Left **Low floor bus** Right **Wheelchair access ramp**

🔟 London for the Disabled

1 Accommodation

Most large, modern hotels have disabled access, but older or small hotels may not, so it is best to check before booking. RADAR (Royal Association for Disability and Rehabilitation), the main organization for the disabled, publishes an annual guide, *Holidays in Britain and Ireland*, which lists recommended accommodation.
Ⓢ *RADAR: 020 7250 3222 • www.radar.org.uk*

2 Public Transport

With long escalators, stairs, walkways and heaving rush hours, it is particularly difficult for the disabled to travel on the Underground. Buses are only marginally better. A useful guide, *Access to the Underground*, is produced by the Access & Mobility service, and on sale at Travel Information Centres at Heathrow airport, main tube and rail stations, as well as some suburban ones. Other guides include *London for All*, published by the London Tourist Board.
Ⓢ *Access & Mobility: 020 7941 4600 • www.transport forlondon.gov.uk*

3 Museums

Most of London's museums and galleries have ramps for wheelchair access and disabled toilets. Recorded "audio tours" can often be hired, which are useful to those with impaired vision.

4 Theater and Movies

By 2004 all theaters in London will have disabled access. Until then call in advance to find out what seating is allocated for disabled visitors – some offer good seats, others not so good. For more information on accessibility in arts venues, call Artsline.
Ⓢ *Artsline: 020 7388 2227 • www.artsline.org.uk*

5 Restaurants

Some restaurants are more accessible than others: even if they have wheelchair access, the dining areas may be on an upper or lower floor, so check when booking a table. Our Top10 listings state if a restaurant does not have disabled access.

6 Guided Tours

Based in Kensington, London W8, Can Be Done specializes in holidays and tours for the disabled. They will put together a package to suit your requirements.
London's open-top sightseeing bus tours offer a relatively easy way of seeing the sights of London without having to walk too far. Access can be difficult for those in wheelchairs, however. The tours last for around 90 minutes and can be joined at various city locations (see p168). Ⓢ *Can Be Done: 020 8907 2400 • www.canbedone.co.uk*

7 Students

SKILL, the National Bureau for Students with Disabilities, offers limited help and information, as does the UK Council for International Education (UKCOSA). Ⓢ *SKILL: 0800 328 5050. www.skill. org.uk • UKCOSA: 020 7226 3762*

8 Impaired Hearing

Many theatres have a sign-language interpreter on duty at all or some performances. Call in advance to check. The Royal National Institute for the Deaf (RNID) may be able to help with some enquiries. Ⓢ *RNID: 0808 808 0123 • www.rnid.org.uk*

9 Impaired Sight

The Royal National Institute for the Blind (RNIB) Recreation and Lifestyle Service can provide useful holiday information. Braille maps of London's transport system are available from Transport for London's Access & Mobility unit. Ⓢ *RNIB: 0845 766 9999. www.rnib.org.com • Transport for London: 020 7222 1234. www.londontrans port.co.uk*

10 Publications

The Greater London Action on Disability (GLAD) is a voluntary organization with fortnightly and monthly publications. *Access in London* is a useful guide to getting around the city. Ⓢ *GLAD: 020 7346 5800*

Left **Bank** Right **Post box**

Banking and Communications

1 Money
The pound sterling (£) is divided into 100 pence (p). Paper notes are in denominations of £5, £10, £20 and £50. Coins are £1 and £2 (yellow-gold); 5p, 10p, 20p, 50p (silver); and 1p and 2p (copper).

2 Banks
Opening hours for banks are generally 9:30am–4:30pm Monday to Friday. Most banks and building societies have cash machines in an outside wall. Some also have lobbies with cash and payment machines – these can be accessed by your cash card at any time of night or day.

3 Bureaux de Change
Bureaux de Change are regulated, and their rates are displayed along with commission charges. These are either flat fees or percentage charges. Many offer exchange without a commission fee, but check their rates as these may be less favourable than those charging a fee. Thomas Cook (part of HSBC bank) is the largest bureau, with many branches throughout London.

4 Credit Cards
Most establishments accept the major credit cards such as Visa and MasterCard (Access). American Express and Diners Club cards are less widely accepted in the UK. Credit cards are particularly useful for hotel and restaurant bills, shopping, car rental and booking theatre or movie tickets by telephone. They can also be used to obtain cash advances, with a PIN number.

5 Postal Services
Post offices and sub-post offices are located throughout London. They are generally open from 9am–5:30pm Monday to Friday and until 12:30pm on Saturday. You can also buy stamps in shops, hotels and other outlets. The main West End post office is near Trafalgar Square. Mail sent *poste restante* to this address will be kept for one month. American Express also provides a *poste restante* service for its customers. ◈ *Post office: 24–28 William IV Street WC2. Map M3 • American Express: 30–31 Haymarket SW1. Map L4 • Royal Mail Customer Help Line: 0845 7222 3344. www.royal mail.co.uk*

6 Telephones
Most phone boxes take coins (20p minimum), phonecards and credit cards. You will need a card with at least £2 credit for an international call. If you have difficulty contacting a number, call the Operator (100) or International Operator (155). In an emergency, dial 999 or 112.

7 Dialing Codes
The code for London is 020, which you omit when dialing within the city. When calling from abroad, dial the access code followed by 20, omitting the initial 0. To call abroad from London, dial 00 followed by the access code of the country you are dialing. To find a number call one of the directory services listed below. ◈ *Directory Enquiries: 192 • International Directory Enquiries: 153*

8 Faxes and Photocopies
There are fax and photocopying shops throughout London, and most of the larger hotels also offer these facilities.

9 Cellular Phones
London is awash with cellular phones. Check before leaving home whether yours will work within the UK, which uses a 900 or 1800 GSM system.

10 Internet
There are a number of Internet bars and cafés throughout London with charges varying from free (if you're buying drinks at the bar) to £5 an hour. The worldwide chain easyEverything has 5 branches in central London, including one at the Trafalgar Square end of the Strand. ◈ *Easy-Everything: 456–59 Strand WC2 • Map M4*

Left **Bow Street police station, Covent Garden** Center **Mounted police** Right **Boots pharmacy**

Security and Health

1 Emergency
For emergency police, fire or ambulance services dial 999 – the operator will ask which service you require. This number is free on any public telephone.

2 Personal Protection
London, like most metropolitan areas, has its share of bagsnatchers and pickpockets. Street crime has increased in recent years and you should be aware of this late at night and in outlying or poorly-populated areas. Look after your possessions, keeping valuable items concealed. In pubs and other public places, keep hold of your handbag – it is not unknown for bags to vanish from between their owners' feet in theaters and bars. Avoid poorly-lit back streets, at night and if you are on your own.

3 Theft
Make sure that your possessions are insured before you arrive and, if possible, leave passports, tickets and travelers' checks in the hotel safe. Report all thefts to the police, especially if you need to make an insurance claim. There is a police presence in such busy areas as Leicester Square and Oxford Street, as well as several central police stations. ◈ *West End Central Police: 27 Savile Row W1 • Map J3 • 020 7437 1212*

4 Lost Property
Anything found on the tube or buses is sent to the London Transport Lost Property Office. Allow three days for lost items to get there. The office is open only to personal callers. For items lost in cabs, call the Black Cab Lost Property office. ◈ *LT Lost Property: 200 Baker Street W1. Map C3. Open 9:30am–2pm Mon–Fri • Black Cab Lost Property: 020 7918 2000*

5 Hospitals
There are a number of hospitals in central London with 24-hour emergency services, including dental hospitals. Emergency accident treatment may be free for visitors (see p160).

6 Pharmacies
Pharmacies (known as Chemists in England) are open during business hours, some until late, and can give advice on minor ailments. Boots is a large, well-respected chain with branches throughout London. ◈ *Boots, 75 Queensway W2. Map B3. Open 10am–10pm daily • Bliss Chemist, 5–6 Marble Arch W1. Map C3. 10am–midnight daily*

7 Dentists
Hotels can usually suggest local dentists, and many are listed in Yellow Pages. For free emergency dental work, go to Guy's Hospital Dental Department.

8 Embassies and Consulates
Overseas embassies and consulates are situated around the West End, Mayfair, Belgravia and Kensington. They will help if you lose your passport, need a visa or legal assistance (see p160).

9 Women Travelers
Women often travel alone in London, but, as always, precautions should be taken. Use busy, well-lit streets at night, don't travel in unoccupied carriages on trains or the tube and always use registered black cabs (see p162).

10 Sexual Health
St. Mary's Hospital, Paddington, and St. Thomas's, Westminster have walk-in clinics that deal with sexually transmitted diseases. ◈ *Aids Helpline: 0800 567 123*

London Hospitals

St. Mary's
Praed Street W2 • Map B3 • 020 7886 6666

St. Thomas's
Lambeth Palace Road SE1 • Map N6 • 020 7928 9292

University College
Gower Street WC1 • Map E2 • 020 7387 9300

Guy's Hospital Dental Department
St. Thomas Street SE1 • Map G4 • 020 7955 4317

Left **Punting, River Cam, Cambridge** Right **Palace Pier, Brighton beach**

TOP 10 Excursions from London

1 Windsor Castle
This ancient bastion of British royalty is well worth a day out. Its state apartments and the 15th-century St. George's Chapel are glorious. As it is still a royal residence, access to some apartments is restricted when the Queen is staying. ◈ Windsor, Berkshire • Train: 40 mins • 01753 831 118 • Open Mar–Oct: 9:45am–5:15pm; Nov–Feb: 9:45am–4:15pm • Admission charge

2 Oxford
Britain's oldest university town is a fascinating place to visit, with ancient colleges, museums and galleries at every turn. For a short introduction to the city, start at The Oxford Story on Broad Street. The most magnificent colleges are Christ Church, Magdalen and Merton. ◈ Train: 1 hr • Tourist Information: 01865 726 871 • www.visit oxford.org

3 Cambridge
Don't miss King's, Queen's and Peterhouse, the oldest college (1284) in Cambridge. Relax on a punt on the river Cam, which runs through the meadows (the Backs) between the colleges. ◈ Train: 45 mins • Tourist Information: 01223 322 640 • www.tourismcambridge.com

4 Brighton
"London-on-Sea" is the nickname of this cosmopolitan city, established as a fashionable resort by the Prince Regent in the late-18th and early-19th centuries when he moved to the extravagant Royal Pavilion. Shop for antiques in The Lanes, have fish and chips on the pier and visit the beach. ◈ Train: 1 hr • Tourist Information: 0906 711 2255 • www.visit brighton.com

5 Stratford-upon-Avon
William Shakespeare's birthplace (1564) is firmly on the tourist map. There are several buildings here associated with the great playwright, as well as the Royal Shakespeare Theatre if you want to catch a performance. ◈ Train: 2 hrs • Tourist Information: 01789 293 127 • www.shakespearecountry.co.uk

6 Canterbury
In 597 CE, this pleasant market town southeast of London became the seat of the primate, the Archbishop of Canterbury. The magnificent cathedral includes the tomb of St. Thomas Becket. ◈ Train: 1½ hrs • Tourist Information: 01227 766 567 • www.canterbury.com

7 Chessington World of Adventures
A vast amusement park that was originally a zoo (it still has animals in its Jungle in a Mist section) will keep children happy all day long. The white-knuckle rides include a terrifying upside-down roller coaster. Tickets bought in advance are cheaper. ◈ Chessington, Surrey • Train: 30 mins • 0870 444 7777 • Open Mar–Oct: 10am–5pm daily • Admission charge

8 Thorpe Park
The highest water ride is Europe is just one of the attractions at this theme park, which is one of the most popular day trips for families. ◈ Chertsey, Surrey • Train to Staines: 30 mins • 0870 444 4466 • Open Apr–Oct: 10am–5pm daily (later in school holidays) • Admission charge

9 Woburn Abbey
Home to the Dukes of Bedford, this 18th-century stately home is one of the best in England. It has a fine collection of paintings and porcelain and large grounds. An added attraction is the adjoining Safari Park. ◈ Woburn, Bedfordshire • Train to Flitwick: 1 hr, then taxi • 01525 290 666 • Open Mar–Oct: daily • Admission charge

10 Leeds Castle
England's most romantic castle is built on two islands in a lake surrounded by 500 acres of Kent parkland. It has a collection of medieval furnishings. ◈ Maidstone, Kent • Train to Bearsted: 1½ hrs, then connecting bus • 01622 765 400 • Open Apr–Oct: 10am–5pm daily; Nov–Feb 10am–3pm daily • Admission charge

Left **Walking tour** Right **London sightseeing bus**

Trips and Tours

1 Sightseeing Bus Tours

Open-top sightseeing buses provide one of the best ways of getting to know London. There are several operators and a number of tours with pick-up points around the city, so you can get on and off all day, wherever you want. Some companies include a river trip from Westminster to Tower Pier. ✆ *The Original Tour: 020 8877 1722 • Big Bus Company: 020 7233 9533*

2 River Trips

There is a choice of boat services on the Thames but they are run by different operators and tickets are not interchangeable. It is best to buy tickets at the piers so that you can find out exactly what is on offer. Westminster and Charing Cross are the principal central London piers. Boats from here go up river to Hampton Court and downriver to Tower Bridge and Greenwich. ✆ *Charing Cross Pier: Map M4 • Westminster Pier: Map M6*

3 Regent's Canal

This is a lovely backwater for idle cruising, between Camden Lock and Little Venice. You can catch the boat at either end, with a stop-off for London Zoo (see p68). ✆ *London Waterbus Co: Warwick Crescent W2 • Map B2 • 020 7482 2550*

4 Themed Walks

Jack the Ripper Haunts, Ghosts of the Old City, Shakespeare's London, Hidden Pubs – there are dozens of such walks on offer from both individuals and companies. The longest established operator, The Original London Walks, offers a wide choice of two-hour walks. ✆ *020 7624 3978 • www.walks.com*

5 Audio Tours

This new, guide-free idea for touring the city involves renting a tour audiopack, which will be delivered to your hotel. The pack includes one or more selected tours for the user to follow on headphones. ✆ *ZigZag Audio Tours: 0800 195 7827 • www.zigzag tours.com.*

6 Backstage

Most of London's historic theatres offer daytime backstage tours. The National Theatre's tour of all three theatres (the Olivier, the Cottesloe and the Lyttleton), as well as of dressing rooms and workshops, lasts about 75 minutes. Call to reserve. (see p56). ✆ *National Theatre: 020 7452 3400*

7 Open House

On one weekend at the end of September, around 550 buildings in London, from city blocks to private homes, open their doors to the public, revealing some hidden architectural gems. The unique event is run by the charity London Open House – look at their website for a taste. ✆ *020 7267 7644 • www.londonopenhouse.org • Free*

8 Air Tours

Several companies offer sightseeing tours by helicopter. Cabair offers a half-hour tour of London that follows the route of the Thames. The flight leaves from Elstree Aerodrome in north London. ✆ *Cabair: Borehamwood, Hertfordshire • Train to Radlett, then taxi • 020 8953 4411*

9 Thames Barges

The magnificent Thames barges that used to fill the Pool of London can now be seen in St. Katherine's Dock (see p71). Topsail Charters rents barges for the day or an overnight stay. Tower Bridge is opened to let them through. ✆ *Topsail Charters: 01621 857567 • www.topsail. co.uk*

10 Out of Town

Several operators run bus trips to well-known sights within an hour or two's drive of London or further afield, including Paris. Some tours are themed, focusing on such topics as gardens, steam trains and Ancient Britain. ✆ *Harrods tours: 020 7581 3603 • Frames Rickards tours: 020 7837 3111*

Liverpool Street Station, the City

🔟 Avoiding the Crowds

1 Rush Hour
Try to avoid traveling in the Monday to Friday morning (8–9:30am) and evening (5–6:30pm) rush hours when tube trains and buses are filled to bursting point and cabs are scarce. If you can, it is often more pleasant and quicker to walk.

2 Lunch Hour
Londoners generally have lunch between 1 and 2pm, when pubs, cafés and fast-food restaurants fill up and sandwich bars have long lines. On the other hand, this can be a good time to go to smarter restaurants which try to attract lunchtime crowds by offering cheap menus. Lunch in the City tends to be earlier: noon–1pm.

3 Dining Out
Although restaurants in the West End and the South Bank are generally packed with theatre-goers taking advantage of the inexpensive pre- and post-theatre dinner menus, many of these become less crowded around 8pm once the curtain has gone up.

4 Early Start
Most sights in the capital – especially the major sights, such as the Tower of London and Madame Tussauds – are least crowded early in the day. You will have to fight the rush hour to get there, however.

5 School Holidays
During school holidays, London's museums and other sights in the capital are filled with families and groups of children. In general, school holidays last six weeks in summer from the end of July to the beginning of September, with additional two–three week breaks at Easter and Christmas. Sights are also crowded during half-terms: the last week in February, May and October.

6 Matinees
Some of the most popular shows and events in London theatres are heavily reserved far in advance. However, they often have seats available for their midweek and Saturday matinees.

7 Booking Ahead
Popular exhibitions operate a system of pre-booked, timed entry tickets in order to prevent overcrowding. Try and book well in advance to secure an early morning, lunchtime or late admission to avoid the biggest crowds.

8 Late Evenings
Shops and galleries in the capital often have late-opening evenings when they are less crowded than during the day. The shops in Oxford Street, for example, open late on Thursday evenings. Major exhibitions at the Royal Academy (see p113) and elsewhere sometimes stay open until late. The V & A (see p119) remains open until 10pm on Wednesday evenings and on the last Friday of each month; Tate Modern (see pp18–19) is open until 10pm on Fridays and Saturdays.

9 Weekends
London is emptier on weekends, without the commuters who stream in to work here from Monday to Friday. The City, in particular, is deserted on weekends. This is a good time to wander around and see its sights, when it is relatively free from crowds and traffic.

10 Public Holidays
The capital is quieter during the holidays as many Londoners leave town over Public Holiday weekends. Apart from Christmas and New Year, the main bank holidays in the UK are at Easter, May Day, Whitsun (end of May) and at the end of August. Be aware that some sights may be closed and that museums and galleries tend to have shorter opening hours at these times. They are unlikely to be closed completely, except for Christmas and Boxing Day (26 Dec). It is becoming increasingly common for shops and supermarkets to remain open for some, if not all of the holidays.

Left **Antiques dealer, Camden Passage** Centre **Harrods** Right **Covent Garden Central Market**

🔟 Shopping Tips

1 Shopping Areas

There are many great places to shop in London, with some areas specializing in particular things. Covent Garden has the most up-to-the-minute clothes, shoes, jewelry and gifts; Oxford Street is best for large department stores, music, and cheaper fashion; Bond Street and Knightsbridge are where you will find all the most expensive designer labels and goods; Mayfair and St. James's have the best art and antiques dealers.

2 Shopping Hours

Shops generally open 9:30am–6pm Mon–Sat, with late-night shopping until 8pm in the West End on Thursdays, and in Kensington and Chelsea on Wednesdays. There are limited Sunday hours.

3 Payment

Most shops accept major credit cards and personal checks endorsed with guarantee cards. VAT (Value Added Tax) is charged at 17.5% and almost always included in the marked price. Stores offering tax-free shopping display a distinctive sign and (for non-EU residents) will provide you with a Global Refund form for customs to validate when you leave the country.

4 Consumer Rights

Shoppers have a right to expect that goods are not faulty or damaged (this isn't always the case with sale items). Always keep receipts so you can return any unsatisfactory items.

5 Sales

Large stores and many fashion outlets usually have end-of-season sales in January and July when there are enormous savings on many items, from furniture to fashions.

6 Fashion

Big-label fashion houses are in Bond Street, Knightsbridge and Sloane Street. Tailored wear for men is in Savile Row and St. James's. Oxford Street is good for mid-range clothes. For street fashion, try the markets: Camden (see p141), Portobello (see p120), Petticoat Lane and Spitalfields (see p154).

7 Music

London is one of the world's music capitals, and its big music stores – HMV, Virgin and Tower Records – have huge selections of CDs and DVDs, including imports. Many specialized second-hand and collectors' shops deal in vinyl, which remains popular. The main opera and concert halls also have music outlets. For sound systems, visit Tottenham Court Road.

8 Gifts and Souvenirs

Covent Garden is great for gifts. The big stores (Selfridges, John Lewis, Liberty, Harvey Nichols, Harrods see pp64–5) have gift departments with bright ideas. Elsewhere around the city, there are shops selling designer jewelry, pottery, ceramics and household goods, many of which are designed in the UK. The main museums, galleries and tourist sites all have interesting gift stores.

9 Art and Antiques

The major commercial galleries are in the West End, around Bond Street and Cork Street (see p116). Phillips and Sotheby's (see p114) auction houses are here, too. You can find inexpensive art and craft throughout London. All kinds of antiques can be sought out in Camden Passage (Islington), Portobello Road, Kensington Church Street and King's Road (Chelsea).

10 Out of Town

If you want to do a lot of shopping under one roof and avoid the city center, there are three huge out-of-town shopping malls. Brent Cross in north London, calls itself "London's North West End". Lakeside Shopping Centre is in Grays, Essex, and Bluewater, Europe's largest shopping complex, is at Greenhithe, Kent. Shops are open until around 8pm, restaurants and entertainments stay open later.

Left **Covent Garden Piazza** Right **St. John's, Smith Square**

London on a Budget

1 Accommodation
There are a number of youth hostels in London, and universities offer accommodation from June to September. International Students House has year-round accommodation. There is also a host of cheap bed and breakfasts *(see p179)*.

2 Travel
Buses are cheaper than the tube (underground). If you are making more than two tube journeys in a day, Travel Cards are good value. They are also valid on buses and the Docklands Light Railway (but not before 9:30am on weekdays). Carnets, with 10 Zone 1 tickets, also saving money *(see p162)*.

3 Eating
It's quite possible to eat a two-course meal with a drink and coffee for under £20 in many places in London. Chinese and Indian restaurants are often inexpensive, and many churches have cheap lunchtime cafés. Expensive restaurants can become affordable with set-lunch or pre-theatre menus.

4 Museums and Galleries
Some museums are free. Others have free late afternoon or evening entry. Special deals can mean that buying a season ticket makes sense if you want to visit more than twice. An International Student Card (ISIC) offers reduced-price entry to many museums. Look out for free lunchtime lectures.

5 Street Entertainment
Covent Garden is the best place for day-long entertainment, and there's always someone to look at or listen to in Leicester Square. At weekends artists hang their work up on the railings in Piccadilly outside Green Park, and by Hyde Park on Bayswater Road.

6 Free Music
London is awash with free music. Free lunchtime concerts are held in churches and at the music colleges (in term time). Music is performed free at The Royal Festival Hall, Royal National Theatre and National Gallery, and in malls such as Hays Galleria and Canary Wharf.

7 Cheap Tickets
The best place for these is the Half-Price Ticket Booth, located in the middle of Leicester Square, which sells tickets for performances on that day only. "Fringe" theatres outside the West End (often in pubs) are considerably cheaper. Bench seats are £5 for all performances at the RSC (Barbican Centre). On Mondays, all seats are £5 at the Royal Court. The Royal Opera House has standing tickets from £6. The Prince Charles cinema in Leicester Place is the cheapest in central London.

8 Fashion
Pick up barely-worn, designer clothes at a dress agency (try The Loft, 38 Monmouth St WC2; L'Homme Designer Exchange, 50 Blandford St W1).

9 Markets
London's markets have bargain antiques, fashions, jewelry and cheap food *(see pp64–5)*.

10 Parks
London's parks offer endless free entertainment, whether watching sports in Regent's Park or listening to bands at St. James's Park bandstand *(see pp28–9)*.

Directory

London Hostel Assoc
54 Eccleston Square SW1 • 020 7834 1545

Youth Hostels Assoc
8 St. Stephen's Hill, St. Albans, Herts, AL1 2DY • 01727 855 215 • www. yha.org.uk

International Students House
229 Gt Portland St W1 • 020 7631 8300

London Bed & Breakfast Agency
71 Fellows Rd NW3 • 020 7586 2768

Left **Elizabeth Hotel** Right **Bar, Brompton Hotel**

Inexpensive Hotels

1 County Hall Travel Inn Capital

London's best inexpensive hotel has a memorable location in the old County Hall near the river and the London Eye. Though basic, facilities are more than adequate, with fold-out beds for children in each of the 313 rooms. It is essential to book well in advance. ❧ *Belvedere Road SE1 • Map N6 • 020 7902 1600 • www.travelinn. co.uk • £*

2 Columbia Hotel

The Columbia has a delightful leafy setting overlooking Kensington Gardens. Originally five mansions, and once used as a US military officers' club, it has magnificent rooms and is much more opulent than its prices suggest. ❧ *95–9 Lancaster Gate W2 • Map B3 • 020 7402 0021 • www.columbia hotel.co.uk • ££*

3 Fielding Hotel

Ideally situated for Covent Garden, this quaint room-only hotel is a warren of oddly shaped rooms, with showers and basins tucked in corners. A token bar is squeezed in and outside there is all of Covent Garden to breakfast in. ❧ *4 Broad Court, Bow St WC2 • Map M2 • 020 7836 8305 • ££*

4 Mabledon Court Hotel

Between St. Pancras and Euston stations, and just around the corner from

the attractive Woburn Walk, this small, com-fortable hotel has tea- and coffee-making facilities in all its rooms and a pleasant breakfast room. ❧ *10–11 Mabledon Place WC1 • Map E2 • 020 7388 3866 • www.smooth hound.co.uk/hotels • ££*

5 Lancaster Court Hotel

Between Paddington station and Hyde Park, Sussex Gardens is a quiet, pleasant street lined with inexpensive hotels. Lancaster Court is just a few minutes walk from Hyde Park. ❧ *202–4 Sussex Gardens W2 • Map B3 • 020 7402 8438 • www.lancaster-court-hotel.co.uk • ££*

6 Craven Gardens Hotel

Located in a quiet, upmarket part of town, this privately run hotel has 43 bedrooms and two executive suites, with 24-hour service, coffee- and tea-making facilities in the rooms and a bar. It has no restaurant but there is a good Greek taverna just a few yards away. ❧ *16 Leinster Terrace W2 • Map B3 • 020 7262 3167 • craven@diecon.co.uk • ££*

7 Brompton Hotel

Situated just by South Kensington tube station and handy for the museums, this typical west London hotel has comfortable private

rooms. Reception is on the first floor. On the ground-floor is an American-style bar (not owned by the hotel) run by New Yorker Janet Evans, which serves great cocktails. ❧ *30–2 Old Brompton Rd SW7 • Map C5 • 020 7584 4517 • www.bromhotel.com • ££*

8 Gresham Hotel

Forty rooms in a row of Georgian townhouses near Bedford Square make this a good, central option. It has a choice of single and double rooms and suites for up to four people. ❧ *36 Bloomsbury Street WC1 • Map L1 • 020 7580 4232 • info@gresham hotellondon.com • ££*

9 Elizabeth Hotel

This handsome town house overlooks a quiet, private square, which is available for guests' use. It is close to Victoria station, and has single, double and family rooms. ❧ *37 Eccleston Square SW1 • Map D5 • 020 7828 6812 • www. elizabeth-hotel.com • ££*

10 Kenwood House Hotel

One of a number of small hotels near Baker Street, Madame Tussaud's and Regent's Park, this friendly establishment has 16 rooms, including five family rooms. ❧ *14 Gloucester Place W1 • Map C3 • 020 7935 3473 • www.hotelconnections. com • ££*

Royal Garden Hotel

Mid-price Hotels

1 Bedford Hotel

One of five large, good-value Bloomsbury hotels run by Imperial London Hotels, the Bedford's advantage is a good restaurant and a sunny lounge and garden. ◈ Southampton Row WC1 • Map M1 • 020 7636 7822 • www.imperial hotels. co.uk • £££

2 St. Giles Hotel

Centrally located near the corner of Tottenham Court Road and Oxford Street, this modern hotel is a good choice for fitness fanatics – guests have free use of a basement fitness center and 83-ft (25-m) pool. ◈ Bedford Ave WC1 • Map L1 • 020 7300 3000 • www. stgiles.com • £££

3 Thistle Trafalgar Square

The Thistle Group has 24 hotels in London, many in prime sites. This one is next door to the National Gallery, so staying here will save on transport costs for much of your sightseeing. ◈ Whitcomb St WC2 • Map L4 • 020 7930 4477 • ££££

4 Regent Palace Hotel

This large, rambling hotel near Piccadilly Circus is good value for its central position. Because it is a popular hotel for London breaks, weekend rates are more expensive. The hotel has no restaurant but there is a large Irish theme bar, Callaghan's. ◈ Piccadilly Circus W1 • Map K3 • 020 7734 0716 • £££

5 Cranley Gardens Hotel

Occupying four large Victorian mansions, this is one of the best of the many South Kensington townhouse hotels. Airy, modern and overlooking a quiet square (some rooms have balconies), this is a relaxed and friendly place to stay. ◈ 8 Cranley Gdns SW7 • Map B6 • 020 7373 3232 • cranleygarden@aol.com • £££

6 Langham Court Hotel

Located in a quiet side street near Oxford Circus, this enticing hotel, with attractive exterior tile work, is as warm and friendly inside as its exterior promises. Rooms are comfortably furnished and there is a good restaurant serving mainly French food. ◈ 31–5 Langham St W1 • Map J1 • 020 7436 6622 • ££££

7 Bryanston Court

This family-run hotel near Marble Arch is well suited for a one- or two-day shopping and sightseeing stopover. Blue awnings outside add a jaunty continental touch, but inside the atmosphere is civilized and old-fashioned. ◈ 56–60 Great Cumberland Pl W1 • Map C3 • 020 7262 3141 • £££

8 Gainsborough Hotel

Named after the English painter Thomas Gainsborough, this hotel aims to recreate the feel of an English country home. it is conveniently located for the museums and Knightsbridge shops. ◈ 7–11 Queensbury Place SW7 • Map B5 • 020 7957 0000 • gainsborough @eeh.co.uk • £££

9 Royal Garden Hotel

This hotel squeezes into the mid-price category for its excellent weekend rate. It is a pleasantly airy modern hotel next to Kensington Gardens and Kensington Palace and close to the shops of Kensington High Street. Facilities include a health centre, spa and gym, 24-hour business center and two restaurants. ◈ 2 Kensington High Sreet W8 • Map B4 • 020 7937 8000 • www.royalgarden hotel.co.uk • ££££.

10 The White House

Close to Regent's Park, this classic hotel was built as a block of model apartments in 1936. Now refurbished as a comfortable 82-room hotel, it has spacious rooms, a restaurant and bar. Prices can vary by 100 percent, the most expensive times being mid-summer and Christmas. ◈ Albany Street NW1 • Map D2 • 020 7387 1200 • www.solmelia.es • ££££

Left **Halkin** Center **One Aldwych** Right **St. Martins Lane**

⁑10 Designer Hotels

1 The Sanderson

London's most stylish hotel is cool, minimalist and thrillingly expensive. Behind a 1950s office-block exterior, plain walls are punctuated by Dali-lips and Louis XV sofas, while wafting curtains and oil paintings decorate the ceilings of the sparse bedrooms. Facilities include a sauna, gym and spa. Check for special break deals. ⊗ *50 Berners Street W1 • Map K1 • 020 7300 1400 • www.ianschragerhotels.com • £££££*

2 One Aldwych

In a former 1908 bank building, this is a relaxing designer hotel with art-filled lobby and corridors, two good restaurants and an 60-ft (18-m) pool with underwater music. ⊗ *Aldwych WC2 • Map N2 • 020 7300 1000 • www.onealdwych.co.uk • £££££*

3 St. Martin's Lane

The Sanderson's sister hotel was designed by Phillipe Starck. Rooms have floor-to-ceiling windows and even the bathrooms (all with big tubs) are 50 percent glass. ⊗ *St Martin's Lane WC2 • Map L3 • 020 7300 5500 • www.ianschrager hotels.com • £££££*

4 myhotel Bloomsbury

Just off Tottenham Court Road, this hotel is an oasis of calm, with a mystical, Oriental style and attentive staff. The rooms are light and feng-shui assured, with white orchids, fishtanks and candles for decoration. ⊗ *11–13 Bayley Street WC1 • Map L1 • 020 7667 6000 • www.myhotels. co.uk • £££££*

5 Charlotte Street Hotel

One of the most tasteful and comfortable hotels in London, where leather armchairs and antiques mix with contemporary works of art, and log fires burn in the drawing room and library. The bustling Oscar bar and brasserie attract Charlotte Street diners. ⊗ *15 Charlotte St W1 • Map K1 • 020 7806 2000 • www.charlottestreet hotel.com • £££££*

6 Mercure London City Bankside

Opened in 2000, and just a stone's throw from Tate Modern, this seven-story hotel has pay TV and video games in every room. ⊗ *75 Southwark Street SE1 • Map R4 • 020 7902 0800 • www.mercure.com • £££*

7 Number Five Maddox Street

Glass, steel and bamboo feature in these high-quality Japanese-style serviced apartments, with on-call chefs to cook for you, Ben and Jerry's ice-cream in the fridge and full Internet facilities. ⊗ *5 Maddox Street W1 • Map J3 • 020 7647 0200 • www.living-rooms.co.uk • £££££*

8 The Hempel

When you walk into this dazzling white, Zen-inspired hotel, you'll think you've reached Nirvana. Immaculate and stylish, it has a central atrium from which five floors radiate. Each room is individually designed in a minimal Japanese style. The restaurant serves Thai-Japanese cuisine. ⊗ *31–5 Craven Hill Gardens W2 • Map B3 • 020 7298 9000 • www.thehempel. co.uk • £££££*

9 Metropolitan

Contemporary and stylish, this was one of the first of the classy modern hotels in London, with black-clad staff, cool interiors and minimalist Asian-style bedrooms. Go celebrity-spotting in the Met Bar or in Nobu, its fashionable Japanese restaurant *(see p117)*. ⊗ *Old Park Lane W1 • Map D4 • 020 7447 1000 • www.metropolitan.co.uk • £££££*

10 Halkin

A startlingly beautiful hotel in a Georgian town house, which has been given a thoroughly modern overhaul with marble, glass and dark woods and oriental details. The restaurant overlooks the garden and the rooms are equipped for communications and sound. ⊗ *5 Halkin Street SW1 • Map D4 • 020 7333 1000 • www.halkin.co.uk • £££££*

Note: *Unless otherwise stated, all hotels accept credit cards and have private bathrooms*

Price Categories

For a standard,		£	under £70
double room per		££	£70–100
night (with breakfast		£££	£100–150
if included), taxes		££££	£150–200
and extra charges.		£££££	over £200

Left **Marriott** Right **Tower Thistle**

TOP10 Business Hotels

1 Great Eastern

Built in 1884 as the railway hotel serving Liverpool Street station, and the only hotel in the City of London, The Great Eastern has recently been brilliantly renovated. Among its delights is a wonderful glass-domed restaurant, the Aurora – one of a number of restaurants and bars. Rooms are designed for business guests with ergonomic desks, ISDN lines and VCRs and DVD players. ✆ *Liverpool Street EC2 • Map H3 • 020 7618 5000 • www.great-eastern-hotel.co.uk • £££££*

2 Jurys

This beautiful Neo-Georgian building was designed by Edwin Lutyens for the YWCA in 1929. The Queen Mary Hall is now a conference centre and the former chapel provides a quiet, discreet meeting room. The suites and rooms have been designed for a mainly business clientele, with modems, voicemail and work desks. ✆ *16–22 Gt Russell Street WC1 • Map L1 • 020 7347 1000 • www.jurysdoyle.com • £££££*

3 Four Seasons Hotel

As smart and stylish as you would expect from a new Canary Wharf hotel, the Four Seasons has a central atrium and good sense of space. Rooms are all well equipped for business needs and there is a good northern Italian restaurant. ✆ *46 Westferry Circus E14 • DLR Westferry • 020 7510 1999 • www.four seasons.com • £££££*

4 London Bridge Hotel

Just over the river from the City, this handsome, modern, independently owned hotel is fully equipped for business guests. Modern French cuisine is served in its Simply Nico restaurant. ✆ *8–18 London Bridge Street SE1 • Map H4 • 020 7855 2200 • www.london-bridge-hotel.co.uk • £££££*

5 Marble Arch Marriott

A modern hotel near the western end of Oxford Street. Facilities include a bar and restaurant, gym, health club and swimming pool. There are full business facilities in the executive lounge. ✆ *134 George Street W1 • Map D3 • 020 7723 1277 • www.marriotthotels.com • £££££*

6 Paddington Court Hotel

Located in a quiet area of west London north of Kensington Gardens, this Best Western hotel has 157 comfortable, spacious rooms, an inexpensive restaurant for residents and a pleasant lounge bar. ✆ *27 Devonshire Terrace W2 • Map B3 • 020 7745 1200 • www.paddington court.com • £££*

7 Sheraton Park Tower

This circular hotel is a Knightsbridge landmark – views get better and more expensive the higher you go. Business guests are well catered for. ✆ *101 Knightsbridge SW1 • Map C4 • 020 7235 8050 • www.sheraton.com • £££££*

8 Tower Thistle

Many of the 800-plus rooms in this vast modern block near Tower Bridge and St. Katharine's Dock have spectacular river views. ✆ *St. Katharine's Way E1 • Map H4 • 020 7481 2575 • www.thistle hotels.com • £££££*

9 Holiday Inn Express

One of a chain of ten, value-for-money London hotels, the London City hotel is not actually in the City, but backs onto newly fashionable Hoxton Square *(see p153)*, an area known more for art than for business. ✆ *275 Old Street EC1 • Map H2 • 0800 897 121 • www.hiexpress.co.uk • ££*

10 City Hotel

Just off Whitechapel High Street, at the bottom of Brick Lane *(see p154)*, this hotel is ideal for business travelers who wish to be close to the City. ✆ *12 Osborne Street E1 • Tube Aldgate East • 020 7247 3313 • www.cityhotel london.co.uk • £££*

Left **Goring Hotel** Right **Durrants Hotel**

Character Hotels

1 Hazlitt's
As much a literary event as a hotel, Hazlitt's is located in the former townhouse of essayist William Hazlitt (1778–1830). The hotel's literary feel is enhanced by its library of books signed by the many authors that have stayed here. ✆ *6 Frith Street W1 • Map L2 • 020 7434 1771 • www.hazlitts hotel.com • ££££*

2 Durrants Hotel
This Georgian hotel, close to Marylebone High Street and Oxford Street, has been in business since 1790. It has a comfortable, old-fashioned style, with oak-panelled rooms, paintings on the walls and comfy leather seats. ✆ *George Street W1 • Map D3 • 020 7935 8131 • www.durrants hotel.co.uk • ££££*

3 Topham's Belgravia
With lace and chintz, hunting prints and horse brasses, this quaint hotel has the feel of a country cottage – though it's just down the road from the Queen's London home, Buckingham Palace. It has a bar and a small brasserie serving modern British dishes. ✆ *28 Ebury Street SW1 • Map D5 • 020 7730 8147 • www. tophams.co.uk • £££*

4 Basil Street Hotel
Creaking slowly into the 21st century, this Edwardian institution has a lost-world charm to its individual rooms. The Parrot Club provides a retreat for women guests. ✆ *Basil Street SW3 • Map C5 • 020 7581 3311 • www.thebasil.com • ££££*

5 Goring Hotel
Decorated throughout in delightful Edwardiana, this gracious, family-run, country-house-style hotel combines comfort with delightful nostalgia. ✆ *15 Beeston Place SW1 • Map D5 • www.goringhotel.co.uk • £££££*

6 Blakes Hotel
A Victorian delight, with sumptuous cushions and drapes, bamboo and birdcages, each room is individually styled with exotica from all over the world. The Chinese Room bar and restaurant in the basement continues the theme with low seating and cushions. ✆ *33 Roland Gardens SW7 • Map B6 • 020 7370 6701 • www.hempel.com • £££££*

7 The Gore
Originally opened in 1892, this hotel retains a relaxed, *fin-de-siècle* feel. Persian rugs, potted palms and paintings are in keeping with the elegance of the building, and rooms are furnished with antiques. The restaurant and bistro are also recommended. ✆ *189 Queen's Gate SW7 • Map B5 • 020 7584 6601 • www.gorehotel.com • ££££*

8 Portobello Hotel
Full of character, full of junk, with each room individually and tastefully cluttered, this is the kind of hotel you would hope to find near London's great antiques market. Food in the restaurant is prepared by the nearby Julie's wine bar. ✆ *21 Stanley Gardens W11 • Map A4 • 020 7727 2777 • www.portobello-hotel. co.uk • ££££*

9 The Rookery
A warren of rooms has been linked together to create a brilliant hotel that evokes Victorian London, with a Gothic touch. It takes its name from the gang of thieves who once haunted this area near Smithfield market, just outside the City. ✆ *12 St. Peter's Lane EC1 • Map Q1 • 020 7336 0931 • www.rookery hotel.com • £££££*

10 Dorset Square Hotel
Located in an elegant square near Regent's Park, this stylish, modern small hotel is decorated in English country style. The theme is continued in its basement restaurant, The Potting Shed, which has live jazz Tuesday to Saturday. Rooms are decorated with antique furniture (two have four-posters) and there is a pleasant small garden. ✆ *39 Dorset Square NW1 • Map C2 • 020 7723 7874 • www.firmdale.com • £££*

Note: Unless otherwise stated, all hotels accept credit cards and have private bathrooms

Palm Court, Ritz

🔟 Luxury Hotels

1 The Lanesborough
In London's most luxurious hotel, the Regency decoration reaches a peak in the Oriental Conservatory restaurant, while all the rooms, with deep pile carpets and gleaming mahogany, are fitted with the latest entertainment and communications technology. There is also a fitness center. ✪ *1 Lanesborough Place SW1 • Map D4 • 020 7259 5599 • www.lanesborough.com • £££££*

2 London Marriott County Hall
A fantastic setting, with unrivaled views over the river to Westminster, is the best part – but the wood-panelled rooms, original library and dining room are magnificent too. Plus a gym, sauna and indoor pool. ✪ *County Hall SE1 • Map N6 • 020 7928 5200 • www.marriott. com/marriott/lonch • £££££*

3 Savoy
Fortunate in its riverside setting, the Savoy is London's top traditional hotel – a dignified, clubby place with few airs and graces. Leisure facilities include a small rooftop pool. ✪ *1 Savoy Hill, Strand WC2 • Map M4 • 020 7836 4343 • www.savoy group. co.uk • £££££*

4 Ritz
One of London's most glamorous hotels, the Ritz is decorated in cream and pink, with gold and silk trimmings, chandeliers and Louis XVI furniture. Afternoon tea in the Palm Court is popular and the restaurant has a garden terrace. ✪ *150 Piccadilly W1 • Map K3 • 020 7493 8181 • www.the ritzhotel.co.uk • £££££*

5 Covent Garden Hotel
London's most innovative new hotel group is distinguished here by modern style and traditional elegance. Rooms are individually designed with luxurious marble bathrooms. A basement screening room is a nod to its showbiz guests. ✪ *10 Monmouth Street WC2 • Map L2 • 020 7806 1000 • www.firmdale.com • £££££*

6 Waldorf Meridian
Not top-class but quite grand enough, this is one of London's great Edwardian hotels. A band plays on a scrolled balcony overlooking the Palm Court lounge for the hotel's famous weekend tea dances. The leisure facilities, however, are right up-to-date. ✪ *Aldwych WC2 • Map N3 • 0870 400 8484 • £££££*

7 Dorchester
Part of the fabric of London, the Dorchester opened in 1931 and was the center of glamorous London life for several decades. It can still outswank most places. Book a "superior executive" for a view over Hyde Park. ✪ *53 Park Lane, W1 • Map D4 • 020 7629 8888 • £££££*

8 Brown's
Since 1837, when this Mayfair hotel was founded by James Brown, valet to Lord Byron, to accommodate country society staying in London for the Season, it has mellowed with grace and style. It is clubby without being exclusive, old with all "mod cons". ✪ *Albemarle Street W1 • Map J4 • 020 7493 6020 • www.browns hotel.com • £££££*

9 The Berners Hotel
Dating from the 19th century, this hotel has a marble-clad lobby with ornate ceilings. The grandeur of this room, and the dazzling Reflections restaurant, are enough to make you want to stay. It has a fully-equipped business center. ✪ *Berners Street W1 • Map K1 • 020 7666 2000 • www.theberners hotel.co.uk • £££££*

10 Grosvenor House Hotel
The first hotel in London to have a swimming pool also once had a skating rink, in what became the Great Room, the largest banqueting room in Europe. The pool has now been joined by new leisure facilities. ✪ *86–90 Park Lane W1 • Map C4 • 020 7499 6363 • £££££*

Left **Hampstead Village Guesthouse** Right **Richmond Hill Hotel pool**

TOP 10 Hotels Out of Town

1 Hampstead Village Guesthouse

This large Victorian family house, located just off the bottom of Hampstead High Street – and still full of the family memorabilia and toys – is now run as a guesthouse. There is a pleasant small garden in which guests can eat breakfast. 🚇 *2 Kemplay Rd NW3 • Tube Hampstead • 020 7435 8679 • www. hampsteadguesthouse.com • ££*

2 Hampstead Posthouse

Located between Camden and Hampstead, this modern 140-bedroom hotel has all the regular facilities of a chain hotel, including a bar and the Marco Pierre White brasserie. It offers very good rates at weekends. 🚇 *215 Haverstock Hill NW3 • Tube Belsize Park • 0870 400 9037 • £££*

3 Richmond Hill Hotel

Dating from 1726, this Georgian mansion at the top of Richmond Hill, close to Richmond Park, has a modern wing. A few select rooms, which are not necessarily more expensive, have river views. Guests have use of such facilities as a pool, sauna and a beauty salon. 🚇 *Richmond Hill, Surrey • Train & tube Richmond • 020 8940 2247 • www.corushotels.com • ££££*

4 Riverside Hotel

Based in an attractive Victorian building, this hotel has a great position near the River Thames and is not far from Richmond Park or the fashionable shops of Richmond. Some of the rooms overlook the river and one has French windows onto the hotel garden. 🚇 *23 Petersham Rd, Richmond, Surrey • Train & tube Richmond • 020 8940 1339 • www. smoothhound. co.uk • ££*

5 Bardon Lodge Hotel

Just a fifteen-minute walk from Blackheath Station, and five minutes from Greenwich Park, location of the Old Royal Observatory *(see p147)*, this large Victorian property has 32 rooms, including some with four-poster beds and jacuzzis. The restaurant has a short menu with mainly English dishes. 🚇 *Stratheden Rd SE3 • Train to Blackheath • 020 8853 7000 • www. bardonlodgehotel.com • ££*

6 Greenwich Parkhouse Hotel

This pleasant townhouse is beside Greenwich Park in the center of Greenwich. There are eight rooms: two triple-bedrooms overlook the park and there is also single accommodation. 🚇 *1 Nevada St SE10 • Train to Greenwich • 020 8305 1478 • www.greenwich-parkhouse-hotel.co.uk • £*

7 Ibis Hotel Docklands

This inexpensive French chain's Docklands hotel is near the river on the east side of Canary Wharf, just off the busy main streets. Rooms are perfectly adequate, and a substantial buffet breakfast is served. 🚇 *Blackwall Way E14 • DLR Blackwall• 020 7517 1100 • www.ibishotel.com • £*

8 Jarvis International

With only 56 rooms and a pleasant garden, this is an alternative to the large Heathrow airport hotels. A courtesy bus leaves for the airport every hour from 7am–10pm and takes around 10 minutes. 🚇 *Bath Rd, Cranford, Middlesex • Tube Hounslow West • 020 8897 2121 • www.jarvis.co.uk • £££*

9 Le Meridien

Walk directly from Gatwick's North Terminal to this elegant hotel, which has a full range of facilities. It is linked to London by the Gatwick Express train service. 🚇 *Gatwick Airport • 01293 555 044 • www.lemeridien-hotels.com • £££££*

10 Hilton

A modern hotel with good, standard facilities, this is the closest hotel to Stansted Airport. Ideal for early flights, it is a short bus journey to the terminal. 🚇 *Stansted Airport • 01279 680 800 • ££*

Note: *Unless otherwise stated, all hotels accept credit cards and have private bathrooms*

Left **City of London Youth Hostel** Right **London City YMCA**

Price Categories

For a standard, £ under £70
double room per £ £70–100
night (with breakfast £ £100–150
if included), taxes £ £150–200
and extra charges. £ over £200

🔟 Budget Accommodations

1 Hotel Strand Continental

Caught in a time warp, this old-fashioned hotel is the cheapest in central London. The India Club restaurant on the second floor is also a bargain. 🚫 *143 Strand WC2 • Map N3 • 020 7836 4880 • No en-suite bathrooms • £*

2 Arosfa

The artist John Everett Millais once lived in this Georgian town house, which is now a pleasant small hotel. It has a garden at the back. 🚫 *83 Gower Street WC1 • Map E2 • 020 7636 2115 • £*

3 Elysée Hotel

In a quiet street opposite one of west London's most attractive corners, Leinster Mews, this small hotel is one of the cheapest in the area. Basic but comfortable, there are various size rooms available, including a family room for up to five people. 🚫 *25–26 Craven Terrace W2 • Map B3 • 020 7402 7633 • www.elyseehotel-london.co.uk • £*

4 The Court Hotel

The Court Hotel is a favourite of Australian and South African backpackers. Basic accommodation is offered in single or shared rooms, and there are reduced weekly rates. Internet facilities. 🚫 *194–196 Earl's Court Road SW5 • Map A5 • 020 7373 0037 • courthotel@hotmail.com • £*

5 The Village

This is the largest of three hostels on this street run by St. Christopher's Inns, which cater for 248 people between them. Other branches are located in Camden, Greenwich and Shepherd's Bush. Double rooms or cheaper dormitories are available. There is a bar, roof terrace, hot tub and sauna. 🚫 *163 Borough High Street SE1 • Map G4 • 020 7407 1856 • www.st-christophers.co.uk • £*

6 Driscoll House Hotel

Visitors from all over the world come to this south London hotel, which has been open since 1913. It offers good food and facilities – including eight pianos for residents to use. All its 200 rooms are for single occupancy only, and the price includes breakfast and dinner. Weekly rates available. 🚫 *172 New Kent Road SE1 • Map G5 • 020 7703 4175 • www.driscoll hotel.co.uk • No credit cards • £*

7 Youth Hostels Association

There are seven youth hostels in London: Oxford Street, City of London, Holland House, St. Pancras, Earl's Court, Hampstead Heath and Rotherhithe (all *en suite*). Not all do breakfast and most have shared facilities. There are various rooms, including family rooms, and cheaper rates for under 18s. 🚫 *8 St Stephen's Hill, St Albans, Herts AL1 2DY • Central booking: 020 7373 3400 • www.yha.org.uk • £*

8 YMCA

There is some nightly accommodation at the London City YMCA (8 Erroll Street EC1) and Barbican YMCA (Fann Street EC2). Otherwise try the German YMCA (35 Craven Terrace W2) or the Indian YMCA (41 Fitzroy Square W1). 🚫 *Central booking: 020 8509 4564 • £*

9 Host and Guest Service

This agency specializes in inexpensive accommodation in about 1,000 homes in London – plus others elsewhere in the UK. A two-night minimum stay is preferred. 🚫 *103 Dawes Road SW6 • Map A6 • 020 7385 9922 • www.host-guest.co.uk • £*

10 International Students House

In university holiday times, some student accommodation becomes available at reasonable rates. This house, though, has space all year. Dormitories, single and twin rooms are available at a range of prices. There is a bar downstairs, a restaurant and internet café. 🚫 *229 Great Portland Street W1 • Map J2 • 020 7631 8300 • www.ish.org.uk • no en-suite bathrooms • £*

General Index

Index

Acknowledgements

The Author

Roger Williams is a London-born journalist and long-time Soho inhabitant. He has written and edited several dozen travel guides, including Dorling Kindersley's Eyewitness guides to Provence and Barcelona. He is also the author of *Time Traveller*, an illustrated history of newspaper and periodical publishing, and his novels include *Lunch With Elizabeth David.*

Project Editor Simon Hall
Art Editor Nicola Rodway
Senior Editor Marcus Hardy
Senior Art Editor Marisa Renzullo
Publishing Manager Kate Poole
Senior Publishing Manager Louise Bostock Lang

Director of Publishing Gillian Allan

Photographer Demetrio Carasco

Illustrator Chris Orr & Associates

Cartography Casper Morris

Maps Tom Coulson, Martin Darlison (Encompass Graphics Ltd)

Editors Michelle de Larrabeiti, Irene Lyford

Researcher
Jessica Doyle

Picture Research Brigitte Arora

Proofreader Stewart J. Wild

Indexer Hilary Bird

DTP
Jason Little

Production
Joanna Bull, Marie Ingledew

Design and Editorial Assistance
James Hall, David Saldanha, Lilly Sellar, Melanie Simmonds, Hayley Smith, Rachael Symons

Additional Photography
Max Alexander, June Buck, Jo Cornish, Michael Dent, Mike Dunning, Philip Enticknap, John Heseltine, Roger Hilton, Ed Ironside, Colin Keates, Dave King, Bob Langrish, Robert O'Dea, Stephen Oliver, John Parker, Rob Reichenfeld, Kim Sayer, Chris Stevens, James Strachan, Doug Traverso, Vincent Oliver, David Ward, Matthew Ward, Steven Wooster

Additional Illustrations
Conrad Van Dyk

Picture Credits
t-top; tl-top left; tlc-top left centre; tc-top centre; tr-top right; cla-centre left above; ca-centre above; cra-centre right above; cl-centre left; c-centre; cr-centre right; clb-centre left below; cb-centre below; crb-centre right below; bl-bottom left, b-bottom; bc-bottom centre; bcl-bottom centre left; br-bottom right; d-detail.

The publishers would like to thank the following individuals, companies and picture libraries for their kind permission to reproduce their photographs.

The work of Henry Moore, *Arch* 1979) in Kensington Gardens, page 28b, has been reproduced by kind permission of the Henry Moore Foundation.
ARCAID: Richard Bryant. Architect: Foster & Partners 11c, 11b, 11t; ARCBLUE: Peter Durant 16l, 18cl.
ARENA IMAGES: Carol Rosegg 60-61b; Colin Willoughby 60tl; Nigel Norrington 61t.

BRIDGEMAN ART LIBRARY, LONDON / NEW YORK: Guildhall Library, Corporation of London 43c; Kenwood House 51t; BRITISH LIBRARY: 107bl; BRITISH MUSEUM: 6tr, 8b, 9tl, 9cb, 9bl, 9cra, 10tr, 10bl; Peter Hayman 8cr; Liz McAulay 10c; BROMPTON HOTEL: 172tr.

CAMERA PRESS: Cecil Beaton 89b; CHRIS CHRISTODOULOU: 57cr; COLLECTIONS: Brian Shuel 66tr; David McGill 80tl, 130cl; James Bartholomew 7crb; John D. Beldom 55br, 66cr, 119br; Keith Pritchard 153bl; Liz Stares 17bl; Nigel Hawkins 129tl; Oliver Benn 150tr; BILL COOPER: 56c; CORBIS: Adam Woolfitt 34cb; Grant Smith 17r; Jeremy Horner 147tl; London Aerial Photo Library 6cl, 16-17c; Robbie Jack 99br; S. Carmona 160t.

THE ENGLISH HERITAGE PHOTO LIBRARY: 148br; MARY EVANS PICTURE LIBRARY: 52c, 72tl, 72tc, 72bl.

FINANCIAL TIMES: 72c; FREUD MUSEUM, LONDON: 52b;

FRIENDS OF HIGHGATE CEMETERY: Doug Traverso 75bl, 143tl.

GETTY IMAGES: Hideo Kurihara 1; Jo Cornish 30-31; SALLY & RICHARD GREENHILL: Sally Greenhill 164tr.

ROBERT HARDING PICTURE LIBRARY: 66tl, 66cl, 84tr, 107br; A. Tovy 126-127; Adam Woolfitt 67cr; D. Hughes 137tl; Ellen Rooney 54tr, 67bl; M.P.H. 26bl; Nigel Francis 28-29c; R. Richardson 34-35c; Simon Harris 36-37c; Walter Rawlings 130br.

LEIGHTON HOUSE MUSEUM: 53bl; THE LONDON AQUARIUM: 68bl.

MADAME TUSSAUD'S, LONDON: 128tl, 129bl; MARINEPICS LTD: Mark Pepper 156tr; MAXWELLS GROUP: 59l; MUSEUM OF LONDON: 44c, 44b, 44t, 45tl, 136cl.

NATIONAL GALLERY, LONDON: 12b, 12t, 13cr, 13cb, 13bl, 13t, 50c; NATIONAL MARITIME MUSEUM: James Stevenson 48b, 149cr; NATIONAL TRUST PHOTOGRAPHIC LIBRARY: Bill Batten 149tl, Michael Boys 52tr; NATIONAL PORTRAIT GALLERY, LONDON: 6c, 14cl, 14bl, 14-15c, 14br, 15tl, 15cl, 15cr, 15b. NATURAL HISTORY MUSEUM, LONDON: 22b, 23tl, 23tr, 23c, 23b, 119bl; Kokoro 22cr. PERETTI COMMUNICATIONS: Chris Gascoigne & Lifschutz Davidson 77tr; PHOTOFUSION: Paul Bigland 153tl, 155br;

Acknowledgements

Paul Doyle 152cr; Ray Roberts 67tr; PICTURES COLOUR LIBRARY: 4-5; POPPERFOTO: Reuters/Greg Bos 72tr; PRIVATE COLLECTION: 43tr.

REX FEATURES: 27b; Andy Watts 67br; Ray Tang 73bl; Tim Rooke 26br, 54tl; RICHMOND HILL HOTEL: 178tr. THE RITZ, LONDON: 177tl; THE ROYAL COLLECTION © 2001 HER MAJESTY QUEEN ELIZABETH II: A. C. Cooper Ltd. 27tl; Crown © HMSO 39cl; Crown © HMSO 39tr; Derry Moore 27tr; ROYAL BOTANIC GARDENS, KEW: 147br; ROYAL GARDEN HOTEL: 173tl.

SCIENCE MUSEUM: 24tr, 24c, 24br, 25cra, 25bl; Antony Pearson 25crb; National Railway Museum/Science & Society 25tl; STRINGFELLOWS: 59r.

© TATE, LONDON 2001: 6bl, 20cl, 20br, 20-21c, 21tl, 21c, 21bl, 21r, 21br, 50tr; *Three Studies for Figures at the Base of a Crucifixion* (one of three panels) (c. 1944), Francis Bacon 21cr; *The Bath* (1925), Pierre Bonnard © ADAGP, Paris and DACS, London 2001 18cb; *Composition (Man and Woman)*, (1927), Alberto Giacometti © ADAGP, Paris and DACS, London 2001 19cb; *England* (1980), © Gilbert and George 19r; *The Three Dancers* (1925), Pablo Picasso © Succession Picasso/DACS 2001 18tr;

Summertime: No. 9A (1948), Jackson Pollock © ARS, New York and DACS, London 2001 18-19b; *Light Red over Black* (1957), Mark Rothko © 1998 Kate Rothko Prizel and Christopher Rothko/DACS 19ca; *Marilyn Diptych* (1962), Andy Warhol © The Andy Warhol Foundation for the Visual Arts, Inc./ARS, NY & DACS, London 2001 18-19c.

TRANSPORT FOR LONDON: 164tl.

COURTESY OF THE TRUSTEES OF THE V&A PICTURE LIBRARY: 119tl; Bethnal Green Museum of Childhood 69t.

WAGAMAMA LTD.: 77bl; THE WALLACE COLLECTION: 50b; PHILIP WAY PHOTOGRAPHY: 40bl, 40-41c, 41cr, 41t, 42c, 42bl, 43b, 80tr; WOODMANSTERNE PICTURE LIBRARY: 40b.

COVER: All photographs specially commissioned except: ARCBLUE: Peter Durant inside flap bcr; CORBIS: Jeremy Horner inside flap br; ROBERT HARDING PICTURE LIBRARY: B/C cl; LONDON TRANSPORT MUSEUM: F/C centre above; THE PHOTOGRAPHERS LIBRARY: F/C main picture.

All other images are © Dorling Kindersley. For further information see www.dkimages.com